D1561183

Sun Rhythm Form

*No one knew exactly when she had begun
to lose her sight. Even in her later years,
when she could no longer get out of bed, it
seemed that she was simply defeated by de-
crepitude, but no one discovered that she
was blind. . . . She did not tell anyone about
it because it would have been a public recognition of her uselessness. She concentrated on a silent schooling in the distances
of things and people's voices. . . . Later on
she was to discover the unforeseen help of
odors. . . . She knew with so much certainty
the location of everything that she herself
forgot that she was blind at times. . . .*

*Sometimes unforeseen accidents would
happen. One afternoon when Amaranta
was embroidering on the porch with the
begonias, Ursula bumped into her.*

*"For heaven's sake," Amaranta protested,
"watch where you are going."*

*"It's your fault," Ursula said. "You're not
sitting where you're supposed to."*

*She was sure of it. But that day she began
to realize something that no one had noticed and it was that with the passage of
the year the sun imperceptibly changed position and those who sat on the porch had
to change their position little by little without being aware of it. From then on Ursula
had only to remember the date in order to
know exactly where Amaranta was sitting.*

Gabriel Garcia Marquez, *One Hundred
Years of Solitude*

Ralph L. Knowles

Sun Rhythm Form

The MIT Press
Cambridge, Massachusetts
London, England

Publication of this volume has been aided by grants from the National Endowment for the Arts and the Department of Energy.

© 1981 by The Massachusetts Institute of Technology

All rights reserved. No part of this book may be reproduced in any form or by any means, electronic or mechanical, including photocopying, recording, or by any information storage and retrieval system, without permission in writing from the publisher.

This book was set in VIP Frutiger by DEKR Corporation and printed and bound by Halliday Lithograph in the United States of America.

Library of Congress Cataloging in Publication Data

Knowles, Ralph L.
  Sun rhythm form.

  Includes bibliographical references and index.
  1. Solar energy. 2. Architecture and solar radiation. I. Title.
TJ810.K56   720'.47   81-16901
ISBN 0-262-11078-4   AACR2

Sun

The sun is fundamental to all life. It is the source of our vision, our warmth, our energy, and the rhythm of our lives. Its movements inform our perceptions of time and space and our scale in the universe.

Assured access to the sun is thus important to the quality of our lives. Without access to the sun, our perceptions of the world and of ourselves are altered. Without the assurance of solar access, we face uncertainty and disorientation. We may lose our sense of who and where we are.

That the quality of life depends upon the sun is the central concern of this work. It will be addressed both directly, by observing desirable conditions, and indirectly, by setting forth the circumstances for solar energy conversion to attain the best quality of life.

The concept of solar access is an abstract notion generalized from particular observations. The natural world appears to abound with examples of arrangements based in some measure on exposure to the sun.

More to the point of this work, observations of the modern built world reveal that we have not followed nature's example in this regard. Our cities are nondirectional; our buildings are undifferentiated by orientation to the sun. They stand static, unresponsive to the rhythms of their surroundings.

If we should wish to follow nature more closely, we must recognize the basic rhythms of solar change when we design and site our buildings. Hence, the concept of solar access must be defined by the paths of daily and seasonal variation in the sun's relationship to earth.

Solar access is a reference to both time and space because there exists an inevitable relationship between when and where access to the sun can be achieved. These twin aspects of its definition may be analyzed separately, but they always coexist where their practical control is concerned. The determination of one cannot be made without the other.

Assured access to the sun is therefore a matter of being in a distinct place during a special period of time. The fact seems ridiculously obvious that we must be talking about a time between sunrise and sunset in order to discuss solar access at all. On the other hand, the fact that we must specify where we are standing on the earth and in relation to what natural or built forms may be less obvious.

For example, the length of our seasons may be determined by our latitude. Where we stand in relation to a tall building or hill that casts shadows can determine the perceptual length of our day.

A clear purpose is required to make sense of all this. Where and when we have access to the sun then becomes a matter of control, related to a purpose. For example, if our purpose is to grow a summer garden, access must be provided from the east and west because most direct summer sun comes from those directions and from almost straight overhead. These observations, and countless others, remind us that the sun moves by day and by season. It is an ever-changing source of heat and light, a source that we can tap only to the degree in which we take account of its dynamic character.

Significance of Solar Access

Without access to the sun, we cannot use it. Current discussions of solar access concentrate on the sun as a replacement for apparently unreliable fuel supplies and as a means for preserving our existing quality of life.

Solar energy is perceived as a direct replacement for artificial light and heat and, through decentralized access to photovoltaic cells, it beckons as a local alternative for electric power grids, which run our air conditioners during hot summer months. The energic potential of the sun is, in fact, a changing perception. Our concepts of how to use the sun may change. Current technologies may not prove durable. But the energy of the sun promises more important contributions to our lives if we retain our access to it.

This work, however, seeks to go beyond the perception of insolation (and therefore solar access) as a replacement for energy to preserve existing conditions. It seeks to extend the concept of solar access to support an improved quality of life, today and tomorrow. This assertion necessarily goes beyond current perceptions of an energy crisis.

If that problem were suddenly solved by some economic, technological, or political breakthrough, and even if our rate of energy conversion could be miraculously doubled or tripled, we would still need to confront the basic issue of life quality. It is improved life quality, rather than a direct concern for the energy situation, that led to this research on solar access. And it is this concern that forms the design context of the work. Assuming any very direct correlation between rates of energy conversion and the quality of life is an incomplete, if not dangerous, basis for national policy.

These convictions derive from a number of sources, including A. E. Parr, formerly Senior Scientist of the American Museum of Natural History, who has stressed the human species' mental, as well as physical, adjustment to the natural environment as a basis for design during an era of unprecedented urbanization. Parr and others have worried about our "ability to alter our surroundings on an order of magnitude that leaves far behind the scale of individual mental and physical performance to which man has become adapted and adjusted by his earlier evolution." *

Parr notes that some progress has "brought about a virtual suspension of the natural laws which would previously have forced a readaptation to the new circumstances of our lives." He then concludes that since we do not appear to have assured mechanisms for continued adaptation and adjustment to modern changing conditions, we must "see to it that the changes themselves are adjusted to the real needs of those who must endure them."

*A. E. Parr, "Mind and Milieu," *Arts and Architecture,* vol. 80, no. 10 (October 1963), p. 21. (Reprinted from *Sociological Inquiry,* Winter 1963.)

Certainly the sun is a primary condition for our mental and physical fitness. Therefore, even in a time when we can theoretically create totally new environments of our own design, I would stress access to the sun as a condition for an improved quality of life in our changing cities. The assurance of solar access can provide the continuity mid change that allows our adjustment to it.

Change is a condition of life, a part of its dynamic. Samuel Butler, the nineteenth-century author of *The Way of All Flesh,* once wrote: "All our lives long, every day and every hour, we are engaged in the process of accommodating our changed and unchanged selves to changed and unchanged surroundings." It is the process of accommodation to change that can define the quality of our lives.

Several components of the quality of life are related to the sun. The first is physical comfort, which may be the easiest to define. It is generally expressed in numerical ranges of temperature, humidity, air movement, light and sound levels, and other properties of the physical environment that impinge directly on our bodies. Access to the sun has a direct impact on at least the thermal and luminous components of this complex set and a secondary relationship to most of the rest. It is important to remember, however, as Parr has said, "a comfortable body is no guarantee of a comfortable mind," which brings us to the second element in the quality of life—choice.

Choice is a harder element of life quality to define. In the broadest sense we generally know when we have choices and when we don't. For the designer, solar access provides a broader range of options because solar heat and light are assured for the future. For the user, solar access keeps future options open in the event that changing technologies and aesthetics make the sun more, not less, valuable. To the extent that solar access provides more designer and user choices, it clearly contributes to the quality of life.

Comfort and choice are inextricably linked to the third element in the quality of life—a sense of well-being. Although somewhat difficult to define, well-being is nonetheless the reason we seek comfort and choice. Well-being is the sense of a condition rather than the condition itself. Yet even with such a vague understanding, we must satisfy ourselves that a sense of well-being is the minimum basis for an aesthetic and for a value system in building. Its superlative form is the fourth element in the quality of life—joy.

We often hear the expression, "the joy of life," and generally understand it in terms of pleasure and delight. It is a special state. We experience joy itself. It may result from external stimuli, but it is inside us and it is excessive! To the extent that solar access provides comfort, choice, and a sense of well-being, it provides the potential for joy. Perhaps joy lies in the sun's warm rays as they strike our outstretched bodies, or it may lie in reflections from a flower or a child's face. But in joy may lie the greatest justification for access to the sun.

Means of Solar Access

Solar access has recently come into focus as a topic of discussion in the United States because more and more we are looking at the sun as a source of energy. Solar access has therefore become a legitimate area of public policy, in which the aim is to regulate how and when neighbors may shadow one another.

A universal covenant has been sought that assures a right to the sun now and in the future. Alternative approaches to this problem have been explored but are largely untested in real communities. They fall into two main categories.

The first category includes a number of recent proposals to use permits, covenants, and easements that have been aimed at guaranteeing solar access for energy conversion. The main advantage is that there are legal precedents; but there are disadvantages. Future access is not assured for structures without present systems. Several permits acting on different, adjacent properties (as well as those on distant sites) may act to stop development completely on one of them.

An alternative to the permit system that applies to the same set of concerns is the solar envelope.* Several versions of this approach are being explored by cities, counties, and states throughout the country, but most share two characteristics. First, they are generally modeled on straightforward zoning regulations, and second, their intent is to assure future rights of access for land parcels.

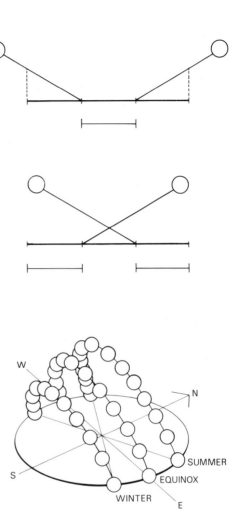

The solar envelope has the additional advantage of being a more neighborly approach to the problem. Instead of restricting the development surrounding a given property, it constrains development on that property to protect the surround. The distinction may appear fine, but the ethical and legal differences can be significant.

The solar envelope as it is conceived in this work is a container to regulate development within limits derived from the sun's relative motion. Development within this container will not shadow its surround during critical periods of the day. The envelope is therefore defined by the passage of time as well as by the constraints of property.

The time involved would be a duration of solar access, a period of direct, line-of-sight approach to solar heat and light. The duration of access is determined by some segment of an arc drawn to represent the sun's path. If year-round access is required, two arcs may be used to represent paths of the sun during summer and winter.

*I first introduced the concept of the solar envelope in *Energy and Form* (Cambridge, Massachusetts: MIT Press, 1974), pp. 118–121.

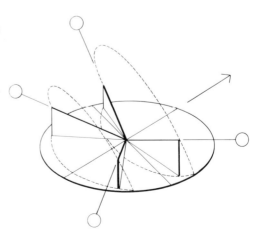

If the resulting angles of the solar azimuth and altitude are transferred to the edges and corners of a land parcel, the consequence is a set of geometric limits that derive their vertical dimensions from the sun's slanting rays.

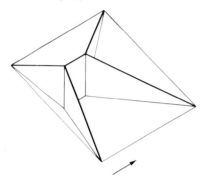

Depending on the duration of desired solar access, the land parcel configuration, and surrounding conditions, the size and shape of the envelope will vary. This work is concerned with exploring the design implications of that diversity and its relationship to the quality of life.

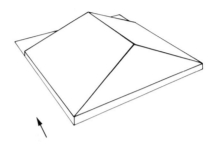

If the entire volume implied by the vertical limits is drawn as an explicit form, the result is a container with surfaces representing the three-dimensional boundaries of development.

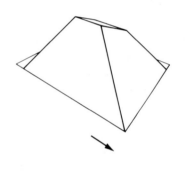

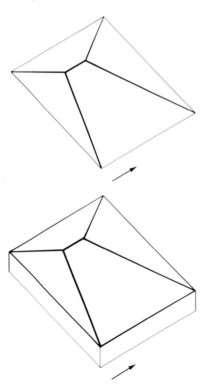

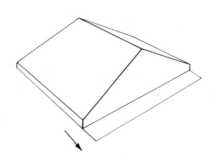

Rhythm

Rhythm is recognized in all natural processes. It appears in our behavior and in our feelings about the world around us. When our environment pulses in natural time, we seem to know and understand it. When we are isolated from natural recurrence, when we cannot feel natural tempos, we lose contact with a basis of our perceptions.

In this book I am proposing that these natural tempos can be linked to a concept of architectural and urban design. Implicit in this is the idea that there is aesthetic potential in rhythm as a perceptual analogy to natural systems. The transformation of rhythm into design provides a visual and behavioral connection between people and their environment that promises humane, as well as diverse and beautiful, environments.

Rhythm links time to the traditional spatial concepts of design. Time is, in this sense, not a linear function, as when a light source moves continuously away. Rather it is recurrent, as reflected in the patterns of season, or day and night. Then, the clear relation between rhythm and form may be easily converted to a relation between energy and form.

This proposition stresses the need for energy self-sufficiency and energy balance. Self-sufficiency and balance mean that built arrangements, like natural systems, cannot use more energy than they exchange with their immediate environment. They must diversify to fit local conditions and not be dependent on large complexes of centralized energy supplies.

A focus on choice resulting from diversity as a condition of life quality is also important, so that a basic proposition for design and research reads: *An artificial system, made in balanced energy response to nature, will exhibit diversity useful in expanding choice for life quality.*

The proposition implies a value of diversity that must be understood against a backdrop of adaptive evolution, in which orientation in space and time was a precondition for survival.

Rhythm and Perception

Nature is the origin of our perceptions. This is true to the extent that our senses have evolved to function in a world richly structured by adaptive processes. People are well adjusted to natural increments of space and time and seem to feel quite comfortable with them. Where they have not suited a population, those people either tried to modify them or tried to move elsewhere.

Nature has sometimes been romanticized, but here, my purpose is simply to emphasize that our modern awareness is rooted beyond comprehensible time. Our ability to gauge duration and distance is ancestral.

One of our remote forerunners just noticed a difference of color and light and saw a predator in the forest; another one just noticed the difference in the wind and escaped the grass fire. The ability to notice the critical difference distinguished unsuccessful individuals from those who were able to escape, and thence to become our progenitors.

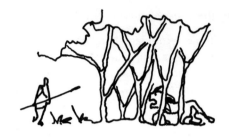

Our forerunners were the result of countless near misses that selectively equipped them to feel those conditions that might have done them harm. The conditions were spatial in the sense that each victim stood at some point in relation to potential danger; the conditions were also temporal in that there was a duration of imminent danger. If danger appeared as an isolated event, the victim might survive, but there was no way to prepare for a one-of-a-kind situation. If the danger were recurring, as with daily periods of predatory activity, or seasonal periods of drought and food shortage, the interval could be anticipated and action might be planned. In the second case, adaptation became rhythmic. Perceptions of the environment had to account for fundamental and contrapuntal beats.

The imperative that has tuned our perceptions is natural variation. Our mind and sense abilities are scaled to the differentiated natural world. When, for whatever reason, we cannot read horizontal change, we may not be able to tell one direction from another, or left from right. When we cannot read vertical change, we may not be able to tell up from down. Finally, when we cannot perceive directional change within a comprehensible interval, we lose the assurance that accompanies natural recurrence.

In some degree, we become disoriented and lose our general sense of well-being. Under similar circumstances, if our ancestors could not modify the situation, they would probably have moved; to stay where they were would have invited disaster.

The pueblos of America's southwest provide a good example of how early settlements recognized natural rhythms in the adaptation of location and form for human comfort. Their ritual celebrations also confirmed the impact of natural variation.*

*See Knowles, *Energy and Form*, pp. 17–46 for a detailed analysis of the pueblos' solar characteristics.

Rhythm and Ritual

The location and form of buildings at Longhouse Pueblo, Mesa Verde, Colorado, provided ancient residents with year-round comfort. The pueblo demonstrates a remarkable ability to mitigate extreme environmental temperature variations by responding to the differential impact of the sun during summer and winter, night and day.

The primary adaptation of the pueblo to the solar dynamic is in its location. The settlement is sited in a large cave that faces south, and the built structures are nestled within. The brow of the cave admits warming rays of the low winter sun but shields the interior of the cave from the rays of the more northern summer sun. Not only the orientation of the cave itself (which measures almost 500 feet across, is 130 feet deep, and arches to 200 feet) but the juxtaposition of the structures within it are responsive to the solar dynamic. The interior structures stay within the summer shadow line, and they are arranged so that one structure steps up from another toward the back of the cave.

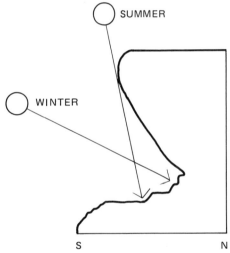

Willa Cather might have had Longhouse in mind when she wrote, "Far above me, a thousand feet or so, set in a great cavern in the face of the cliff, I saw a little city of stone, asleep." (Willa Cather, The Professor's House. New York: Knopf, 1925).

It is thus the location of the cave itself and the siting of structures within the cave that ensured the comfort of the pueblo dwellers. Because of orientation, the irradiation of the cave on a winter day is equivalent to that on a summer day. The performance of buildings within the cave is 56 percent more effective as a solar collector in winter than in summer, providing winter heat and summer coolness with remarkable efficiency. Longhouse is one of many pueblos built after A.D. 1100, at Mesa Verde, but is one of only a few facing south. Those facing east are much colder in winter; those facing west are too hot in summer.

The seasonal adaptation at Longhouse is complemented by the pueblo's response to a daily rhythm as the sun moves from the eastern to the western sky, casting morning rays inside the west end of the cave and twilight rays inside the east end. The thermal mass of the cave itself, as well as the structure of buildings within, helped to mitigate extreme daily variations, but a main adaptation for comfort may be best understood in the rhythms of people's lives.

The tempo of life may have been an effective adaptation to the solar environment. A closer examination of this tempo suggests important clues to the relationship between solar access and life quality and will move us toward the emergence of rhythm as a design strategy.

It is reasonably well documented that the cave dwellers of Mesa Verde tended to migrate in and out of the cave in response to the north-south seasonal migrations of the sun. The way they worked suggests that they moved deeper into the cave for shelter during summer and spread further to the south in winter, using their terraces for work and play with full exposure to the warm solar rays.

This north-south migration coincided with the shadows and thus the thermal variations of exactly one year's interval. It is possible to speculate on a transverse migration of a much shorter duration that might very well have occurred in response to the daily, rather than the seasonal, rhythm of the sun's movement.

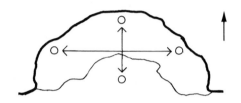

There is not much documentation of the tempo of daily life at Longhouse, but the following scenario helps to provide a useful image. During much of the year, morning light entered the dark cave from the east and outlined those buildings at the western end. All of the families in the pueblo kept turkeys, but only the turkeys first struck by the morning rays of sunlight would awake and become noisy. The turkeys roused the children who, in turn, disturbed their parents. Those first pulses of activity would then travel 500 feet finally to echo against the eastern walls of the Longhouse cave.

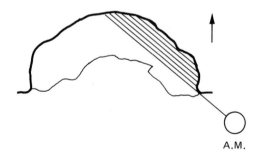

A.M.

The day passed with fairly general activity distributed throughout the cave. As late afternoon approached, twilight first came to the western end of the cave and subdued the turkeys, then the children. Their parents could breathe those last sighs of relief, while parents in the eastern end of the cave still had time to go before their day was done. As their light disappeared, the last turkeys uttered a quiet gobble and the children of the eastern cave let that day finally go.

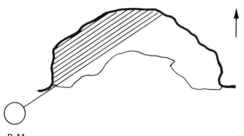

P.M.

The foregoing sequences are imaginary, but not without historical foundation. The fact is that such a scene could very well have taken place. And what is more important, it could have occurred every day with seasonal variations as I have described—suggesting a strategic rhythm for thermal comfort and for life quality.

Pueblo Bonito, in Chaco Canyon, New Mexico, relied primarily on its form to respond to solar access and to provide comfort for people dwelling within it. Only ruins remain, but the original forms are clear.

Bonito is like an amphitheater, with a stage surrounded by curving rows of seats too big for people—the Greek theatre of Epidauros transplanted and scaled for gods. Even today, one can sense in the powerful half forms of Bonito's ruins some pulsing affirmation of life.

In earlier times, these forms helped mitigate the extreme effects of summer and winter, with a considerably higher percentage of winter solar gain and minimal exposure to the summer sun. Not only the plan but the structure of the buildings within Bonito adapted to the solar dynamic. The summer sun falls primarily on horizontal surfaces with low storage capacity and winter sun falls more on vertical surfaces with heat retention characteristics, allowing stored heat to reradiate to the interior of the dwellings during cold winter days.

The evidence for seeing Bonito as a designed response to solar access is strong. The buildings in Bonito step in terraces from a high circular wall around the north, east, and west boundaries. These terraces descend toward the center of the plan to two courts, separated by a building and wall arrangement.

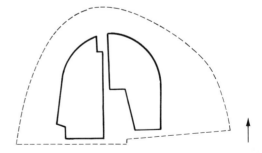

Not only its physical form, but its culture and traditions, point toward a life tempo in which solar access was clearly equated with life quality. This conscious response to conditions of solar access further suggests rhythm as a design strategy.

Pueblo Bonito, in addition to being an early trading center of considerable importance, was probably designed as a temple to honor the sun and was very likely a background for ritual celebrations that occurred not only at special times of the year but perhaps every morning and evening with the rising and setting of the sun. Daily and seasonal rhythm was not only a condition of pueblo life, it was a cause for celebration.

Using heliodon and model studies at the University of Southern California, I established in 1968 that Bonito might have served as an astronomical observatory, as it accurately identified the seasonal extremes of summer and winter solstice by shadow relationships to sunrise and sunset on those days.* Subsequent work by others, primarily specialists in archeoastronomy, has further identified window openings within the pueblo that have special relationships to astronomical phenomena.†

During those studies, I could sense the rhythm of light changes on Bonito's forms and start to share the deep feeling that people often express about Bonito after experiencing, even for short periods of time, its transformation as the sun moves. This transformation is rhythmic, repeating by day and season.

*Knowles, *Energy and Form*, pp. 38–39.

†Anthony F. Aveni, ed., *Archaeoastronomy in Pre-Columbian America* (Austin and London: University of Texas Press, 1975).

Some sense of this can be conveyed by a short description of changes in sunlight on the main court floor. The result of the sun's daily migration is a shift in the shadowed portions of the courts and a related shift in the sunlit portions. That shift always takes place in the east-west direction. The summer-winter shift occurs in a north-south direction.

P.M.   SUMMER   A.M.

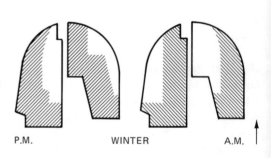

P.M.   WINTER   A.M.

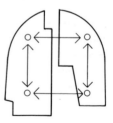

The daily shift in the shadows from east to west occurs at all times of the year, but the shadowing of the north and south portions of the court varies with season. Daily and seasonal cycles can be diagrammed as at Longhouse with arrows pointing north and south to suggest a seasonal migration of shadow patterns and with other arrows pointing east and west to indicate the daily migrations of shadows.

The result is a kind of segmentation of each court into spotlighted areas where it is easy to imagine ritual activities taking place at different locations in the courts at different times of the day and year. Such rituals occur today on the terraces and in the courtyards of modern pueblos.*

This practice was probably well developed by the time of Bonito. Morning ritual dances might have taken place in the glaring light of the western portion of each court, while evening dances would have shifted their stage to the east. Summer celebrations might have occurred in the southern portions of each court, while the winter celebrations shifted north to gain exposure to the sun.

Historically, ritual has served to intensify our awareness of recurring natural events. The rites of spring, fall, and Thanksgiving, morning flags and evening trumpets, all remind us of natural time. Of course, Bonito may not have functioned precisely as described, but the images are strong. The notion that ritual activities may have migrated upon Bonito's stage, following the movement of the sun, only strengthens the conviction that solar access is a condition of life quality.

*For a moving and image-filled discussion of ritual dances as they presently occur in pueblo settlements, see Vincent J. Scully, *Pueblo: Mountain, Village, Dance* (New York: Viking, 1975).

Form

Form in nature bears the imprint of rhythmic variation. Primitive human shelters and early settlements also express rhythmic variation in their shapes and structures. Buildings in our modern industrial cities are subject to the same recurring forces that act to structure nature and that caused purposive adaptations at Longhouse and Bonito.

Despite this fact, we continue to build and perceive our cities as nonresponsive to recurring natural forces. There are few indications of natural rhythm in our urban forms. The modern city is a place where time is read from the face of a clock, not from natural cues. Days and seasons are counted along a single thread. They are not perceived as part of a deep tapestry of rhythms.

The city is not a place where we easily find our way. The clues that are normal to our perceptions are missing. We should not be surprised, then, if city dwellers become disoriented and lack a general sense of well-being.

We do not have to be threatened, as our ancestors might have been, to realize that our cities are sometimes unrewarding as physical places. If we are not free to move, perhaps we can change our urban environments by gradually rebuilding them in a way that more graphically displays their responsiveness to the directional forces of nature. But first we must ask why buildings look as they do and why they tend to march across the land with apparent indifference to natural variation.

Natural Variation and Buildings

The same forces that act to differentiate nature are at work on buildings. The sun, for example, acts differently on the faces of a building, just as it does on the various slopes of a hill. James Marston Fitch, author of *American Building,* has asserted that the climatic differences between the north and south side of a building can be equivalent to 1,500 miles—the distance from Boston to Miami Beach.

A cube-like building oriented on the cardinal points will receive different amounts of solar energy from one face to another. Over time, the irradiation levels upon any given face will vary. In winter, at 35 degrees north latitude, no energy will fall on the north face. The south face will receive the most energy, while east, west, and top faces receive moderate amounts. In summer, a small amount of energy will be received by the north face in the early morning and late afternoon; a small amount will also be received on the south face. But the lion's share will be received on the top face, with somewhat smaller amounts on the east and west. Overlay on the picture the variable impact of ambient temperature and wind, and the results can be startling.

A warped and torn corner of a building near Anchorage is a good example of differential climatic impact. Constructed of metal panels during a recent summer, the building got only part way through its first Alaskan winter. On a bright and windy November day, when the ambient air temperature dropped to about −30°F, the intense sun struck the south, west, and top surfaces of the building. Where the panels met at the southeast corner, the warming south face met the wind-chilled east. The combination of the expanding south and the contracting east literally exploded the corner,

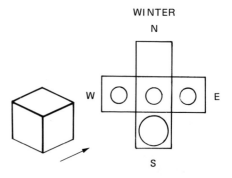

WINTER

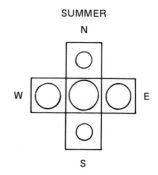

SUMMER

proving that at least where faces meet, buildings are certainly susceptible to natural variation.

The cynic may resist my regional example because it is too extreme. Perhaps it is the strong image of those bent panels that makes me defend my example. The Alaskan case may not be generally applicable to paneled corners, but certainly it characterizes the differential impact of sunlight and heat on the luminous and thermal state of the spaces inside buildings. How is it that buildings usually look the same on all sides in spite of such differential impacts? For the answer to this question, we must go back to conditions that followed World War II.

After World War II, rapid growth was the order of the day. The war years almost completely diverted our energy and resources abroad, so that by 1945 there was a backlog of building need. Our population was increasing; it had shifted from the farms to the cities and much of our building stock needed to be replaced.

The result was a postwar period of exuberant urban expansion. Because we could depend upon the automobile for transportation, we could and did build outward onto our agricultural land and onto the raw land beyond. Such rapid growth could not really be planned. Changes took place so fast that planners could barely keep their maps up to date. We were busy applying American know-how, turning out buildings in assembly-line fashion.

We had older models of buildings that fit into their environments quite well. There were the indigenous American buildings that varied with climate, the cracker-box of New England, the dog-trot house of Arkansas, and the adobe of Arizona. There were elegant later designs by the Greene brothers, Richardson, and Wright that not only varied with climate but conformed to their specific sites in a way that came to be called "organic."

The indigenous types and the later designs depended on principles that related the building in an evident way to natural variation. But the application of those principles took more time than the postwar building boom could allow. The environmental uncertainty that results from rapid development was not generally a problem confronted by either the early builders or the early twentieth-century architects.

When future conditions surrounding a building are subject to rapid change and when the building cannot be fit to its environment with any certainty about its future performance, one solution is to build an indifferent box, seal it up, and supply it internally with life-support systems. Based on a cheap supply of fossil fuels, such systems were developed and used to such an extent that today, something in excess of 35 percent of our total annual energy consumption goes to light, heat, and cool our buildings. (About 33 percent goes to transportation, although this figure is declining; the remainder goes to industry, including the building industry itself.)

One may conclude from this that the maintenance bill for what we built is high indeed, and certainly the conclusion would be justified. But in addition, what of the visual characteristics, the forms of these buildings that have depended on high rates of energy consumption? After all, it is possible to imagine a time when revolutionary modes of energy conversion multiply the energy available to each of us many times. There must still be concern for the quality of our environment.

The Non-Image of the City

In 1960 Kevin Lynch wrote *The Image of the City.* This classic work considered the visual quality of the city by studying the mental image held by its citizens. Lynch said, "We are not accustomed to organizing and imaging an artificial environment on such a large scale." He was concerned that the disorientation resulting from an unclear urban image might leave us without a sense of balance and well-being. He asserted that "legibility is crucial in the city setting."

The American city's legibility suffered during the thirty-year period of growth from 1945 to 1975. In great part this was the result of rapid development. We did not have time to plan. Rather than take the time to fit our development to a varied environment, we often modified the environment to fit repeated units of construction.

The now-famous subdivision pads that cover many of Southern California's hillsides are an example of gross environmental modification. The subsequent costs of such major tampering with the natural land forms need not be detailed here. The long-term maintenance costs have been exorbitant.

But what of the repetitious character of buildings? How were we able to sustain assembly-line products in a richly varied world? The answer is simple enough: we used sufficient energy to allow their indifferent behavior and aspect. Energy broke the bonds of place and time.

Dominion over nature was heady stuff, but it had at least one unforeseen consequence. Our urban environments became, in a sense, aspatial and atemporal. Our large buildings were often built to appear the same from side to side and from top to bottom. Large and small buildings were often built alike from block to block and even from one geographical region to another, regardless of energy costs.

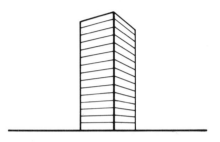

Buildings took on a flat two-dimensional character that was repeated like the receding images between two opposing mirrors. Certainly, this was not Lynch's "crucial legibility."

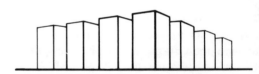

Our buildings no longer responded architecturally to real time. They could mechanically peak-load off-site energy sources and be independent from the older adaptations of location and form. Because designers depended almost exclusively on mechanical rather than architectural support systems, time became nonimageable.

Designers did not often address the passage of time. Only their plate glass windows gave witness to daily and seasonal intervals. The location and form of buildings provided no cues. Our constructions stood faceless in their ranks and still do. How different the modern built world often is from that of our ancestors. Our senses evolved in nature, but they must often function without the essential differences of the natural world—without the legibility Lynch asserted was crucial to our balance and sense of well-being.*

*Kevin Lynch, *The Image of the City* (Cambridge, Massachusetts: MIT Press, 1960).

The Transformation of Cities

Our period of exuberant growth has come to an end. This statement is more easily supported in the northern than in the southern United States. Certainly there is no argument for it in the northeastern part of the country. The statement is less credible in the southwest, but the signs are there too. The reasons are economic, demographic, and climatic. There is a general economic cooling from the white heat of postwar demand; the major war and postwar regional population shifts are slowing, and even reversing in some cases. Finally, while the attractive warmer climates are still moving people south, and particularly southwest, a one-two punch of fewer jobs and too many people in those areas has overburdened state and local relief systems and generated taxpayer revolts. Governors and mayors are saying "think small" and "vacation here but don't stay."

Does this mean that we are at an end of growth or just at an end of growth as usual? I would pick the second option. There are many indications that we are entering a period of growth with different characteristics. If the previous phase can be called "expansionary" by processes of land subdivision, I think the new phase can be called "transformational" by selective processes of land assemblage.

It may seem optimistic to use a term that implies a fundamental change in the physical environment, but surely the signs of rebuilding are present and clear. If a basic purpose can be lent to the process, the result may well be transformed cities.

Serious questions of social displacement are already being heard around the country. But, unlike the great displacements attending World War II, the modern ones are proceeding at a slower rate and at the grass-roots level. There are presently no immense infusions of federal money that displace thousands of people overnight from one region of the country to another. Now people often move from one district to another within the same city. These local migrations may be analyzed as smaller-scale adjustments to changing conditions of the recent past. Surely there will be problems of social service. There will also be a need to provide a different disposition of housing, commerce, and industry.

The question raised here is whether additional purposes can be assigned to this urban rebuilding. Can our cities slowly be transformed to use solar energy and thereby to improve the quality of life?

The answer is a conditional "yes." The condition is that we must spend more human energy designing a framework for urban growth so that less machine energy need be spent to maintain what we build.

A part of the framework for urban growth is already in place, in the network of streets that define the urban grid. If solar envelope zoning provides another part of the framework, a careful look at street orientation is useful.

Street Orientation

The solar envelope's size, shape, and orientation are greatly dependent on the patterns of urban settlement. In the United States, that context is usually influenced by orderly subdivisions that have geometricized the land. Typically, throughout the midwest and the west, streets run with the cardinal points so that rectangular blocks extend in the east-west and north-south direction of the Jeffersonian grid.

Other grid orientations derive from climate, topography, and geology. In Los Angeles, for example, the old Spanish grid is oriented nearly 45 degrees off the cardinal points. This diagonal orientation, an adaptation to sea breezes, was ordered by the King of Spain. It now extends from the old pueblo over the land that is modern downtown Los Angeles.

Before discussing the street grid's influence on the solar envelope, and hence on development, there should be some mention of the important qualitative differences of streets themselves as derived from orientation. A comparison of the Jeffersonian and Spanish grids serves to demonstrate inherent properties related to shadows.

For example, streets that run east-west in a built-up urban area will tend to be shadowed during all of a winter day. In most parts of this country, including Los Angeles at 34 degrees north latitude, the streets thus remain dark and cold. By contrast, streets that run north-south are lighted and warmed during the midday and are consequently more pleasant during the busy noontime shopping period.

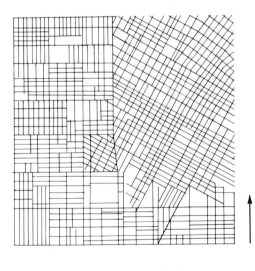

WINTER   SUMMER

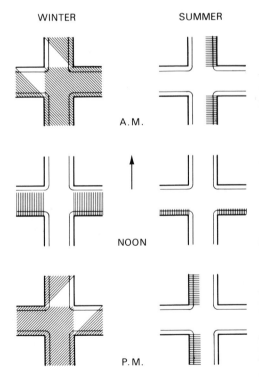

A.M.

NOON

P.M.

Summer presents an entirely different picture. Unlike winter, when the sun's rays come from the southern sky, the summer sun comes more directly from the east in the morning and from the west in the afternoon. At midday, it is nearly overhead. Streets that run east-west will receive a little shadow at midday, much less in the morning and afternoon—a critical factor on a hot afternoon. Streets that run north-south will be shadowed in the morning and afternoon, but will receive the full force of summer's midday sun.

From the viewpoint of solar orientation, the Jeffersonian grid leaves something to be desired. Its east-west streets are too dark and cold in winter; its north-south streets too bright and hot in summer. In Los Angeles, the older Spanish grid seems to have advantages regarding street qualities of light and heat.

During the winter, every street on the Spanish grid receives direct light and heat from the sun sometime between 9 A.M. and 3 P.M., the six hours of greatest irradiation. It is true that at midday all streets have shadows, but because of the diagonal orientation, the effective street width is very much increased, leaving more of the street in sunlight than would be the case for a street that ran directly east-west.

While every street in the Spanish grid receives direct sunlight and heat at some period of a winter day, every street has the advantage of some shadow during most of the summer day. Shadows are cast into every street all day long, with the exception of a short period during late morning and early afternoon when the sun passes quickly over the diagonal streets.

These differences in street quality that result from solar exposure are felt, if only subconsciously, by people, and they are even acknowledged by real estate experts. But street orientation is almost never considered as a basis for land-use and planning decisions.

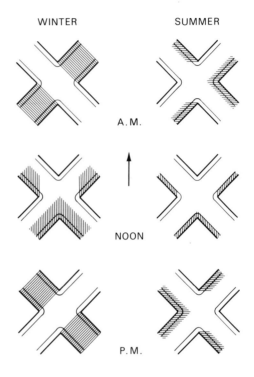

WINTER   SUMMER

A.M.

NOON

P.M.

The Influence of Street Orientation on the Solar Envelope

Street orientation influences the solar envelope in two ways. The first of these has important consequences for development; the second relates more to issues of urban design.

The solar envelope over a city block oriented on the cardinal points will contain more developable volume than one over a diagonal block. This relation between grid orientation and envelope height will be discussed later in more detail. Generally, the most height, and hence volume, are attainable at either of the two possible block orientations within the Jeffersonian grid, and the least volume is attainable at about the angular orientation of the Spanish grid. The street's gain in sunlight thus appears to be the developer's loss; this has made downtown Los Angeles a challenging problem from the viewpoint of development.

The urban design consequences of street orientation are important because they relate to legibility. Pathways, districts, and directions take on clear perceptual meaning when the solar envelope becomes a framework for urban development. Another way of saying the same thing is that urban cues to orientation come more readily if solar access is included as a development criterion.

The foregoing assertions can be shown to be true by comparing three different block orientations; immediately evident are not only different envelope sizes but different shapes as well. These differences will result in street asymmetries, district variety, and clear directionality along streets. Such differences tend to occur systematically, not randomly. They therefore serve as dependable cues to orientation.

For example, solar envelopes over blocks that run long in the east-west direction contain the most bulk and have the highest ridges, generally located near the south boundary. Development that respects the envelope will occur symmetrically along the short dimension of the block, and asymmetrically on the long dimension, with high buildings on the north and low ones on the south to admit winter sun. Buildings along the north side of the street will vary in height. They will appear low at corners and gradually rise toward a high, level section at mid-block.

Solar envelopes on long north-south blocks will have less bulk and a somewhat lower ridge running lengthwise down the middle of the block. North-south streets will be symmetrical, while the shorter, east-west streets will be higher on the north than on the south side. Those to the north will rise to an abrupt peak mid-block.

A third orientation, that of the diagonal Spanish grid as in downtown Los Angeles, produces envelopes with the least bulk and a ridge along the southeast boundary. All streets will be developed asymmetrically, with the northwest and northeast sides of the street higher, and the southeast and southwest sides lower to admit the winter sun all day long. Intersections will, where the envelope is respected, be marked with a high building on the north corner surrounded by lower ones on each of the other three corners.

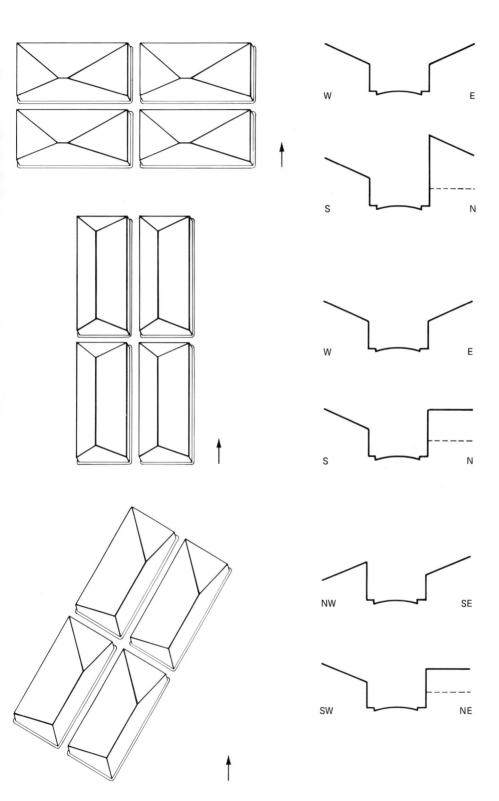

We thus see that development within the solar envelope is highly legible. Streets become qualitatively as well as quantitatively different. They have a predictable one-sidedness. Under the envelope, a change of street orientation always signals a change of aspect. Corners become unique events and are visually announced as one approaches by car or on foot. Street asymmetries, directional differences of streets, and differentiation along streets all add to the definition of pathways, districts, and directions.

Form in Time

In the following chapters, I shall first explore regulatory issues and then move beyond them to the form implications of solar access. In so doing, I am mindful that an important criterion for regulation must be simplicity of concept and of applications; several means have been devised that answer those requirements.

What has compelled me to explore the solar envelope so rigorously in all its diversity is that, more than any other means of regulation, it evokes form. The more diversified the context of its application, the richer become the form possibilities.

Some of the richest form possibilities arise from the dynamic aspects of the solar envelope and its existence as a descriptor of time. Far from being a statical container that preempts design freedom, the envelope suggests new properties of design that respond to both solar rhythms and changes of urban context.

In its organization this book progresses from solar access to envelope, from solar envelope to rhythm, and from solar rhythm to building form. But a more direct connection between rhythm and form can clearly be drawn independently of the envelope or public policies assuring solar access. From the designer's viewpoint, it might finally be this more direct connection that leads to explorations of a new concept of form.

I hope that designers will rise to this challenge. At the same time, I hope they will not fail to understand the aesthetic, as well as the ethical and energic implications of the envelope, and to consider it not as a shackle on their imagination but rather as a concept that can help them to uncover unique and significant architectural form.

Where programmatic requirements of development cause the design to push against the limits of the envelope, the shape of those limits can play an important aesthetic role. If the designer values the sun as a basis for architectural and urban form, the envelope will be a tool that helps to translate that value into form, while providing its neighbors with the opportunity to do the same.

The complex movements of the sun are difficult to see and impossible to quantify without a reference. The envelope provides both that reference and a formal expression of the effects of the sun's motion. It thereby introduces the designer to the concept of form in time and provides a basis for thinking of time as a medium of design. Time, as well as space, then becomes the basis for a new aesthetic.

2 *Solar Policy*

To use the sun, you must have access to it. To have access, there must be a public recognition of the right of access—a solar policy. Access can be achieved by private design or development initiatives, but a commitment expressed as public policy best assures access on an equitable, comprehensive, and long-term basis. The process of developing a public policy also provides a forum for public expression of the value of urban solar access.

A solar policy may be based on a modification of traditional zoning principles, resulting in the solar envelope described in chapter 1. Since given conditions of climate and land use vary from place to place, the specific solar policy selected for particular locations will also vary.

To assure solar access without misunderstanding and conflict among neighbors, the access policy must be fair, unambiguous, and applied evenhandedly. A balance must be struck between the right to develop property and the right of access to the sun.*

*Some of the material in chapter 2 has appeared previously in slightly different form in Ralph L. Knowles, "The Solar Envelope," *Solar Law Reporter*, vol. 2 (July/August 1980), pp. 263–297.

Ethical Background

There is no established solar ethic in the United States. Examples abound wherein solar access has been denied and energy-conscious designs that achieve their efficiency goals at the expense of neighboring buildings' rights to the sun are clearly questionable on moral grounds. Thus, it is worth noting that when the Tennessee Valley Authority sought to make its new office complex in Chattanooga, Tennessee, a national model for energy-conscious design, it called for advanced solar design *and* for protection of its neighbors' sun rights.

In Los Angeles, a typical pattern of urban development is a strip of high-rise commercial buildings that cast shadows north over residential neighborhoods. In one area of the city, for example, 14-story apartments were built just to the south of existing, stable neighborhoods of detached, single-family houses.

The impact of such new development is complex and cannot be viewed in isolation; nevertheless, certain changes were clear and measurable. For example, long north shadows were cast on existing gardens and outdoor recreation areas. The quality of light within adjacent houses was diminished. Increased traffic noise and lack of privacy must have taken their toll, along with the new shadowing.* Over subsequent months, the number of for-sale signs increased dramatically.

---

*Throughout this book, the architectural convention of distinguishing between shade and shadow will be followed. A shaded area is one that is oriented away from the sun; for example, the north side of a building. A shadowed area is one that is oriented toward the sun but is deprived of sunlight by another object; for example, the ground adjacent to the north side of a building.

The ecology of the houses immediately to the north changed drastically. Yards changed character because different species of plants had to replace those that could not survive the shadow. Where sunning terraces could not be relocated, they fell into disuse. The high-rise developers' failure to consider adjacent environmental impacts illustrates the need for a comprehensive solar policy. In the opening lines of his treatise *On Free Choice of the Will,* Saint Augustine notes two aspects of action: what someone does and what someone suffers. Every action that affects another person can be viewed from two perspectives, that of the actor and that of the affected person. In the context of solar access, the two people are you and your neighbor.

Your neighbor's actions—the placement of his house, outbuildings, and vegetation, and their size and height—will determine the extent of your access to sunlight. Similarly, your actions will determine your neighbor's access. These two perspectives represent not only different ethical foundations but different legal and design issues as well.

Selecting a regulatory policy requires a choice between these perspectives. The permit, covenant, and easement approaches, for example, limit your neighbor's freedom of action to protect you, while solar envelope zoning limits your freedom of action to protect your neighbor. Since zoning applies over a specified area, solar envelope zoning has the advantage of producing the same effect on both you and your neighbor.

Legal Background

If solar access is to be guaranteed, some legal experts feel there will need to be a clarification or change of existing laws or even the formulation of new laws. This raises an interesting question of legal precedents. The most commonly cited law outside the United States is the English Doctrine of Ancient Lights. William Thomas of the American Bar Foundation has written extensively about this doctrine.* However, Thomas and other legal experts point to the fact that this doctrine has been repeatedly disavowed in the United States. Some, like Mary R. White, writing in the *Colorado Law Review,* suggest that water law may offer a useful precedent.†

*William Thomas, "Access to Sunlight," *Solar Radiation Considerations in Building Planning and Design: Proceedings of a Working Conference* (National Academy of Sciences, Washington, D.C., 1976), pp. 14–18.

†Mary R. White, "The Allocation of Sunlight: Solar Rights and the Prior Appropriation Doctrine," *Colorado Law Review,* vol. 47 (1976), pp. 421–427.

Water Law

White makes two salient points in comparing sunlight and water. First, both are used rather than captured and sold; both may be consumed, but both are renewable. In addition, there is an equivalence between upstream and downstream in water law and the geometry of solar shadowing. To clarify this last point, I would like to review briefly the two basic approaches to water law that states use: first, the prior appropriation doctrine used in the arid West and, second, the riparian doctrine derived from English common law and used in humid states with ample supplies of water.

The doctrine of prior appropriation is a formalization of the general practice among early Western settlers of apportioning available water according to who first put it to beneficial use. Simply put, "He who gets there first, gets the most." It was the frontier's answer to the exigencies of pioneer settlement.

A rough example of how the law worked can be described as follows: Settler A establishes his residence along a river and puts the water to beneficial use by diverting some of it for irrigation. Subsequently, settler B takes up residence downstream while settler C locates upstream from A. Under the prior appropriation doctrine, both B and C, who presumably settle with foreknowledge of A's prior claim to the river, do so acknowledging that claim and agreeing to endure without protest A's continued use of the river. On the other hand, A has some responsibilities in the matter and cannot significantly change the conditions accepted by B and C when they first settled. There the matter lies, unless some prior agreement among the three or subsequent court action taken by one of the parties effects a change in the pattern of use.

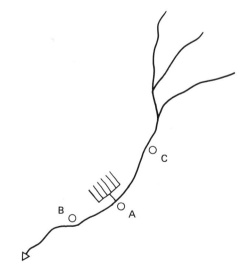

The second water law discussed by White is the riparian doctrine. In humid states with a lot of water, the first settlers brought with them the law of England, where the abundance of water made the right-of-use seem to belong appropriately to ownership of land along a stream. Again, the doctrine can be simply put: "Everybody has an equal share."

Each riparian owner had a right to use the plentiful water that flowed past his property. It made no difference where or when A, B, or C acquired ownership along the river. Of course, a plentiful supply must be understood. This doctrine makes little sense where a resource is scarce or has been modified by the pollution of prior users.

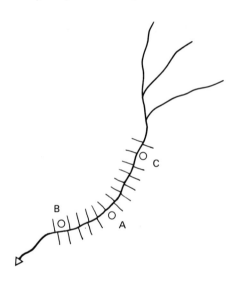

Solar Applications of Water Law

Neither prior appropriation nor riparian-like doctrines are likely to be applied to solar allocation in any simple way. This point has been made abundantly clear in the writings of such legal experts as Gail Boyer Hayes who point out serious weaknesses in any attempt to move directly from water law to solar law.* She points especially to the need for more local administration of rules affecting the allocation of sunlight, and therefore to the greater appropriateness of fairly straightforward zoning approaches to the problem. Therefore, it is more an application of the spirit of these two doctrines than of any close adherence to the letter of the law with which I have approached the matter of drawing analogies between solar allocation and water law. With that important condition, I will proceed with the analogies.

Consider first the solar analogy to prior appropriation. Developer A sites a building that casts shadows to the north. Sometime later developer B locates his building to the north (downstream). Developer B, like settler B in our frontier example, must contend in some way with an a priori appropriation of the resource. Under present law, B would have no right to receive solar energy that crossed A's airspace. His only right would have been to sunlight falling perpendicularly onto his land.

*Gail Boyer Hayes, *Solar Access Law* (Cambridge, Massachusetts: Ballinger, 1979), pp. 106–108.

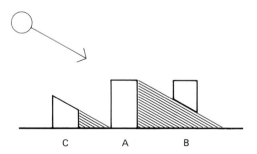

If the doctrine of prior appropriation were applied, this condition would not change. Consequently, if direct access to solar energy on building surfaces is an essential condition for development, if solar energy is the building's raison d'être, the envelope of buildable volume meeting that condition may have a top and no bottom. On the other hand, A cannot change B's condition in the future by building higher. For anyone who may be stymied by the image of a bottomless building, let me offer the alternative of differentiating function so that the lower portion of the building is designed to perform differently from the upper portion.

To continue the analogy, there is a somewhat different situation to the south (upstream). If A's prior appropriation of the sun is guaranteed by law, developer C, who comes along later, would have to accept the limitations of a building envelope with a bottom and no top. Unfortunately, I cannot offer to C the same option of differentiating function to fill in the missing portion of volume, because however this were done would deny A's access to the sun.

Obviously this is a limited example and does not consider what goes on in the world beyond the sites of A, B, and C. What is made clear is that the influence of existing buildings on their surroundings can be addressed in a way somewhat analogous to the settlement along a river covered by the doctrine of prior appropriation. If that doctrine were to be applied, it would probably find greatest use where there is existing settlement and where the exigencies of shadowing from existing buildings must somehow be responded to favorably by reducing uncertainty in a complex situation. People need to know where they stand. They may have to settle for less than total exposure to sunlight; but, where buildings exist, there may be no choice. On the other hand, to conclude that all is lost because there are situations where existing buildings shadow their surroundings is to give up on most urban development in the United States. The situation is really more hopeful than that.

Heretofore our urban development has been of rather low density; much of this is now being rebuilt at higher densities. Where rebuilding occurs, there is a chance to apply zoning regulations that require different performance for solar access.

There is an apparent suitability of prior appropriation where uncertain circumstances accompany existing cityscapes. The applications of prior appropriation may be especially promising where rebuilding is taking place.

But yet there may be benefit in the application of riparian-like doctrine to new development and to those situations where older buildings are being removed from large areas in the city. Under either circumstance, the complexities due to already-built form will not exist. Shadowing can either be avoided altogether or can be controlled by the designer.

Under such new-building conditions, the application of riparian-like doctrine could be accompanied by a three-dimensional approach to zoning that does not now exist. Each piece of property could be assured equal access under the law. The result would be an envelope of developable volume that would derive its size and shape from the size, shape, slope, and orientation of the property. In a conventional subdivision, where housing lots are relatively small

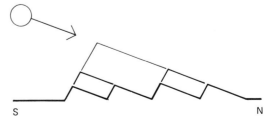

S   N

and repetitive, envelopes of buildable volume will be similarly small and repetitive.
There will not be much height variation,
but, in the hands of the skillful designer,
the envelopes will still offer broad latitude
and the possibility of new design types.

Under such circumstances of equal access, if
larger buildings are to be required to fulfill
community needs, larger land parcels will
have to be developed through some process
of land assemblage. Since all relationships
in such a progression are proportional, each
larger building will require an appropriately
larger assemblage of land. Hence, over
time, small envelopes could merge into
larger ones.

Where the uncertainties of existing development do not interfere, and where new
buildings are being arranged in completely
new combinations to form new communities, the riparian-like doctrine seems to hold
the greatest promise.

My point in describing these two analogies
in some detail is that different kinds of
users will undoubtedly require different
rules to govern solar allocation. As the
problem of solar access is confronted
around the country, different legal approaches will doubtless be tested.

Later in this book I will show examples of
urban design studies that extend the spirit
of these two doctrines through application
of the solar envelope. The first involves mid-
density housing where *equal access for all*
becomes the issue and where the spirit of
riparian doctrine is clearly at work. The second study is of commercial development on
several properties surrounded by existing
buildings. Here the question of *who got
there first* is an issue. And, finally, on the
third project we will see that aspects of
both doctrines combine to balance the requirements of neighbors.

Taken together, these three examples argue
strongly for the defense of local zoning.
Such local zoning is the legal foundation for
the rest of this work.

Solar Policy in the Context of Development

Implementing a policy of solar access requires not only a sufficient ethical and legal
foundation but also a strategy responsive to
existing patterns of land use and regulation. This section therefore examines traditional development patterns and controls,
and introduces the concepts of solar access
and orientation as new development
criteria.

The foregoing discussions of solar access
and its legal precedents have been concerned with the relationship of one parcel
of land to another. Policies have been described that control the development of
one property in order to protect the solar
access of a neighboring property.

In this section, the discussion of solar access is extended to include the design implications of orientation within a parcel of land as well as between parcels of land. In this way the planning and policy issues related to solar access are integrated. The decision to protect solar access by policy is complemented by understanding the variations in land use suggested by solar access.

If a property has access to the sun, it may then be developed in a way that is responsive to the sun. The site will exhibit certain characteristics based on the daily and seasonal migration of the sun that the designer may count on to provide sun and shade as people and activities need or desire it, rather than requiring them to adapt arbitrarily. Without assured solar access these design choices will, in most cases, be denied.

Over the years land use and zoning mechanisms have been formulated and applied without consideration of solar access or orientation as development criteria. The relationship of development to the sun is therefore random, as are the opportunities to use the sun beneficially.

Existing land use and zoning mechanisms may, however, be modified to accommodate solar access. These modifications are also discussed in the following pages.

Orientation as a Planning Criterion

Modern subdivisions have generally been planned without regard for solar access and orientation. We shadow our own land and our neighbor's house and land in ways that interfere with land use. The nature and extent of the interference varies with orientation and with the time of day and year.

A long north-south block accentuates daily variations of shadow impact and of land use. Winter morning shadows are in the front yards of the western row of houses and in the back yards of the eastern row. Afternoon shadows are in the back yards of the western row and in the front yards of those houses along the eastern edge of the block. Summer shadows act in a similar way on this block.

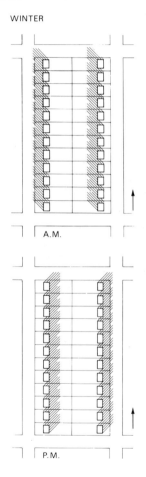

WINTER

A.M.

P.M.

The result can be a kind of daily migration of outdoor and indoor activities from east to west, depending on whether one seeks sunshine or shadow. The cycle repeats itself each morning to the front and each afternoon to the back, or perhaps the reverse, depending on how the house faces the street. Decisions about where to locate a sandbox, a child's swing, or where to get a suntan, will be influenced by such a cycle. Inside the house, the daily tempo will be reflected as first one end, then the other end of the house receives its share of morning or afternoon sunlight. These solar conditions can influence everyday living patterns.

Residents have a very different set of solar conditions if they live on a block that runs long in the east-west direction, and their behavior will vary accordingly. On this block, the winter shadows always stay to the north of the houses. In the morning, they are cast to the northwest; in the afternoon they are cast to the northeast. Instead of alternating between the front and back of the house on a daily tempo, the shadows will stay in the front yards of the northern row and the back yards of the southern row all day and all winter long.

DAILY MIGRATION

WINTER

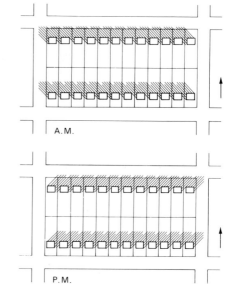

A.M.

P.M.

The long east-west development is subject to a seasonal tempo. Summer shadows, unlike winter shadows, are cast to the south of a house. Morning shadows are cast to the southwest and afternoon shadows to the southeast. Only at midday do they fall slightly to the north. The result of this shift in direction will be a seasonal migration of activities from north to south and back again.

The difference of tempo based on orientation raises many questions that fall under the general heading of "quality of life," and that affect land use at the scale of front, back, and side yards. Orientation influences the rhythms of light and heat, and therefore the way the built arrangements are going to perform.

Daily rhythm is accentuated in a long north-south block, seasonal rhythm in a long east-west block. Such basic differences are not usually taken into account by those responsible for subdivisions. Consequently, land use at that scale becomes an adaptive proposition in which people use their yards and the interiors of their houses as best they can.

Perhaps this behavior can be taken as evidence of variety; but the fact that the behavior is enforced, not freely chosen, raises several questions. First, can policies be developed that make the performance of a building and site more predictable in relation to the sun? Can arrangements be developed that allow people a more informed choice of behavior? And, finally, can designers develop strategies that draw on the correlation between orientation and rhythm in order to enhance the quality of life? These policy, development, and design questions can be addressed only when solar access is guaranteed.

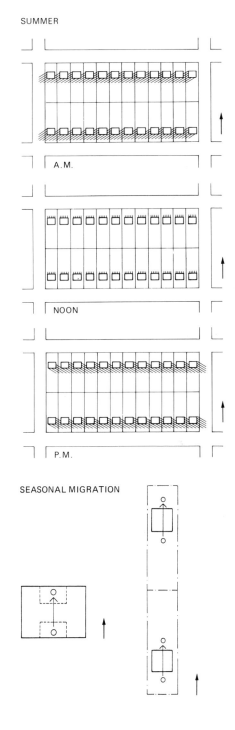

SUMMER

A.M.

NOON

P.M.

SEASONAL MIGRATION

The Jeffersonian Grid

The standard system of subdivision in the United States is, as I have noted, the Jeffersonian grid, that regular geometrizing of the land laid out on the cardinal points of the compass.

After the Louisiana Purchase, Jefferson realized that an effective way to secure the territory was to make sure that Americans settled the land. In order for that settlement to proceed in an orderly fashion, he needed to have a systematic way of allowing growth to occur with minimal complications. The answer seemed to be the establishment of a unit of settlement that was surveyed and laid out according to simple rules.

Congress provided Jefferson with a unit of land called a "township." Based on measures of latitude and longitude, the township was a square, six miles on each side.

Thirty-six square miles, however, turned out to be too large for frontier settlement. People did not rush to settle in great numbers, and when they settled, the groups tended to be smaller than was anticipated by the original township idea. Consequently, in order to meet the exigencies of the frontier, the township became subdivided into smaller units.

The first subdivision was the Agricultural Section. It was a unit measuring one mile by one mile, or 640 acres, and served originally as a single farm. But over time, even this size turned out to be larger than was sometimes necessary to support a single family, so that Congress was petitioned, over the years, to reduce the minimum size of the land parcel.

Each successive petitioning resulted in a smaller unit of land. Starting with the Agricultural Section, the first subdivision produced the Quarter Section, of 160 acres. Next there was one-half of a Quarter Section, containing 80 acres and measuring one-quarter mile by one-half mile. And finally there was the quarter of a Quarter Section, containing 40 acres and measuring one-quarter mile by one-quarter mile.

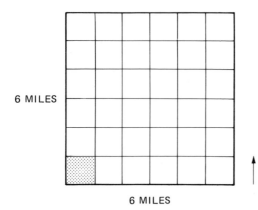

6 MILES

6 MILES

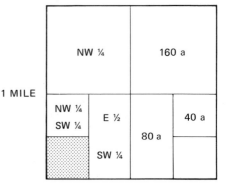

1 MILE

1 MILE

The agricultural section is subdivided into quarter-sections, half-quarter-sections, one-quarter-quarter-sections. Each designation contains directional identification, such as the northwest quarter (NW¼) of the southwest quarter-section (SW¼).

Here the processes of subdivision stopped for agricultural purposes, but not for settlement. If the smallest agricultural unit of one-quarter of a Quarter Section is further subdivided to produce first a twenty-acre section, then a ten-acre section, and finally a five-acre section, we see a unit of land that approximates the modern city block. By four quarterings of the original Agricultural Section, we are down to dimensions that recur with local variations in almost every American city west of the Appalachian Mountains.

The city block is further subdivided into parcels in a range of frontage dimensions, the most common of which is about 50 feet in a city such as Los Angeles. In depth, these lots average about 140 feet, providing an alley that runs longitudinally through the block. This process of subdivision so characterizes American urbanization that we refer to large planned unit developments as "subdivisions," and special sections of our zoning laws address the question of this subdividing of land for purposes of settlement.

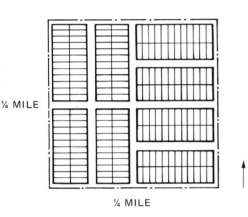

¼ MILE

¼ MILE

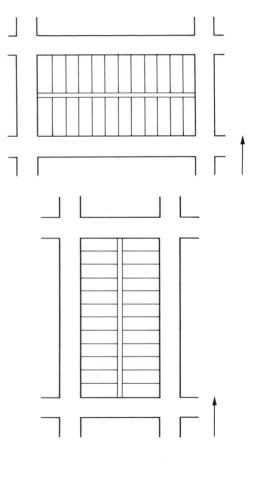

The five-acre parcel that we call a "city block" has been the unit of American urbanization. It measures 330 by 660 feet on its sides. When streets are laid out on the grid lines, the developable area inside measures somewhere around 300 by 600 feet. These blocks can generally be found in both orientations. Their long dimension is sometimes in the east-west direction, and sometimes in the north-south direction. Where other orientations are found, they likely relate to established roads or railroads and to land features. And more recently, subdivisions have been popularly laid out on other geometries, including curves, to produce interest and to slow traffic. However, the most common arrangement is that of the grid.

Orientation as a Development Criterion

Within our grid-like developments, the orientation of houses is toward the street rather than toward the sun. We think of the front of our houses as facing the street, and, therefore, the organization of the house tends to place major living spaces toward the front or toward the street, with service spaces on the back or away from the street. This arrangement is traditional in the United States, and, for the most part, it is an unquestioned tradition with considerable cultural inertia. Houses that are individually designed by architects often seem to break with this tradition, but the majority of speculative development follows this pattern of frontness and backness.

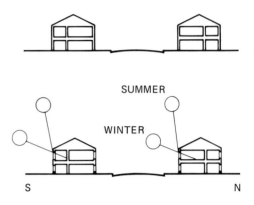

The difficulty with this arrangement occurs when orientation to the sun is considered. The sun irradiates the house in ways that sometimes contradict the formal relation to the street. When houses line an east-west running street, service spaces have the desirable south orientation on the southern row of houses, while living spaces have the desirable south orientation on the northern row of houses.

This inconsistency was resolved in the colonial towns of ancient Greece. Planners made orderly arrangements that took maximum advantage of the sun. Blocks that ran long in the east-west direction generally contained ten houses, five on each side. The houses varied in their size and in their configuration, but they were consistently built around a south-facing court. Consequently, while the house was always entered from the street, and in that sense had a street front, the house was also oriented to the sun and had a *sun front.*

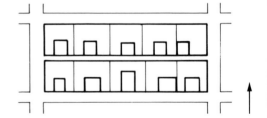

Whatever conflicts may have resulted from this two-fronted approach were resolved internally. Those houses that faced south on the street and south to the sun were entered through the court, while those houses that faced north to the street and south to the sun were entered through passageways that led from the street through the main body of the house and into the court, from which access was gained to all other spaces.

Similar resolutions of this problem of two-frontedness can be found in countries throughout the world. We may safely conclude, therefore, that our lack of resolution of the problem thus far in the United States does not bind us in the future.

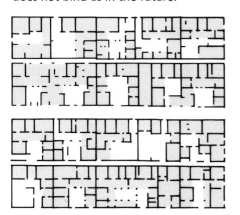

Based on a drawing by J. Walter Graham from plans by Donald N. Wilber in Excavations at Olynthus: The Hellenic House *by David M. Robinson and J. Walter Graham (Baltimore: Johns Hopkins University Press, 1938).*

Advantages of a Zoning Approach

There are two compelling advantages to assuring solar access through zoning rather than through other legal approaches.

First, zoning is a form of local governmental control that is necessarily sensitive to specific local conditions. Since the envelope for any land parcel is intimately based on surrounding conditions that exist or that may exist in the future, a local focus seems essential.

Second, solar zoning can be formulated as a relatively simple modification of present zoning precedences that govern building height and bulk. Both concepts are concerned with defining the limits of development by means of a regulating container or envelope. The solar envelope may even simplify setback and height restrictions that now complicate present zoning and render it insensitive to any but major differences in land use.

Although zoning has not considered solar orientation, it is based on a concept that can be adapted for solar access. Virtually all modern zoning uses an envelope to prescribe developable space. Conventionally, the envelope has vertical sides and derives from the ancient Latin maxim *cujus est solum ejus est usque ad coelum*: whose is the soil his it is to the sky.* The horizontal top of the envelope derives from restrictions set by local zoning ordinances.

*No lid on the ownership of airspace above a property was recognized until *United States* v. *Causby,* 328 U.S. 256 (1946). See Ball, "The Vertical Extent of Ownership in Land," *University of Pennsylvania Law Review,* vol. 76, (1928), p. 634.

Geometry of Zoning

The geometry of modern zoning derives from the grid and from setbacks within the grid. Depending on land use, setbacks may be required on all sides of a property. There can be front yard and back yard setbacks. Generally, as densities and land coverage increase, setbacks tend to disappear. For example, a land-use designation for detached single-family houses will require setbacks on all sides of the property, while land-use designations for higher-density housing and for commercial development may not specifically require setbacks. In every case, developable land is the area lying within the setback limits, so that the developable bulk rises from the setbacks.

The volume that rises from the developable base of the zoning envelope is generally rectilinear, derived from the grid-like framework used in most planning. If the set of imaginary boxes of developable volume comprising the zoning envelopes in a modern city could be seen, they would tend to stack themselves along our streets in some rough approximation of the buildings that will later fill them. Obviously, the larger those boxes, the more the potential buildings are likely to conflict with each other by shadowing.

Methods of Height Restriction

Modern zoning generally uses two methods of defining the height of the envelope of developable volume. The first establishes a fixed-height district. In such a zoning district, the envelope height is set in feet, numbers of floors, or both. In Los Angeles, limited-height districts vary with land use and fall in two categories: The first applies to housing and is limited to three stories or 45 feet; the second applies to higher-density housing or commercial development and is limited to six stories or 75 feet.

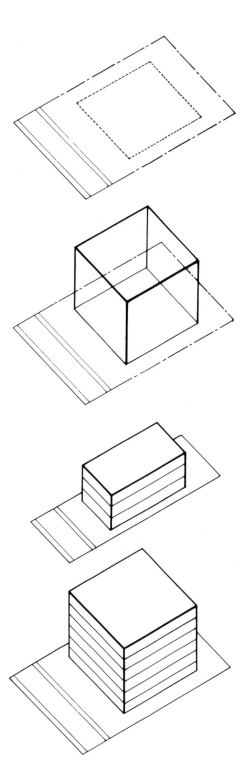

The correlation of a fixed-height limit with
land use rather than with site conditions
leads to difficulty when the land use is
abruptly changed. For example, when an
area of the city that has been detached single-family housing is rezoned, the height
and bulk of the envelope can change dramatically to produce a scale shift that is disruptive to neighborhoods. Small bungalows
can suddenly find 45-foot walls ten feet
from their windows. The result is not only
visually disruptive of the scale of a neighborhood, it is socially and economically disruptive as well.

A second, much more flexible application of
the envelope occurs in what are called unlimited-height districts. The term is somewhat misleading in suggesting no limit at
all. In fact, the limit is based on a ratio between developable land area and floor area
within the buildings on that land. This
floor-area ratio (FAR) allows considerable
flexibility for the developer to change the
building shape, providing he does not exceed the FAR. A FAR of 13, for example,
limits the square footage of the building to
thirteen times the developable square footage of the land within the setbacks. That
FAR may be achieved by covering the entire
developable site with a 13-story building. It
may also be attained by covering only half
the site and building twice as high, to 26
stories, or by covering only a quarter of the
site and building four times as high, to 52
stories. Obviously there are limits on this
progression, related to the technology of
construction, vertical access, and the economics of internal circulation and service;
but within those limits, the owner may have
design options that would be especially valuable in high-density commercial
development.

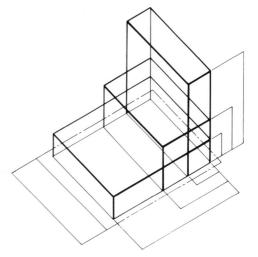

Zoning and Solar Orientation

As far as solar access is concerned, the difficulty with unrestricted-height zoning, especially as applied to high-density commercial land use, is that it does not control building orientation for its solar impact on either building surfaces or the surroundings. As the building gets higher, it becomes more slab-like, and the orientation of this slab determines its shadowing characteristics. A slab oriented broadside north and south will produce a shadow to the north much greater than a building oriented broadside east and west. This difference of orientation to the sun has not generally been taken as a factor in unlimited-height district development.

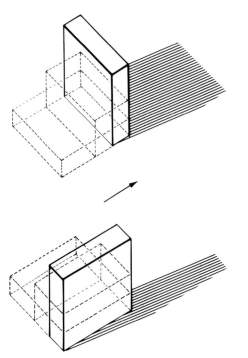

American zoning techniques have traditionally aimed at encouraging development. Consequently, there has been a correlation between land values and allowable FAR. Land values are usually a direct function of development opportunities, paying little heed to climate or solar considerations.

New values emphasizing energy conservation and the effective use of solar resources require a new kind of zoning envelope based on the geometry of the sun's path.

A solar envelope implies a change of spatial constraints from those of present-day zoning. The sun's path does not describe a rectangular form. Present zoning geometry is based on stacking boxes of fixed height on one another, determining the FAR. In a simple modular way, small boxes are used to make larger ones, almost always without reference to the surroundings.

Solar zoning borrows the envelope concept and recognizes the development imperative in our economy. The geometry of developable volume is simply shaped differently. Although it is not clear whether zoning can provide an absolute guarantee of solar access,* zoning at least provides that solar planning will be part of other land-use goals. A further legal guarantee may or may not be necessary. If needed, it could be provided by a solar recordation ordinance,† permit system,§ or some similar legal device.

A solar envelope must take into account the temporal variation of sunlight. Protecting only the south boundary of a site, for example, may forfeit winter rays that cross long

*See Dale Goble, "Siting ≠ Protection: A Note on Solar Access," *Solar Law Reporter,* vol. 2, no. 25 (1980), pp. 41–42.

†See, for example, the recordation ordinance proposed by Gail Boyer Hayes, *Solar Access Law* (Cambridge, Massachusetts: Ballinger, 1979, for the Environmental Law Institute), p. 148.

§See Goble, pp. 31–41.

east and west boundaries and summer rays that cross all boundaries, including those on the north.

Such an envelope could, and perhaps should, replace the accumulated setback regulations of most zoning with a simple prescription of space with certain performance characteristics over time. Whether the luminous and thermal properties of that volume are used immediately or not is up to the property owner. The right to use them should not be diminished or curtailed either now or in the future. This protects both the current and future owners.

Of course, equality of access to the sun does not assure equality of result. The solar envelope does not assure successful development and good design, but guaranteed solar access does assure opportunity.

Zoning for the Solar Envelope

As we shall see in more detail in the following chapter, the solar envelope is a set of volumetric limits that govern building on a particular site. Unlike present zoning envelopes, the solar envelope is modified by the sun's daily and seasonal movements. These similarities and differences are derived from the basic premises of the envelope concept.

The solar envelope is a construct of space and time based on two premises. First, it assures solar access to the property *surrounding* a given site. The envelope accomplishes this by limiting on-site building heights, thus avoiding the casting of unacceptable shadows. The issue may not arise for relatively small constructions, but market pressures will usually force the largest practical volume. This brings us to the second premise.

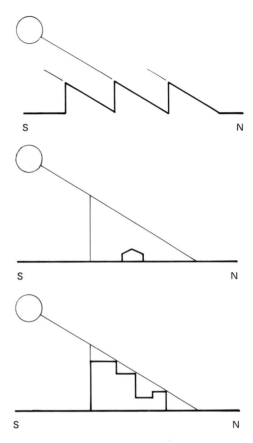

The solar envelope provides the largest developable volume within time constraints. The envelope accomplishes this by defining the largest container of space that would not cast shadows off-site at specified times of the day. We can call these specified times of day the *cutoff times.*

The cutoff times affect development potential. The longer the daily period of solar access, the smaller the developable volume under the envelope. Asymmetrical cutoff times (either side of noon) will affect the form of the envelope asymmetrically. In addition, specified seasons for solar access will affect development potential. Because the winter sun is low in the sky, a winter envelope will generally contain less volume than a summer envelope, given the same latitude and daily cutoff times.

The premise of conventional zoning favors the largest practical volume on a land parcel with usually no consideration of solar access. The solar envelope regulates the shape of that volume. The resulting question is critical. Does the solar envelope reduce the developable volume to the point of overly constraining development and limiting design options? The question must be approached with the understanding that while the envelope is a regulatory device, its limits can be set to balance solar access and development needs. As we shall see in chapter 10, dealing with urban applications, time constraints and edge conditions are controllable and can respond to local requirements of climate, land use, and economics.

Old and New Limits

The envelope's dual function of providing both solar access and the largest developable volume provides a link with the past and a view to the future. The solar envelope accomplishes this by combining new with old limits when it is applied as a zoning tool. The old limits are, as they have always been, related to the site's geometry.

The new limits are based in time—the duration of solar access. The combination produces envelopes of developable volume that have both vertical and sloping faces. Setbacks do not occur arbitrarily, but result from the meeting of rectangular construction with sloping construction limits.

Certain applications of the solar envelope would very likely combine old zoning with new solar limits. This combination would seem most likely to occur where rebuilding or new building takes place in existing development.

Old limits on development space have already been described as deriving from ancient doctrine. These limits are vertical and separate public from private land or one private land parcel from another.

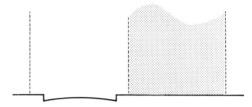

While ownership includes all space to vertical limits at land parcel boundaries, buildable space is much more precisely limited in height. To provide for light and access, buildable limits have generally been set back from ownership limits. The result is generally a rectangular container with traditional vertical and horizontal faces.

The new solar limits that derive from the sun's movement are more likely to be sloping, because they are related to the sun's geometry.

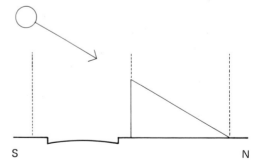

S   N

Where the rays of the sun pass through the vertical limits defining a land parcel, the resulting container or envelope of volume would have both vertical and sloping limits. The vertical limits would derive from older practices for defining land ownership, while the new sloping limits would relate to the sun's altitude angles at those times of day when unacceptable shadows would be cast upon the neighbor. Building below the sloping limit could occur without casting shadows, while building above the sloping limits would shadow the neighbor.

Setbacks that have been used in our culture to gain light and access to the building might occur automatically within such an envelope. The intersection between normal story heights and a sloping envelope would produce terrace-like arrangements that automatically step back from land boundaries. In other words, setbacks would occur automatically and would not have to be set or modified by some relatively arbitrary practice.

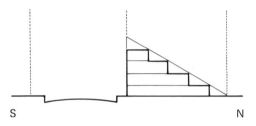

The solar envelope can be applied as a simple prescription of volume in a variety of climatic and development conditions. The prescription would be especially straightforward in new subdivisions, because there are no existing buildings to interfere and cast shadows. Assurance of solar access during specified times of the day could be easily accomplished by an envelope that touches ground or some vertical reference, such as a privacy fence, along the perimeter of each land parcel.

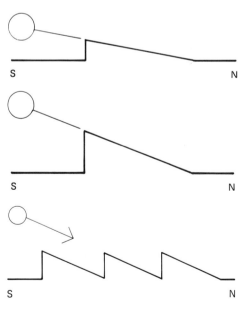

The application of solar envelopes to existing development would be more difficult
but not impossible, especially with low- to
medium-density development. In older
parts of a city as buildings become obsolete
and as land use changes, the normal processes of land assemblage that accompany
change would make the application of solar
zoning quite easy. A variety of existing
building conditions at the property line may
require alternatives to meet edge conditions, but the principle of shaping an envelope in relation to the sun's movement
would still hold true.

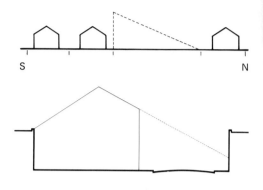

Modes of Energy Conversion

The energy-conversion requirements for solar access can be conveniently categorized
under three modes of energy conversion.
Each distinguishes interrelationships among
development potential, solar access, energy
conversion, and land use.

The first mode, termed *roof-top conversion,*
characterizes solar access to only the roofs
of buildings. Consequently the solar envelope would provide the maximum development potential on any given set of sites but
the minimum potential for energy conversion per unit of built volume. Regulation
pertaining to the envelope would only need
to distinguish between tall buildings that
cast large shadows and small buildings that
don't. The sun's direct radiant energy would
be assured only to building roofs, and shadowing on the outside walls would not be
taken into account. If light were also a desired component of solar irradiation, however, the shadowing might imply a need for
different uses between the upper and lower
floors of a building.

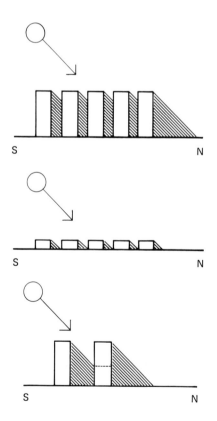

Use of the roof-top conversion approach
obviously has the greatest applicability in
high-density urban areas and would provide
the greatest potential for commercial development. (Single-family residences would

reverse the relationship between development potential and energy conversion; but
such residences are not included in the present study, which is confined to urban applications of the solar envelope concept.)* In
many high-density commercial districts,
roof-top access might well be sufficient to
allow for the use of flat-plate solar energy
collectors in either new or existing structures. But such limited access would not
provide for the broader options of using
the whole building for energy conversion.

The second approach to solar energy conversion does involve the whole building.
Every building is an energy converter by virtue of the specific heat and density of its
materials. Those material properties can be
organized to receive radiant energy as heat,
to be stored and given up over an appropriate period and at a useful rate. The potential for responding to daylighting needs
also increases in this second approach,
which is termed the *whole-building conversion* mode. If this attitude toward energy
conversion were to be followed, differences
in building form must be recognized in generating solar envelopes and in regulating
solar access. For example, small buildings
sited to the south of large buildings would
allow closer packing than the other way
around. Large buildings would have to be
spaced farther apart than smaller ones. The
certainty the designer or developer would
have in planning uses for the roof would, of
course, be extended to the whole building,
or at least to those portions dependent on
the sun for irradiation.

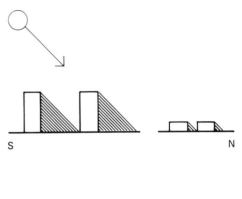

---

*For an overview of solar access to single-family
residences, see Martin Jaffe and Duncan Erley,
*Protecting Solar Access for Residential Develop-
ment* (U.S. Dept. of Housing and Urban Development in cooperation with the Dept. of Energy,
n.d.)

The potential building volume attainable from this approach is less than for roof-top conversion, but the potential uses of solar energy are increased. The whole building's shape and structure could be adapted to conditions of light and heat for improved quality of life. This approach is probably most applicable to mid-density commercial and residential development.

The third approach would allow for *whole-site conversion* and therefore requires a guarantee of solar access to the ground surface of adjacent sites. This approach is the one that would provide the greatest potential for energy conversion and probably the least volume for development. The premise of this approach is that all possible users of solar energy—the ground itself, plants, insects, animals, people, as well as buildings—would be guaranteed direct radiant solar energy.

Under this most inclusive approach, solar envelopes would tend to differentiate themselves according to difference of land parcel size. This would result from providing access to the land itself. In general, larger land parcels could be used for larger buildings because the envelopes would be larger.

In cases where more than one building is to be placed on a single site, as in a planned unit development, the proportional relationship between any single building and its immediate surrounds will result in complex sets of buildings in which size, shape, and even the sequence of development might need to be regulated. For example, as the volume of a solar envelope increases, the

potential for deep space increases, with consequences for energy conversion and environmental quality. This kind of situation raises the issue of intervention by public policy, perhaps in the form of regulation encouraging small-to-moderate-size sites. More probably, however, shadowing within a site and the access of its occupants to the sun will be determined by the designer and developer, both of whom would seem to bear some moral responsibility to value solar access within a project that is regulated overall by a public policy of solar access to surrounding properties.

The singular advantage of this whole-site approach lies in the generous number of design options that it provides for improving the quality of life, making it especially appropriate to housing in the low- to mid-density range.

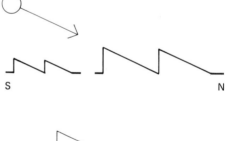

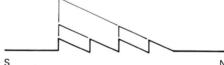

Implications for Development

The development potential of a solar envelope can be calculated much as a conventional FAR: The sum of plan areas at floor-
height intervals, divided by the area of
developable land under the envelope. This
measure, more commonly applied to commercial than to residential development,
can prove deceptive in some cases. For example, when a solar envelope is small, the
FAR will appear less than it is; this reflects
the relationship between the vertical increment and the low envelope height. In practice, however, a roof may be sloped to take
advantage of the lower space toward the
envelope's edge, making the workable floor
area larger than the theoretical one.

The FAR may also be deceptive in a different way when the envelope gets quite
large. As the envelope's volume increases,
ways must be devised to use the inside
space efficiently. Perimeter volume may
have to be cut away systematically, or
courtyards may be introduced. In either
case, volume is lost and the workable floor
area is reduced below that derived from the
FAR. Even with such difficulties, the FAR,
thus defined, is a generally useful description of the relative potential for
development.

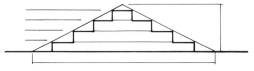

Significant variations in development potential are related to the orientation as well
as to the size of a property. The relation between envelope ridge height and orientation has already been discussed. When
applied to FAR, the impact of orientation
can be significant.

Consider an envelope with a plan ratio of
1:2 oriented with its ridge running north-
south. If the plan is shifted 90°, that is, to an
east-west orientation, the ridge height will
increase by 30 to 40 percent. If the original
envelope could accommodate three stories,
the new one could accommodate four. This
difference in orientation can provide a significantly increased development potential
on larger land parcels.

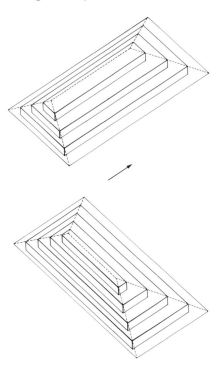

Changing the size of a land parcel without changing its proportions and orientation can also have a significant effect on development potential. This is a result of the geometric relationship between linear, plane, and volume measures; a doubling of plan dimensions will square the land area and cube the envelope volume. Since the FAR depends upon the envelope volume, doubling the site's edge dimensions can theoretically cube the potential for development.

If solar zoning is to be generally accepted, its proponents must recognize the realities of land economics in providing a fair return to a developer. This means that the relationship between what is commonly built in practice, what could be built under standard zoning, and, finally, what might be built under solar zoning, should not substantially disagree. What constitutes substantial disagreement is obviously a matter of interpretation.

A comparison of three sets of FARs on a given land parcel can reveal some interesting facts. The following example is based on a random selection of real buildings representing most of the residential and commercial land-use classifications listed in the zoning regulation. Only buildings less than ten years old are included to avoid obsolete zoning. Comparisons are made, first, for the actual building on the site; second, for what might have been built under present zoning in that district; and, finally, for what could be built under the most stringent solar zoning conditions, where the envelope slopes right down to touch the ground. A word of warning should be inserted here that the samples are small, were taken only in Los Angeles, and that further sampling is necessary. But with that said, the results show some interesting relationships for further study.

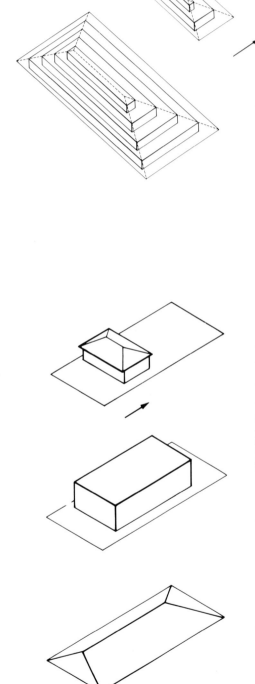

In neighborhoods of both one-family and two-family dwellings, potential floor areas within the envelope are less than what was zoned but, surprisingly, in most cases more than what was actually built.

This situation changes where development pressure increases. In the older neighborhoods of Los Angeles, detached single-family housing is being replaced by multifamily dwellings, especially three-story apartments and condominiums. Here the average built floor areas actually exceed what was zoned.

How the developers managed to exceed zoning is an interesting question in itself, but economics is obviously a strong motivating factor. If solar zoning is to be practical under such high-pressure conditions, ways must be found to increase envelope volume, while providing adequate solar access.

These increases may be achieved in three ways: land parcels larger than the 50-to-100-foot frontages now being used can be assembled; larger land parcels provide larger volumes within the solar envelope.

A second way to increase volume is by starting the solar envelope above the ground, especially where fences are commonly used. Or one might employ other contextual criteria, such as allowing the envelope to cross the street. An extension of this idea in built-up areas might allow the shadowing of adjacent firewalls or even the partial shadowing of window walls. The greatest benefit to development would probably be gained if the solar envelope were extended over adjacent land parcels, so that different land owners would share a wall and each would gain volume.

The third way to increase volume is by reducing the period of solar access. This would add height and some volume to the envelope. Beyond a certain point, of course, this strategy defeats our initial purpose. In addition, the resulting high and pointed envelopes may be less useful, especially for commercial development, than are flatter shapes.

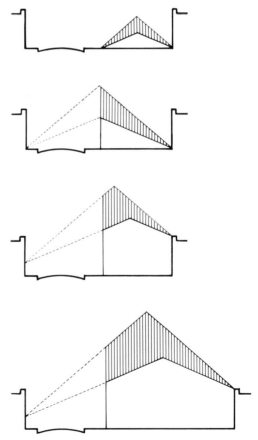

Before leaving the Los Angeles example, I would like to comment on an interesting and somewhat surprising fact about commercial development in that city. Tabulations from randomly selected buildings (including some as small as 15,000 sq. ft. and ranging to others as large as 600,000 sq. ft.) generally parallel those for low-density housing. The average floor area within the solar envelope is less than what was zoned, but considerably more than what was built. This was true across the entire size range.

The excessive surface and above-grade parking common to Los Angeles probably account for the unexpected findings for commercial development. The bad news is that there are a lot of cars. The good news is that such low-density development in cities throughout the country may be more appropriate to future solar zoning, although overall energy tradeoffs must be considered. It should also be noted that since the sample figures were taken, Los Angeles has rolled back its downtown FAR from 13 to 6, a hopeful sign for solar zoning and for the general quality of the city.

3   *Solar Envelope*

As the solar envelope describes the volumetric limits of building that will not shadow surroundings at specified times, it must be constructed from data based on the sun's movement (time) relative to the location and geometry of a site (space). The solar envelope is thus a constructed synthesis of time and space.

The time data appear as specific periods of solar access related to climate and land use. These time data translate into a volumetric description of the solar envelope. Specifically, the daily and seasonal paths of the sun as it appears to move across the sky describe the east, west, north, and south limits for development within a solar envelope.

The space data appear as the specifics of a site, or the area to be included within a solar envelope. The data relate to the latitude, size, shape, slope, and orientation of a given site.

The synthesis of time and space data can best be perceived with the help of a heliodon, which can be used to simulate the dynamic relationship synthesized by the solar envelope. By putting planes on a model site as a basis for analysis, the limits of development may be tested. When the shadows extend beyond the selected perimeter conditions at the prescribed cutoff times, the height and therefore the developable volume must be reduced. If the shadows do not reach the boundaries, more height and volume may be added. The heliodon thus provides a dynamic perception of building and urban design in time and space.

This chapter describes the temporal and spatial concepts underlying the solar envelope, and it may be useful to visualize their simulation on a heliodon. Later, in chapter 4, an example of mathematical simulation will be shown.

The idea of the solar envelope moves beyond concepts of conventional zoning because the latter traditionally delimit space in static terms. But the space within the solar envelope, and hence the implications for design and development, is defined dynamically by the rhythms of solar movement at daily and seasonal intervals.

The use of time as a determinant of space carries with it a whole set of questions that have not been raised since we were an agricultural people concerned with the sun as source of food and life. For the farmer, a response to the rhythm of the sun is essential. The orientation of a sloping field, for example, must be reckoned with if the crop is to survive and be plentiful. How the field performs is related to its time-space exposure.

Today, these responses to time and space are again critical to development in order to take full advantage of the sun as a resource. How we want our land and buildings to perform requires that we add time to our definition of urban space.

Time

The time data for constructing a solar envelope derive from the perceived movement of the sun from one celestial region to another. This movement is defined by a daily path, from east in the morning to west in the afternoon, and by a seasonal path, from south in the winter to north in the summer. These apparent solar migrations by day and season describe the boundaries of the solar envelope and therefore the limits of development within.

Solar Path by Day and Season

The relationship between the paths of the sun and the boundaries of the solar envelope can be understood easily by plotting the sun's path by coordinates. The sun's path over a site is measured in angles of azimuth, or bearing angles, measured clockwise from true north. It is convenient to presume that all solar phenomena occur on the surface of a hemisphere. The great circle forming the base of the hemisphere represents the horizon. The center of the circle represents that point on the earth that concerns us; the center lies at the intersection of two normal lines running north-south and east-west. In this construction, the sun moves in circular paths on the surface of the hemisphere.

In summer, the sun rises to the north of east. As the morning progresses, its altitude angle (taken from the center of the circle) increases. At noon, the sun appears at the greatest altitude angle and its furthest position south for the day. Then, as afternoon progresses, the sun drops along its circular path to disappear on the western horizon, north of west. During this daily migration, the sun's rays appear to define a conical shape, opening to the north.

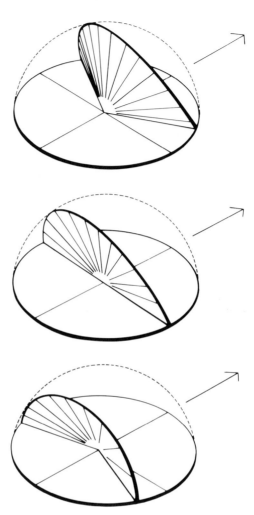

At the fall and spring equinoxes, sunrise occurs due east. The sun's rays then strike the circle's center from a path that takes the sun from due east to due west. At equinoctial noon, the sun's altitude angle is much less than in summer. The daily accumulation of the sun's rays appears to define a plane. For sites (center of the circle) north of the equator, this plane is tilted to the south.

In the winter season the sun rises south of east. At noon its rays reach the center of the circle from the smallest altitude angle of the year. And from there it progresses to sunset along the southwestern edge of the circle. The sun's rays now define a conical shape opening, cave-like, to the south.

The foregoing description of apparent solar motion is easy to fix in the mind because it is based on our perception that the sun moves and we stay still. Though it is contrary to what astronomers tell us, this geocentric view of the sun's path is the one best suited to our design purposes.

Daily Limits

The apparent migration of the sun from east to west at daily intervals describes the east and west boundaries of the solar envelope. If we put a flag in the center of our circle, we can start to make use of these east-west boundaries.

First, we need to define the useful hours of solar access, or the hours during which we want to avoid casting shadows on adjacent land. This issue of useful solar access will be discussed more fully in a following section, but understanding the concept is helpful here in describing a solar envelope for a given piece of land.

In the morning hours, the shadows from the flag will be cast to the west; in the afternoon hours, the shadows will be cast to the east. The upper limits of developable volume slope down from the top of the flag to intersect a western boundary in the morning; they slope down to the east in the afternoon.

In order to define the upper limits of developable volume lying between parallel east and west boundaries, it is necessary to use a plane that casts shadows in both directions. Morning shadows cast from the top edge of the vertical plane then intersect the western edge of the property, while afternoon shadows cast from the top of the plane intersect the eastern boundary. The combination of morning and afternoon limits results in an enclosure that resembles a tent, open at the north and south ends.

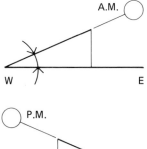

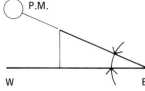

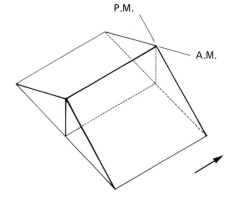

Yearly Limits

The yearly, or seasonal, migration of the sun describes the north and south boundaries of the envelope. The winter sun casts shadows to the north of the flag in the center of the circle. The summer sun, higher in the sky and more northward in its path, casts shadows to the south at certain times of day. For example, in Los Angeles, at 34° north latitude, summer shadows are cast south before 9 A.M. and after 3 P.M. (Between 9 A.M. and 3 P.M., shadows are cast north from the flag.)

The winter shadows, therefore, determine the north limits of the envelope; the summer shadows determine the south limits of the envelope. The north face of the envelope is more gently sloped than the south face because it is determined by winter when the sun is lower in the sky. The combination of summer and winter faces on a rectilinear property is again a tent-like structure, this time open at the east and west ends.

Integration of Daily and Yearly Limits

The combined effect of daily and seasonal migrations of the sun would result in shadows that define sloping limits to all the boundaries of a rectilinear site. The combined effect of those limits would be a solar envelope enclosed on all four sides.

The shape of the envelope is defined by the rhythms of the sun's movements and by the orientation of the site. Using the specified time and latitude of these studies, the daily (north-south) ridge of the envelope intersects the seasonal (east-west) ridge. The resulting envelope is pyramidal if the site is relatively square. The vertex lies halfway between the east and west boundaries of the base, but closer to the south boundary than to the north boundary of the site. The

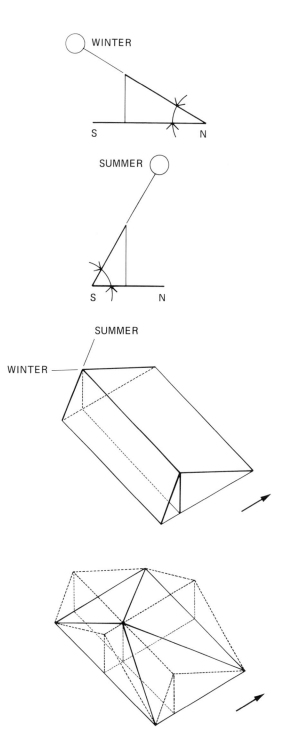

daily path of the sun, therefore, has a symmetrical effect on the geometry of the envelope; the seasonal path has an asymmetrical effect.

If vertical planes are passed through each edge of the triangular faces of the pyramid, they will define ridges from the vertex to each corner of the base.

This method of representing the upper limits of developable volume is a good description of how the movement of the sun can delineate space. It has the advantage of simplicity and clarity and provides images useful for further understanding.

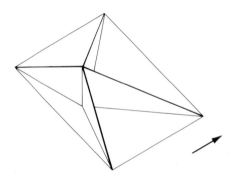

Periods of Useful Insolation

The functional time period for a solar envelope must be specified in response to a clear purpose. Time periods seem easier to specify for energy purposes than for quality of life. As society increasingly values solar access as a right, however, we may find that our purposes for solar access are more clearly qualitative.

This discussion relates useful periods of solar access to energy, which requires definition of the term "useful" in relation to the technology of energy conversion and to the movement of the sun.

Consider first that energy technology is rapidly changing. We are more knowledgeable about passive design strategies every day. And the present state of the art for heating water and air with flat-plate collectors and concentrating collectors may dramatically change. Manufacturing innovations may allow the economical production of photovoltaic cells that convert sunlight directly into electricity. Or perhaps there is a chemical process that is less well known but allows the collection, conversion, and storage of energy in ways that may quickly improve the state of the art and significantly reduce the duration of access essential for useful conversion. As things now stand, a minimum period of about six hours a day is considered practical.

Our ideas about energy technology may also respond to changing perceptions of natural resources and their value. Such concepts as edible landscaping, home gardening for food production, and better understanding of such phenomena as photosynthesis as an energy source may alter our current definitions of solar utilization. These concepts of energy, which are tied to the land, argue for a broader concern with solar access than buildings alone.

However we may wish to use the sun, certain principles of solar radiation must be understood. Consider that the sun's energy is not equally distributed throughout the day and year, because of atmospheric attenuation. Everyone has had the experience of receiving reduced heat and light from the rising and setting sun. The first red glow of sunrise is usually a promise of heat that is not fulfilled until later in the day. This is because the sunlight penetrates less atmosphere as the sun rises toward the zenith.

At sunrise and sunset, the rays of light are tangent to the earth at the site. Consequently, they pass through so much atmosphere that one may safely stare directly into them. But later in the day, don't try it. A brilliant glare replaces the soft red glow. Even a short sighting can make your eyes water. Longer exposure may permanently damage the eye.

This perceived difference in the amount of energy that gets through the atmosphere can be approximated by the sine of the sun's altitude α. At sunrise, $\sin \alpha = \sin 0° = 0.0$. If the sine function is used as a multiplier of the maximum possible irradiation, the product is then 0 at sunrise and sunset. As the sun rises overhead, the altitude angle approaches 90°, as $\sin \alpha = \sin 90° = 1.0$. Used as a multiplier, the received energy would be closer to 100 percent of the maximum possible.

Assuming that the minimum duration of access is about six hours for useful energy conversion, access would be required from 9 A.M. to 3 P.M. each day of the year. The hours before and after are less useful for energy conversion and are therefore excluded from periods of assured solar access.

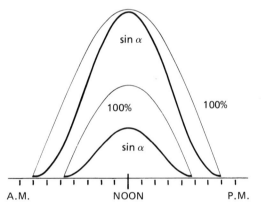

sin α

100%   100%

sin α

A.M.   NOON   P.M.

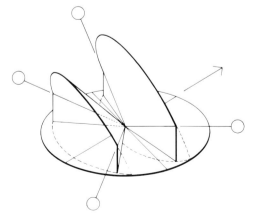

On the other hand, the sun's altitude angle at 9 A.M. in the summer is greater than during the same time in winter. Only 52 percent of the sun's energy is available at noon on a winter day (sin 31.5° = 0.52) compared with 98 percent of the sun's energy at noon on a summer day (sin 78.5° = 0.98).

If access were to be determined by some fixed percentage of available energy, cutoff times would change over the course of the year. Those hours when less useful amounts of energy can penetrate the atmosphere would be excluded from periods of assured access. For example, if the desired energy level were 30 percent of maximum available energy at 34 N, the sun would have to rise 17.46° above the horizon on any day of the year. When the sun passed below that angle in the afternoon, we might also be willing to give up access. The times of the day that correspond to $\alpha = 17.46°$ would then limit the duration of access. For Los Angeles, those times are 6:24 A.M. and 5:36 P.M. in summer and 8:54 A.M. and 3:06 P.M. in winter.

It is again important to note that useful amounts of energy are available for more hours of the summer than the winter day. If we define "useful" to be 40 percent of maximum available solar energy instead of 30 percent, we reduce the period of assured access by about 50 minutes in summer. But we reduce it by about twice that amount in winter, or about 110 minutes.

Higher irradiation levels can be achieved at the start and finish of the period, but the period for each day will be shorter. This is the result of the different rates at which the seasonal curves of the solar path rise and fall. If, for example, the useful amount of energy were defined as 20 percent of maximum available solar energy, the period of access would be longer.

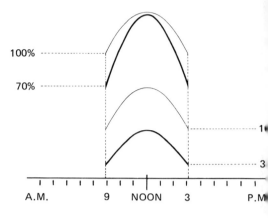

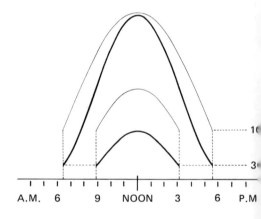

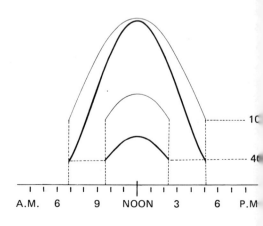

The question of whether to set duration of access by energy levels or by hours of access is very much open to debate. It may finally be settled in different ways in different places. Measuring the percentage of maximum solar energy, however, does provide a more rigorous and precise basis for setting cutoff times.

It is conceivable that some seasons may require higher percentages than others. If only 30 percent is required at cutoff in summer and 40 percent in winter, the period of critical solar access will be much greater in summer than in winter.

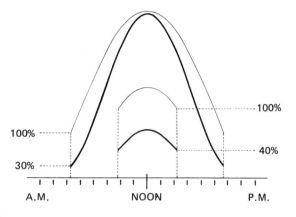

If higher percentages are required for morning cutoff than for the afternoon, the period will start later in the morning and end later in the afternoon.

The idea that cutoff times may vary with season and time of day is intriguing because it extends the purpose of solar access to include the possibility of mitigating daily and seasonal variation by varying the duration of solar access. For example, lengthening the duration of winter access while shortening the duration of summer access may act to mitigate the seasonal effect of thermal variation. Similarly, increasing the duration of morning access while decreasing the duration of afternoon access may act to mitigate daily thermal variation. It may also overcome some of the adverse effects of high ambient air temperatures during the afternoon, especially during the summer season.

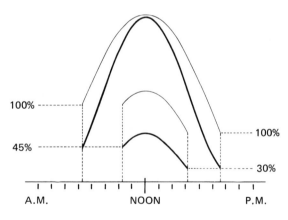

Varying cutoff times to mitigate natural variation implies modes of location, form, and energy conversion beyond that provided by present-day solar collectors. It includes the passive-design and thermal-conversion properties of whole buildings and even entire sites. And it suggests that buildings may be sited purposely to shadow one another, as well as to provide exposure to the sun.

Still another variable that will be discussed later is the inclusion of landscaping elements as energy design strategies. In this case, the leafing patterns of trees, which vary seasonally with deciduous trees, and varying densities and heights of growth may work in combination with the solar envelope to mitigate natural variation.

Residential and Commercial Applications

Dissimilar functions suggest different periods of solar access. Housing seems to lead the list of functions requiring access to the sun, which may relate to perceived as well as actual need. People behave differently when they are at home. Their attitudes about where they live, opposed to where they shop or work, are more proprietary and they exercise more control. Their perceived and actual rights are defended more vociferously where they live. This is true regardless of the actual time spent at home.

Shopping and working, at least in our culture, are perceived to be independent of the outside world. Consequently, our sense of the sun's importance to these pursuits is less well developed.

The greater value of solar access for housing suggests the possibility of vertical differentiation in mixed-use development. For example, within the pyramidal shape of a solar envelope, a greater duration of solar access can be attained toward the top. This fact, in combination with other design criteria for good housing, may be used to distinguish function.

HOUSING

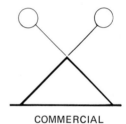

COMMERCIAL

MIXED—USE DEVELOPMENT

Housing can be zoned in the upper regions of the envelope in urban areas where land is at a premium, while commercial functions occupy those regions farther down. Of course, this arrangement assumes a certain notion about housing and commerce and their relationship to each other. Such notions may vary regionally, but in instances where they are acceptable, they form a basis for interesting prototypes.

A counterargument is that many residences are unoccupied during daylight hours, while work, recreation, commercial, and institutional spaces are occupied mostly during that time. This assumes a different notion about housing that may, under certain conditions, require regions of the solar envelope to be carefully planned three-dimensionally for mixed-use access to the sun. This is a particularly useful concept when the envelope is of urban-design scale.

The consideration of useful solar access, particularly at urban scale, must also be sensitive to surrounding development. The land uses surrounding a site, the type of buildings, and the nature of human activities and desires obviously affect decisions about optimum periods and uses of solar energy.

Cutoff Times and Envelope Shape

Once useful periods of solar access are defined, it is important to consider their effect on the geometry of the solar envelope. An obvious and somewhat frustrating fact about solar envelopes is that the longer the period of solar access, the more volumetrically constrained the envelope. More simply put, less time means more volume; more time means less volume. This, of course, is because the sun's angle defines the slopes of the envelope. Early morning and late afternoon sun angles are relatively low, while midday angles are steeper, at all seasons of the year. Hence, on a daily basis,

progressively increasing the hours of solar access will set cutoff times that provide progressively less and less building volume under the envelope.

Determining exactly what cutoff times might be used, then, will depend not only on desired insolation but also on how much building volume is required to accommodate development needs. Some comparisons are useful to clarify this inverse space-time relationship, which is unique to the solar envelope.

Suppose, for example, that six hours of access were needed, and that the requisite
cutoff times were kept symmetrical so that
sunlight was assured between 9 A.M. and
3 P.M., the six hours of solar access that contain most of the useful insolation of the
day. The resulting envelope will be defined
and the developable space regulated by the
sun's rays as they strike the site from the
east in the morning and from the west in
the afternoon.

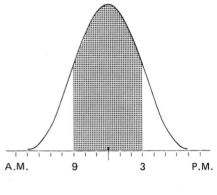

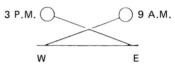

If a shorter period of solar access sufficed,
say from 10 A.M. to 2 P.M., the area under
the insolation curve defines less total energy than did the six-hour period. But, because the period of access starts later in the
morning and ends earlier in the afternoon,
the sun's rays will strike the site from higher
in the sky at the cutoff times. The resulting
envelope consequently will contain more
volume. The less the duration of solar access, the more space provided by the
envelope.

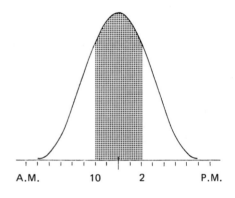

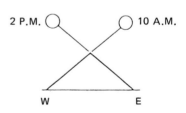

When the period of assured solar access is asymmetrical around noon, the solar envelope will have unequal slopes on the east and west. For example, if the period were taken from 9 A.M. to 2 P.M., the envelope would be steeper on the east because the sun is higher at 2 P.M. Just the reverse is true if the same duration of access is shifted to extend from 10 A.M. to 3 P.M. To keep this relationship clear may require the reminder that it is the morning sun that defines the envelope's western limits; the afternoon sun defines its eastern limits.

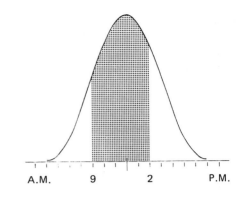

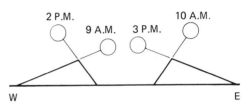

There is also a seasonal counterpart of the relationship between the duration of solar access and volume under the envelope. This is also an inverse time-space relationship. The larger the number of cold months of a year for which solar access is provided, the smaller the volume of the envelope. For example, if access were required for a full twelve months of the year, the envelope would contain less volume than if access were required for only six months, say from spring equinox through summer to fall equinox. This results from the much lower angles of the sun's rays in winter than at the equinox.

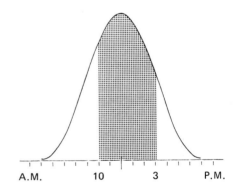

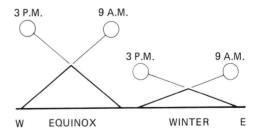

When a site's shape and orientation are known, the impact of cutoff times upon the envelope's geometry can be determined. Take the example of a rectangular site oriented long in the north-south direction.

Winter cutoff times will set the envelope's northern boundaries, with morning periods setting the northwest and afternoon periods setting the northeast limits of the envelope. Summer cutoff times set the southern boundaries. Morning hours set the southwest and afternoon hours the southeast boundaries.

There is no guarantee that cutoff times selected for purposes of energy conversion and quality of life will necessarily produce simple envelope shapes. The long north-south ridge of the preceding example may occur at one elevation if set at the south end of the envelope and a different elevation if set at the north. In other words, the two ridges would not coincide, in which case the lower ridge would necessarily control. A more complete discussion of this principle of generation follows in chapter 4.

In general, it is more convenient to set cutoff times that produce simple envelope shapes. The convention I have adopted here for showing all limits of an envelope appears in plan view as a kind of hip roof with times designated on their appropriate limits.

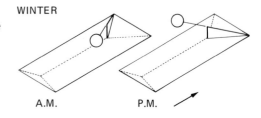

WINTER

A.M.　　　　　P.M.

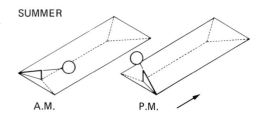

SUMMER

A.M.　　　　　P.M.

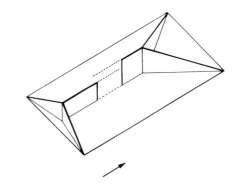

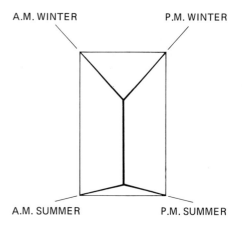

A.M. WINTER　　　　　P.M. WINTER

A.M. SUMMER　　　　　P.M. SUMMER

Space

In addition to the temporal constraints derived from daily and seasonal movements of the sun, there are five generalized spatial constraints delimiting the solar envelope. They are the site's latitude, size, shape, slope, and orientation.

Latitude

Latitude affects the height, and therefore the volume, of a given solar envelope for a site of a given size and shape. If the cutoff times are held constant, the envelope height decreases as the latitude increases, primarily because of the critical effect of winter sun on the envelope's north slope. Consequently, the volume of a solar envelope increases with proximity to the equator; the volume decreases toward the north and south poles.

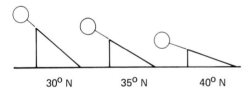

| 30° N | 35° N | 40° N |

In cold areas of the United States, where the volume of the solar envelope is decreased by latitude, greater design emphasis on east and west exposures offers potential compensation. Parcels with a long north-south orientation would facilitate this approach.

Size

Sites of different size but similar proportions will have solar envelopes of different size but similar proportions, given the same time constraints.

Doubling the edge of a site will thus double the envelope height. Other things being equal, sites with the long dimension running north-south will all have envelopes with corresponding faces proportional. The ridges that run north-south will vary in length as the length of the sites vary. A doubling of plan dimensions will produce a doubling of ridge length.

Increasing the size of the envelope will also decrease its surface-to-volume ratio, with resulting design implications for building development and energy performance within.

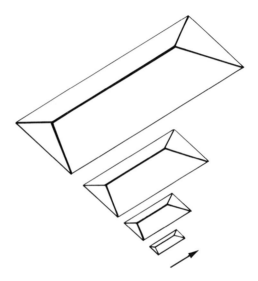

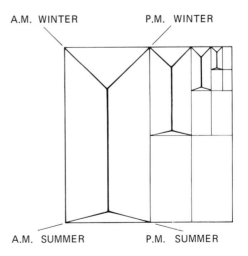

A.M. WINTER   P.M. WINTER

A.M. SUMMER   P.M. SUMMER

Shape

A change in the shape of the site will change the envelope shape, even when time constraints are the same. Generally, the ridge of the envelope will parallel the long dimensions of the site, but each change in the proportion of the site will result in a change in the envelope size and shape. Irregular sites, however, produce irregular and sometimes very complex envelope shapes.

The nearly square envelope, with four triangular facets that meet a single vertex, was described earlier. But it is a situation that does not occur often in practice. A more common situation involves a site considerably longer in one direction than another.

If the longer dimension of the site runs north-south, the solar envelope's ridge will also. The reason for this can be seen by reviewing separately the daily and seasonal movements of the sun.

The east-west (daily) migration of the sun can be described by casting shadows to the long edges of the site from a vertical plane running north-south. There result the "daily" faces of the envelope.

The north-south (seasonal) migration can be described with a vertical plane running east-west that casts shadows to the north and south. There result the "seasonal" faces of the envelope.

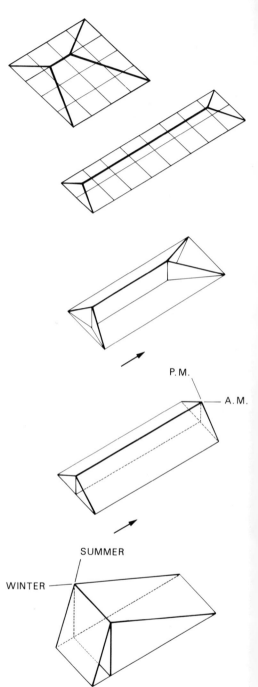

P.M.

A.M.

SUMMER

WINTER

When the daily and seasonal envelopes are combined, the lower, or the daily, envelope controls. Any attempt to build above the north-south (daily) ridge would cast shadows off the site to an adjacent property.

The final envelope can be described with a set of vertical planes representing the largest amount of volume that can be developed without casting shadows off the land parcel within specified times. The daily ridge is clearly the dominant ridge in limiting developable volume because it is the lowest ridge.

If the longest dimension of the site is east-west, the ridge conditions change. In this orientation, the shadows will be cast longer to the east and west than to the north and south. The vertical plane casting daily shadows will be higher than the plane casting seasonal shadows.

As with the preceding example, the mismatch in ridge heights can be resolved by using the lower plane as the dominant one to produce an envelope effective every day of the year. In this case, however, the seasonal ridge dominates. It runs east-west, but asymmetrically closer to the southern than the northern boundary.

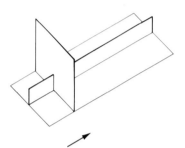

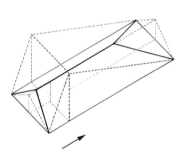

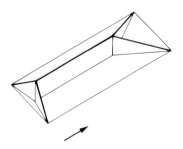

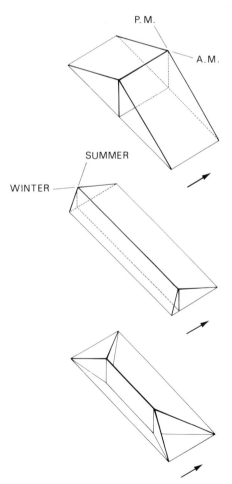

P. M.

A.M.

SUMMER

WINTER

Note that if the sites have the same dimensions and if the time constraints are the same in each case, the season-dominated envelope contains more developable volume than the day-dominated envelope. At the latitude of Los Angeles, the seasonal envelope has a ridge about 30 percent higher.

A refinement in the concept of envelope shape is its relationship to the urban surround and the specified relationships to adjacent streets and buildings. This will be discussed in more detail later on, but the basic concept is worth noting here. The site for the envelope may differ from the legal building site within it because the envelope may be defined to cross streets and alleys or to shadow specified portions of adjacent structures, including fences and buildings. These parameters, which may be determined by policy in the case of solar zoning, can be manipulated to achieve maximum development potential while protecting solar access.

Slope

Although I have been treating each of the spatial constraints separately, for clarity, they do not work in isolation. In discussing shape, I also discussed orientation. In discussing slope, I must also discuss its orientation.

The slope of the site affects both the height and shape of the envelope. First, a site of constant dimension produces envelopes of different heights as the slope changes. If we begin with a flat site and gradually increase the slope toward the south, we see that we increase the envelope's height and, therefore, its volume. Of course, as the slope approaches the vertical, volume is again lost.

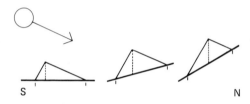

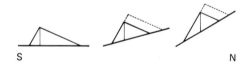

A second way to observe this change is to hold constant the height of the envelope and to increase the slope of the site. In this case, a gradual increase of slope is seen to diminish the envelope's plan dimension in the north-south direction and, therefore, to decrease its developable volume. And again, as the vertical is approached, volume disappears.

These basic concepts may now be examined in more detail in the context of different orientations. The orientation of the slope affects both the height and shape of the solar envelope. This can be demonstrated in two ways, similar to the ways we just examined the impact of slope on the envelope.

The first method is to hold the site dimension constant but vary the orientation of a fixed slope to produce envelopes of different heights. The envelopes over south-facing sites will generally be much higher and contain more volume than those on north slopes. Envelopes over east and west sites are somewhat more dependent on parcel shape, but they generally contain a moderate height and volume.

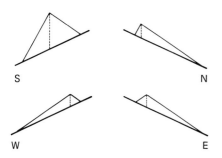

The second method is to fix the height of the envelope and vary slope orientation. Here the faces of the envelope remain at constant angles because shadows are cast in a fixed direction, given fixed times and latitudes. Shadows cast uphill, however, are foreshortened, while shadows cast downhill are elongated.

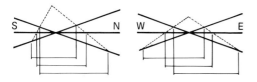

The result is that from a fixed height reference, the shape of the envelope will be different with each orientation. On south slopes, the envelope's south face will elongate, while its north face will foreshorten. On north slopes, the south face will foreshorten, while the north face will elongate. The same phenomenon will produce similar differences on east and west slopes.

The solar basis for these observations is clear from the angle of the sun's rays as they reach different directions of slope. For example, south slopes tend to equalize summer and winter insolation because the direction of the slope is toward the sun. The winter angle of approach more nearly equals the summer angle.

The areas between the dotted lines represent assured energy on the solar envelope. Note the mitigation of seasonal variation because a greater percentage of E_{winter} is assured than E_{summer}.

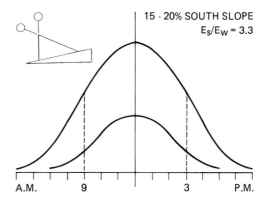

15 - 20% SOUTH SLOPE

$E_S/E_W = 3.3$

North slopes have the opposite effect. The winter sun approaches at an angle smaller than if the site had been flat. Since the summer sun is high enough to be less affected, the ratio between summer and winter insolation is increased.

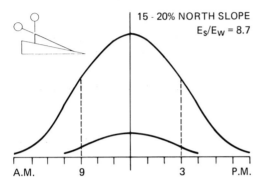

15 - 20% NORTH SLOPE

$E_s/E_w = 8.7$

A.M.   9   3   P.M.

West slopes accentuate daily variation by receiving the afternoon sun's rays more directly and the morning rays at a significantly lower angle; east sites favor the morning sun. The insolation ratio on both lies between a north and a south slope ratio.

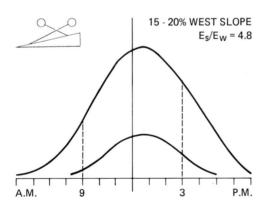

15 - 20% WEST SLOPE

$E_s/E_w = 4.8$

A.M.   9   3   P.M.

Orientation

Some aspects of orientation have already been discussed. The purpose of this section is to illustrate how the angular rotation of a site, aside from the issue of slope, must be considered when a site is not oriented along the cardinal points.

An angular rotation of the grid will change the height and therefore the developable volume described by a solar envelope. This significant change can be demonstrated by incrementally rotating a model site, of constant size and shape.

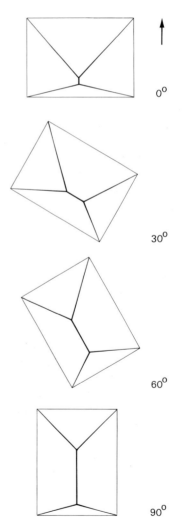

0°

30°

60°

90°

To demonstrate the effect of such rotation, I have defined an arbitrary site. The lot is flat and measures 150 ft. in the north-south direction and 205 ft. east-west. I also have assumed the latitude of Los Angeles and the time constraints of 9 A.M. to 3 P.M. in winter and 7 A.M. to 5 P.M. in summer. Under these conditions, the height of the solar envelope is 48.5 ft.

A clockwise rotation of this model site at 15° intervals successively reduces envelope height up to an angular rotation of 60°, when this particular solar envelope has its minimum height (30.3 ft.). Beyond that, rotation increases the envelope height until, at 90°, the envelope height is 35.5 ft.

There are two important observations to be made here. First, an orientation of approximately 60° off the cardinal points does not offer the volumetric possibilities of any other site orientation. Second, sites oriented long in the east-west direction allow a greater volume of development under the solar envelope than sites running north-south.

As will be discussed in chapter 10, other design values can dictate grid orientation but, for volume alone, the Jeffersonian grid has the advantage.

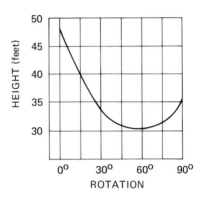

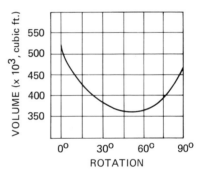

4 *Envelope Generation Techniques*

The significance of envelope generation lies in the suggestion of control for given conditions of change. Control, in turn, suggests a purpose or intention concerning that change. If our purpose requires the assurance of a period of solar access, the conditions of change are established by the sun's movement.

Access to the moving sun must be prescribed differently from access to a still object, such as a distant mountain peak. In the case of a mountain view, only statical determination of the sight line is required; the mountain does not move around relative to my window. Viewing the sun through my window is quite a different matter. I must specify exactly *when* I want to see it and consider whether I want the view from sunrise to sunset all year long, or whether some shorter period of the day during certain seasons is enough for my purposes. Certainly, if anybody else is to exist in my near world, time constraints must be clearly established on the duration of my view. Otherwise, nobody will be able to build within my horizon. Furthermore, I am my neighbor's neighbor. He may also want to view the sun!

General Discussion of Alternative Techniques

In order to generate a solar envelope, some way must be found to convert data about the sun's movement into a fixed geometry. A means is required to trace the envelope's perimeter by moving points, lines, or surfaces. Either descriptive or computational techniques may be used; each method has its own advantages and disadvantages.

Descriptive techniques use physical models on the heliodon and therefore have the advantage of being easily visualized and "read." They have the disadvantage of slow and painstaking generation work when the envelope has a complicated shape.

Computational techniques have the advantage of speed and precision in dealing with large and complicated sites, but machine processes are generally not easily visualized. This is a critical disadvantage for the designer whose perceptions of the sun's movement may be conditioned as much by the process of working with a model as by the final results.

Descriptive Techniques of Envelope Generation

The simplest and most descriptive technique is based on the flag, or fixed-position shadow generator, which casts a shadow on the ground. This method falls into a general class of descriptive modes of generation that can be used to characterize sites of different slope and orientation, either on a model or on a site. Within time constraints, a flag will cast shadows that can be used to both site and design buildings. This method leads to a quick understanding of different site characteristics.

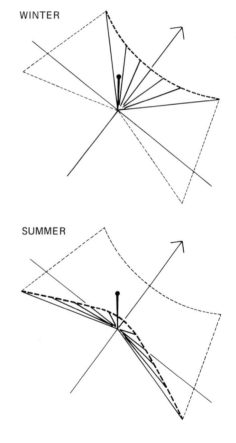

WINTER

SUMMER

A second method is really only a different way of looking at the first. In the first case, we looked at ground shadows. In the second, we are interested in the shadow ray that extends from the flag head. This method develops the shadow surface as it is projected from the head of the flag. The method both defines a space, or volume, and generates a surface whose shape reflects both the time of day and season of the year.

This second method can be used to generate envelopes of shapes that receive solar irradiation in controlled amounts and times. The technique can be used to determine a building or land form in specific relation to the sun.

A third technique presumes a fixed focal point for the sun's rays and generates a surface for those rays. As shown, the surface has been arbitrarily limited by a circular segment, although the edge of the surface may have other kinds of limits, depending on the purpose for which the surface is generated. Like the surface generated from the head of the flag, this technique can be used to generate shapes with controllable properties.

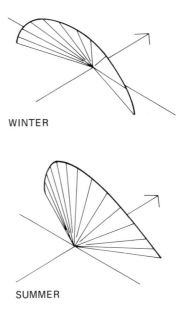

WINTER

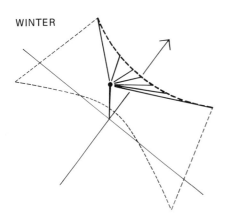

WINTER

SUMMER

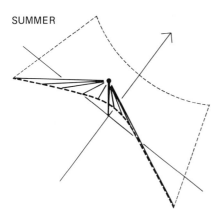

SUMMER

Computational Techniques of Envelope Generation

Computers can be programmed to accomplish the tedious generation processes required for complex problems or for simple problems that must be done quickly. A suggested program can be described in three steps.*

---

*This program was suggested by Charles S. Dwyer of the School of Architecture, University of Southern California.

Step 1: Define Edge of Site
The edge of the site is defined by a series of straight-line segments in a three-dimensional, Cartesian space. Then the coordinates of a terminal point of any line segment of the site's boundary are given by three numbers, x and y (horizontal) and z (vertical) coordinates. This method allows the site boundary to follow any topography. (Topographic features within the site can be ignored if they do not affect the envelope by rising above it.)

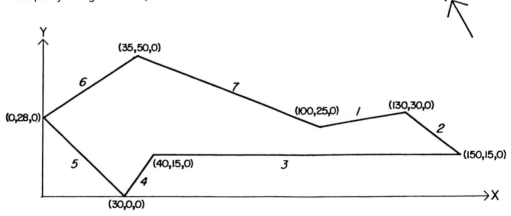

Definition of site by straight-line segments in Cartesian coordinate system.

Step 2: Application of Grid
Next, a rectangular grid is superimposed on
the site as defined by the boundary segments. The grid may have any orientation,
and may be as fine as required by the precision of the measurements to be made.

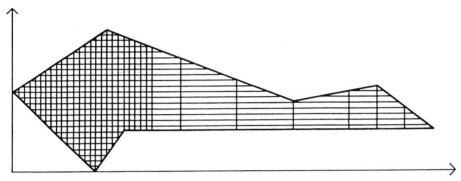

Superimposition of grid on site.

Step 3: Calculation of Vertical Heights
Third, specified sequential sun positions
must be supplied that do not cast shadows
beyond the site boundary. Then, from each
grid intersection, the largest height is calculated for a vertical element that does not
cast a shadow beyond the site boundaries
during specified times. The result is a matrix
of elevation values, each of which touches
the envelope at some instant in the sequence of specified times.

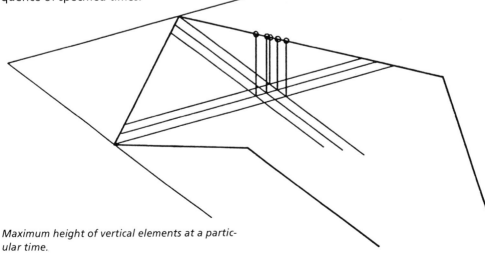

*Maximum height of vertical elements at a partic-
ular time.*

If the process were plotted at hourly intervals from the sun's viewpoint, a series of twisting images would appear with vertical elements that change height with each turn. As time passes, the envelope's final shape is set by the shortest height attained for each vertical element.

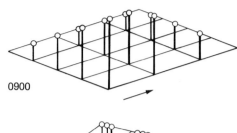

0900

Plotted in this way, the resulting matrix can be seen as only an approximation of the true solar envelope. The true envelope and its calculated approximation do, however, coincide exactly at the grid intersections. Inaccuracies can occur only between grid intersections.

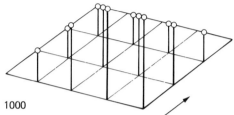

1000

Any degree of precision can be approached, however, by making the grid finer. The finer the grid, the more accurately a complex envelope can be represented.

1100

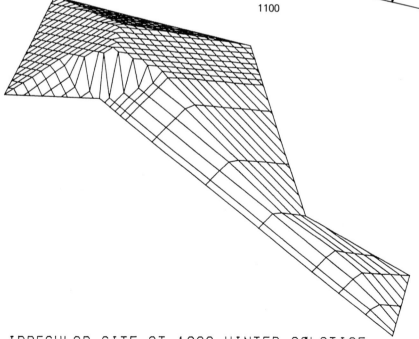

IRREGULAR SITE AT 1000 WINTER SOLSTICE

Solar Zoning Charts

The practical application of solar zoning is very likely to require simple charts that translate all solar data into envelope slope angles that could be laid out on the site, normal to property lines. Such tables could be easily devised for any given latitude. They would contain an array of envelope angles based on the compass bearing of property lines and predetermined by the cutoff times for solar access. With such a table, any developer or designer could determine constructional limits in the field or on the drawing board.

Descriptive Geometry Exemplar

The descriptive technique that will now be demonstrated in drawings has both laboratory and site applications. It is analogous to both heliodon and surveying procedures because it is based on a simple transfer of solar angles, as mentioned in chapter 1.

The method depends on intersecting the site with vertical planes. Each plane is systematically located and shaped in accordance with solar azimuth and altitude angles between the cutoff times.

In each drawing, the top edge of a plane represents a solar ray that passes over the site to intersect a predetermined boundary. A number of planes represent selected times of the day and year. When the heights of planes are compared, the lower ones will determine the envelope's limits; any taller segment of plane is then removed. The result is a systematic definition of the envelope's volumetric boundaries.

The presentation strategy is to demonstrate the steps of generation on several different sites.*

First, a rectangular site is rotated to demonstrate the effect of orientation on the solar envelope. Next, the site shape is made irregular to determine what changes this makes in the envelope's form. Finally, party walls are added to the site's perimeter to demonstrate how the envelope may systemically gain volume in urban conditions but, at the same time, reduce the extent of solar access.

*Some of the following material has appeared in slightly different form in Ralph L. Knowles and Richard D. Berry, *Solar Envelope Concepts: Moderate Density Building Applications* (Golden, Colorado: Solar Energy Research Institute, 1980), pp. 17–78.

While the grid orientation, site shape, and surround are varied for this demonstration, the duration of solar access is held constant. The consequence of holding the period of solar access constant is that the sun's angles of approach to the earth remain a fixed set. The selected cutoff times, the altitude angles α, and the azimuth angles θ are as follows: 0900–1500 winter ($\alpha = 17.6°$, $\theta = 137°$ and 223°); 0700–1700 summer ($\alpha = 25°$, $\theta = 78°$ and 282°). Two azimuth angles are given for each season, but only one altitude angle need be given. This is because the selected cutoff times are symmetrical around noon, making the morning and afternoon angles constant at a given season.

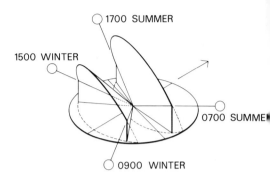

The consequence of varying site geometry and surroundings is that different combinations of the cutoff times establish the envelope's shape and bulk. To demonstrate this point, we begin with a grid oriented on the cardinal points, and then rotate the grid, thus generating a new envelope with each fractional turn. Each envelope will initially be shown in a plan-oblique drawing for easy visual reference. Vertical planes will be shown extended from the site to describe the envelope's four sloping hips and single horizontal ridge.

Grid Orientation 0°

The first envelope is generated over a land parcel 205 ft. east-west and 150 ft. north-south. This orientation is referred to as 0°. The envelope is seen to be symmetrical in the east-west direction and asymmetrical in the north-south direction. Its four sloping hips rise to a horizontal ridge, 48.5 feet high. The enclosed volume of the envelope contains 5.3×10^5 cu. ft.

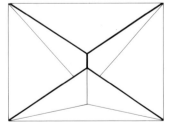

The descriptive steps that follow are all based on measures of the sun's position at those cutoff times for which the envelope is to be generated. As mentioned earlier, it is convenient to presume that all solar phenomena occur on the surface of a hemisphere. Where the hemisphere intersects the earth, a circle results, forming the horizon. The center of the circle is the point on the earth that concerns us, and is identified by the intersection of lines running north-south and east-west. In this construct, the sun moves in circular paths across the surface of the hemisphere. Its position at the cutoff times is shown by triangular planes set vertically; these planes all meet at the center of the circle. The base of each triangle marks the azimuth angle θ, measured clockwise from north. The hypotenuse of each triangle marks the sun's altitude angle α, measured above the horizon.

These measures will now be applied to a site using an unsymmetrical dimetric drawing. (Later demonstrations will all use plan-oblique drawings that make measurement easier; but for this first demonstration, the unsymmetrical dimetric gives a clearer picture.)

The triangles that represent each cutoff time will be directly transferred from the solar hemisphere to the edges and corners of the site. First morning, then afternoon cutoff times will be transferred. Then the descriptive triangles that mark each time will be systematically combined to define the envelope's upper limits.

To make the sun's measures even clearer, a second description has been included for the first two steps. This second description makes use of vertical planes cut, as from the sides of a box, to cast shadows precisely covering the site.

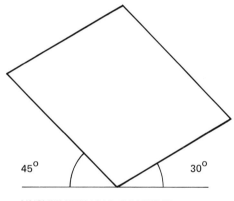

45° 30°

UNSYMMETRICAL DIMETRIC

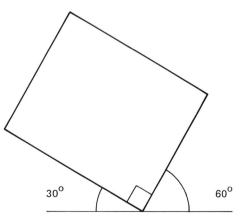

30° 60°

PLAN OBLIQUE

Step 1: Use the Morning Cutoff Times
The summer morning rays (0700 summer;
$\alpha = 25°$, $\theta = 78°$) approach the site across its
north and east boundaries.

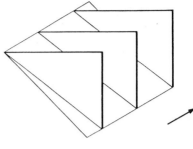

Planes located at those boundaries and cut
to precisely intersect the sun's rays as they
enter over the site cast shadows to the opposing south and west boundaries.

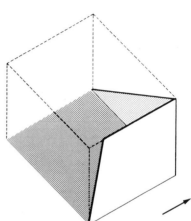

The winter morning rays (0900 winter;
$\alpha = 17.6°$, $\theta = 137°$) approach the site from
the south and east.

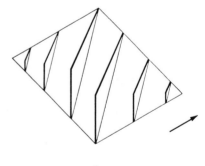

Planes located at those boundaries are
shaped to cast shadows to the opposing
north and west boundaries.

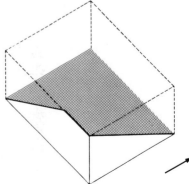

Step 2: Use the Afternoon Cutoff Times
The summer afternoon rays (1700 summer;
$\alpha = 25°$, $\theta = 282°$) approach the site across
its north and west boundaries.

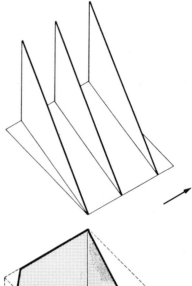

Vertical planes at those boundaries are
shaped to cast shadows to the opposing
south and east boundaries.

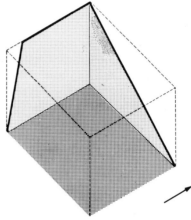

The winter afternoon rays (1500 winter;
$\alpha = 17.6°$, $\theta = 223°$) approach the site across
its south and west boundaries.

Vertical planes at those boundaries are
shaped to cast shadows to the opposing
north and east boundaries.

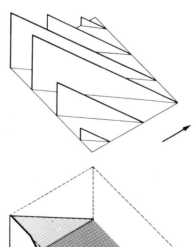

Step 3: Combine the Effects of the Morning and Afternoon Cutoff Times
The combination of summer rays slopes across the site to strike the south and west boundaries in the morning, the south and east boundaries in the afternoon. The planes all intersect at the same height, midway in the site.

The combination of winter rays slopes across the site to strike the north and west boundaries in the morning, the north and east boundaries in the afternoon. The planes intersect at different heights across the site.

Step 4: Indicate Redundancy
That portion of any triangular plane that rises above an intersecting plane casts shadows off the site at one or another of the cutoff times. Such portions, which are descriptively redundant, are shown above the dotted lines in the two accompanying drawings.

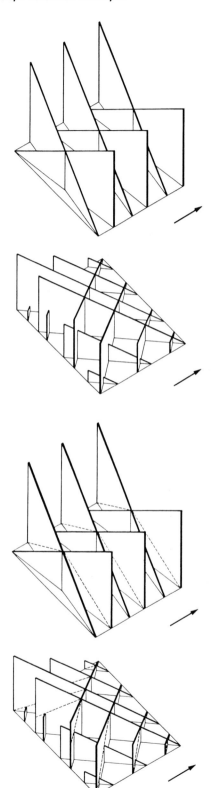

Step 5: Eliminate Redundancy
When redundant portions of triangular
planes are cut away, the result is a tent-like
shape for the summer solstice and an irregular pyramid for the winter solstice. Each is
a solar envelope that functions perfectly for
one day of the year.

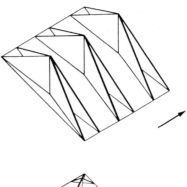

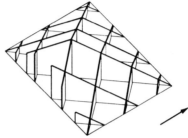

Step 6: Find the Envelope Hips
External angles, or hips, are defined where
two sloping faces of the envelope meet.
The triangles that define summer faces also
indicate two hips that slope from a vertex
ridge to the site's southeast and southwest
corners.

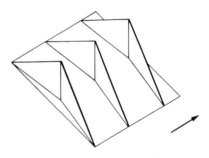

The triangles that define winter faces also
indicate two hips that slope from a vertex
to the site's northeast and northwest
corners.

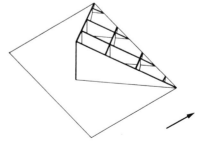

Step 7: Delineate Envelope Ridges
A ridge appears where opposing east and west slopes meet at the envelope's top.

One ridge extends north from the vertex of two intersecting summer hips.

A second ridge extends south from the vertex of two intersecting winter hips.

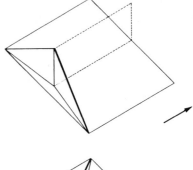

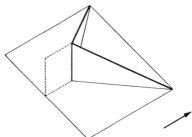

Step 8: Allow the Ridges to Converge
When the summer and winter ridges are superposed, they precisely contact each other. These summer and winter ridges lie in the same plane. Of course, the plane differs for differing cutoff times and site geometry.

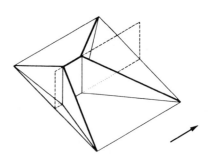

Step 9: Exhibit the Complete Solar Envelope
The final envelope emerges with four hips that meet at a short, north-south ridge.

Two hips appear at the site's southern corners. Their top edges follow the sun's rays at the two summer cutoff times.

Similarly, two hips appear at the site's northern corners. Their top edges follow the sun's rays at the two winter cutoff times.

The volume thus generated could not be larger without casting unwanted shadows.

Grid Orientation 30°

The second solar envelope is generated for a site of dimensions equal to the foregoing, but rotated clockwise 30°. Its four sloping hips rise asymmetrically to a horizontal ridge, 34.1 ft. high, that parallels the site's long edges. The envelope loses volume in this orientation; its volume is 3.8×10^5 cu. ft., compared with 5.3×10^5 cu. ft. for the first case.

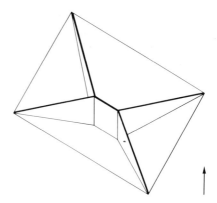

In this and the following cases, information is, as in the 0° case, transferred from the solar hemisphere drawing, but the drawing is henceforth plan-oblique, in which north is always at the top of the page. Other than this change, which makes measurement easier, the generation procedure is identical with the first six steps shown in the first example. In steps 7 and 8, the procedure is slightly modified because the change of orientation causes a transformation of the envelope geometry. This transformation occurs because the sun's rays approach the site's edges asymmetrically at the cutoff times (which, of course, remain constant for all of the examples). The envelope in these cases is generated in eleven steps, rather than nine; steps 9 through 11 follow the original procedure.

Step 1: Use the Morning Cutoff Times
Summer morning rays approach the site
across its northeast and southeast
boundaries.

Vertical planes at those boundaries are precisely cut to cast shadows across the site to
the opposing northwest and southwest
boundaries.

Winter morning rays approach the site
across its southeast and southwest
boundaries.

Vertical planes at those boundaries are cut
to cast shadows across the site to the opposing northeast and northwest
boundaries.

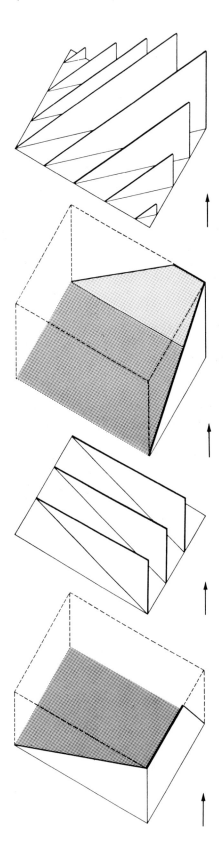

Step 2: Use the Afternoon Cutoff Times
Summer afternoon rays approach the site
across its northwest and southwest
boundaries.

Shadows are cast to the opposing northeast
and southeast boundaries.

Winter afternoon rays approach the site
across its northwest and southwest
boundaries.

Shadows are cast to the opposing northeast
and southeast boundaries.

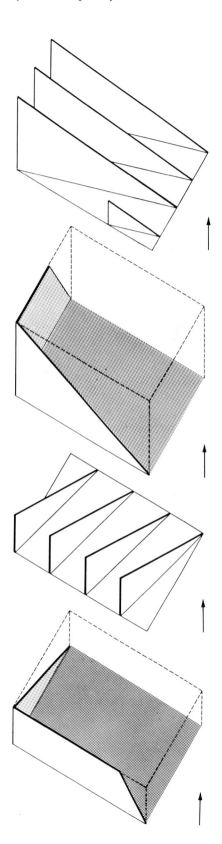

Step 3: Combine the Effects of the Morning and Afternoon Cutoff Times
The combination of summer rays slopes across the site to strike the northwest and southwest boundaries in the morning, the northeast and southeast boundaries in the afternoon.

The combination of winter rays slopes across the site to strike the northwest and northeast boundaries in the morning, the northeast and southeast boundaries in the afternoon. No rays cross the site in such a way that they strike the southwest boundary.

Step 4: Indicate Redundancy
That portion of any triangular plane that rises above an intersecting plane casts shadows off the site at one or another of the cutoff times. Such portions, which are descriptively redundant, are shown above the dotted lines in the two accompanying drawings.

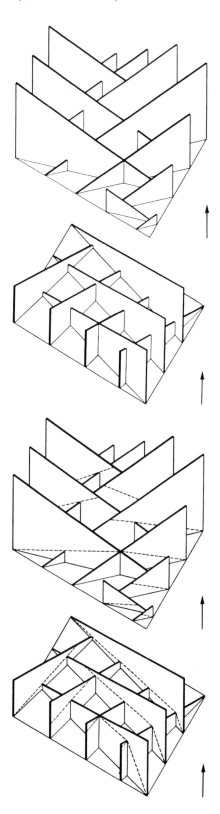

Step 5: Eliminate Redundancy
When the redundant portions of triangular
planes are removed, two different solar envelopes appear: one provides solar access at
the summer solstice; the other provides solar access at winter solstice.

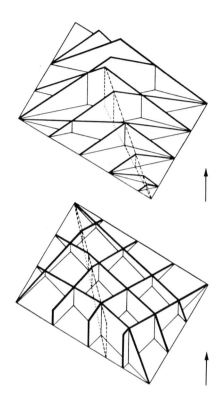

The shapes of the two seasonal envelopes
are somewhat more complicated than those
for the 0° case. An understanding of the differences between summer and winter envelopes is critical in order to carry out the next
few steps for this 30° site.

The summer envelope differs from the winter envelope in two important respects.
First, solar rays cross the site so as to meet
all four boundaries of the summer envelope, but the rays meet only three boundaries of the winter envelope, leaving the
southwest boundary unresolved. Second,
the locations of the hips occur over different regions of each envelope.

The rotation of this site produces a single
hip at the southernmost corner of the summer envelope, rather than the two hips
seen in the 0° case. Comparison of the summer and winter envelopes here also shows
that the summer hip is below the winter
hip. Therefore, the summer sun controls the
envelope's height for solar access over the
site's southern region. In other words, the
winter envelope is superseded by the
summer.

The reverse condition occurs at the site's
northernmost corner. Here the winter hip
controls the envelope's height because of
the lower angles of the winter sun in the
southern sky.

Step 6: Define the Envelope Hips
The two hips that appeared in the last step are now isolated so that the next step can be taken. The summer hip is shown extended to the site's northern limits.

The winter hip is shown in the same way, extended to the southern limit.

Step 7: Determine the Summer and Winter Intersections
This step has no counterpart in the 0° site demonstration. It is based on the simultaneous application of measures derived from the two seasons. The summer hip is intersected by the rays of the winter afternoon sun.

The winter hip is intersected by the summer morning rays.

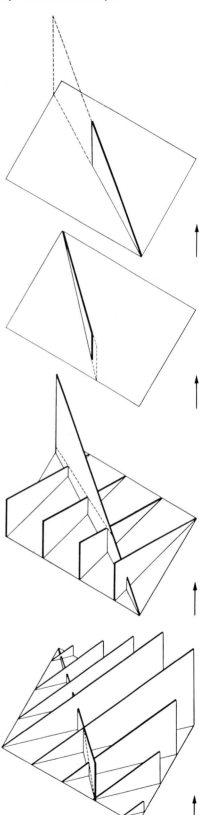

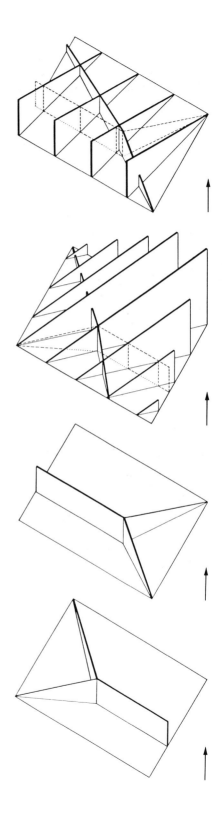

Step 8: Find the Two-Season Hips
When the redundant portion that would produce shadowing is removed from each seasonal hip, a vertex appears. A second hip must then descend from this vertex to the adjacent corner of the site where a summer face of the envelope will meet a winter face. This becomes a two-season hip, occurring on the east corner after intersecting the summer hip.

It occurs on the west corner after intersecting the winter hip.

An unresolved horizontal ridge extends from each of these intersections.

Step 9: Find the Envelope Hips and Ridges
Each final set of hips and ridges requires two seasons to establish. The southernmost hip is set by summer sun's morning and afternoon rays; the easternmost hip and the ridge require the addition of the winter afternoon's rays.

The northernmost hip is set by winter morning and afternoon; and the westernmost hip and the ridge require the addition of summer morning rays.

Step 10: Allow the Ridges to Converge
When the two ridges are superposed, they precisely contact each other, as occurred in the first demonstrations on the 0° site.

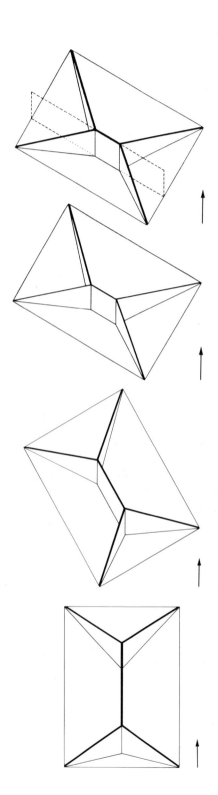

Step 11: Exhibit the Complete Solar Envelope
The completed envelope for the 30° site appears to be similar to the envelope for the 0° site, having similar hips and a ridge which define its form. But this envelope contains 30 percent less volume than the first one; it is the result of a more complex construction than the first.

Grid Orientation 60° and 90°

For the third rotation, the envelope is generated for the same-size site, but rotated 60°. Its horizontal ridge is 30 ft. high; volume is only 3.6×10^5. Both measures are significantly less than for the prior two cases. The drawing and generation techniques for this case are identical to those used for the 30° site.

The fourth rotation brings the site to a 90° position. In this case, the envelope is again symmetrical over the site; the height (36 ft.) and volume (4.6×10^5 cu. ft.) are increased over those for the 60° site.

Irregular Site at 60°

The site of the fifth solar envelope is like
the third in all respects except that its
southwestern boundary is skewed, making
the site nonrectangular. This condition is
not uncommon, and is of special interest
because it is similar to sites in the moderate-
density housing study reported later in this
work.

This single change in the site affects both
the envelope's basic shape and the generation procedure. The envelope's shape becomes much less regular on this site,
principally because the ridge does not lie
parallel to any boundary and, furthermore,
it is not horizontal.

Some differences also appear in the generation procedure. They are pointed out where
they occur in the following exposition.

Drawings of each step are grouped as a set.

Step 1: Use the Morning Cutoff Times
Summer, same as 30° and 60° sites.

Shadow-casting vertical planes at the northeast and southeast boundaries only touch
the horizontal top of the box-like reference
at a single point.

Winter morning rays approach the site across three, rather than two, boundaries. This difference from the 30° and 60° sites is the direct result of the skewed southwestern boundary.

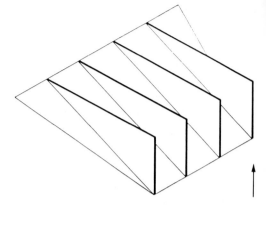

Vertical planes at the northeast, southeast, and southwest boundaries cast shadows across the site to the remaining boundary on the northwest.

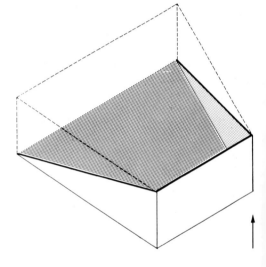

Step 2: Use the Afternoon Cutoff Times
Summer, same as 30° and 60° sites.

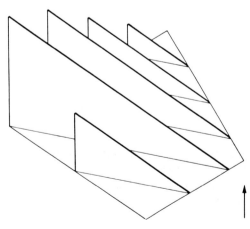

Same as for 30° and 60° sites.

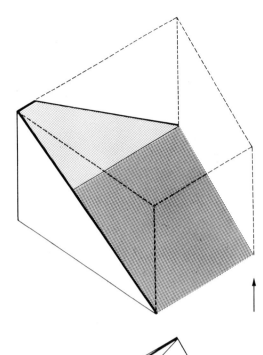

Winter, same as 30° and 60° sites.

Shadow-casting vertical planes at the south-east and southwest boundaries only touch the upper horizontal reference at a single point.

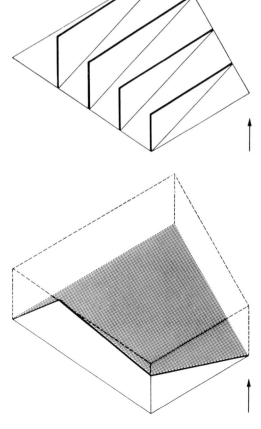

Step 3: Combine the Effects of the Morning and Afternoon Cutoff Times
Summer, same as 30° and 60° sites.

Step 4: Indicate Redundancy
Same as 30° and 60° sites.

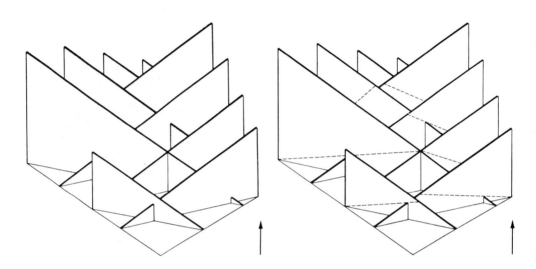

Winter, the combination of morning and afternoon rays slope across the site to strike only the northwest and northeast boundaries.

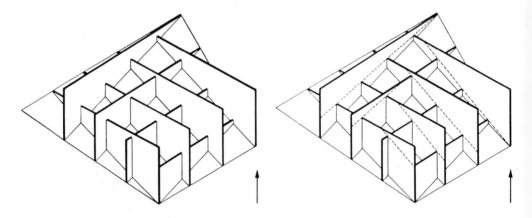

Step 5: Eliminate Redundancy
Summer, same as 30° and 60° sites.

Step 6: Find the Envelope Hips
Same as 30° and 60° sites.

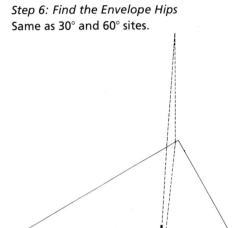

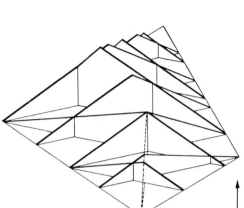

In winter the envelope has two unresolved
edges that occur where the sun's rays do
not strike the southeast and southwest
boundaries.

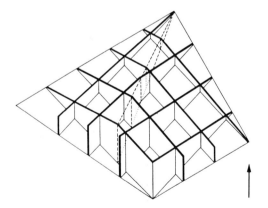

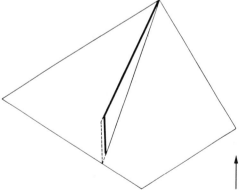

Step 7: Find the Summer and Winter Intersections
Same as 30° and 60° sites.

Step 8: Find the Two-Season Hips
Same as 30° and 60° sites.

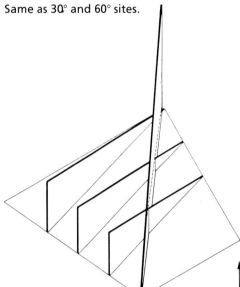

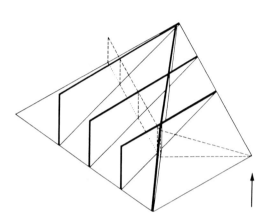

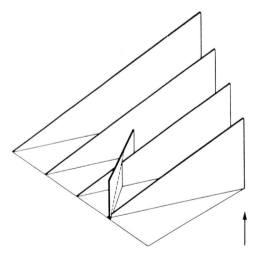

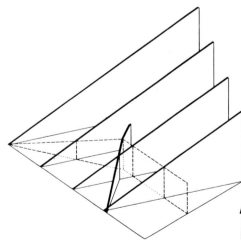

Step 9: Indicate the Hips and Ridges
Same as 30° and 60° sites.

Step 10: Allow the Ridges to Converge
When the two different sets of hips and
ridges are superposed, the ridges do not
contact each other. Their azimuth angles
and height are different.

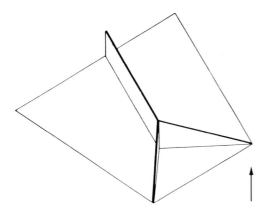

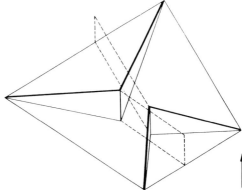

*Step 11: Exhibit the Complete Solar
Envelope*
The ridge mismatch is easily resolved in the
final step by directly connecting the two
vertexes. The two individually derived
ridges are replaced with a composite ridge
that functions year round during the specified hours of solar access.

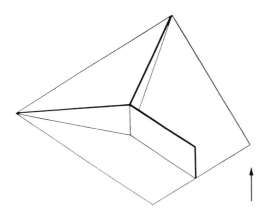

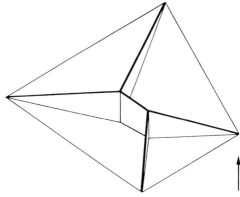

With this final step in the generation of an envelope for the irregular site at 60°, the demonstration of a descriptive geometry exemplar is complete. The principles of this technique will be applied in chapters 5 and 10 to generate, respectively, solar envelopes for hillsides and for large, urban sites with a complicated boundary condition.

5 *Building Site Applications*

Various conditions at the boundary of a site can affect the envelope's size and shape. These conditions include such things as setbacks and fences, traditional features of our neighborhoods. Topography and adjacent streets and buildings also affect the envelope. The extent of their impact is determined by our attitudes about private and public space, as well as about solar access. In this chapter I discuss different attitudes and apply the envelope construction to a variety of building sites.

Setbacks and Fences

Setbacks are a traditional part of development in our culture. Normally there are setbacks on all four sides of a house, especially in subdivisions. The resulting front, back, and side yards have become an integral part of our attitudes about housing.

Strong proprietary feelings often develop about these areas between houses. Fences are used to establish boundaries. But even without fences, individual landscaping usually establishes the boundary. Consequently, any consideration of solar access makes an issue of the relationship between shadows and setbacks.

Different Attitudes About Setbacks

The solar envelope will vary significantly with differences of attitude about setbacks as shadow limits. For example, the envelope height will increase if shadows are allowed to extend to the neighbor's traditional setbacks rather than being constrained by the property's own setbacks during the period of specified access.

Community attitudes may vary to produce a range of possible limits. The most constraining attitude would limit shadows to the property's own setback. The solar envelope would, in that case, assure a period of solar access to the owner's front, back, and side yards.

A second attitude might allow shadowing of the owner's yard, but not the neighbor's. The envelope of developable volume would expand in all plan dimensions and its height would increase.

A third attitude might allow shadowing to the center of streets and alleys. The envelope would then expand in only one plan dimension and may not increase its height if expansion is parallel to the ridge orientation.

A fourth extension may allow shadows to cross the street and alley, but forbid any effect beyond the property lines. Like the third approach, this one does not add much volume for development because the ridge height does not increase.

Community attitudes may also allow shadows to fall upon a neighbor's yard up to the traditional setbacks. Envelope height would then increase because of expansion normal to ridge orientation. This last approach may also be applicable to landscaping. Shadows from a neighbor's trees may be acceptable on your yard, but not acceptable on your house.

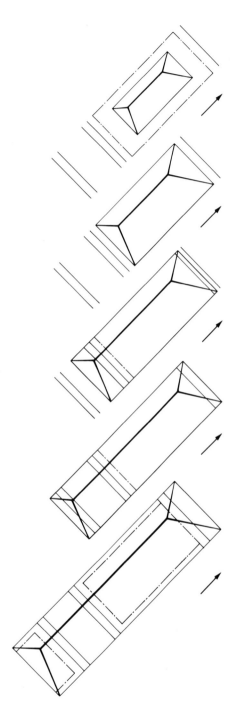

This progression of expanding shadow limits may continue finally to include designated parts of the neighbor's building. Such an approach could be used to increase volume in high-density areas or to rebuild within the constraints of existing development. Such an approach, however, would require a systematic correlation with land use and building function.

The Effect of Privacy Fences

Many communities include the option of a privacy fence at the property line. While there are local variations, an allowed height of six feet is common in Los Angeles.

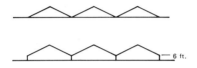

Obviously, a fence casts shadows. Integrating the fence into the solar envelope adds developable volume and still provides the same specified period of access to each site, but starting at six feet above grade. Below that, access is decreased toward ground level, where the original altitude angles for access reach a maximum deviation, measured from the envelope's ridge. The deviation produces a shorter period of access— one starting later in the morning and ending earlier in the afternoon—than the original envelope.

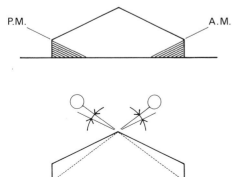

This relation between elevation and duration of access within the envelope will be further developed later as a useful design idea for differentiating function within the building. At a planning scale, it may also act to organize land use vertically.

Streets

How streets are related to the sun can characterize a society both geographically and culturally. For example, the arcaded streets of Latin America and Spain derive partly from hot, sunny climates. By contrast, the simple, open streets of New England, much of the eastern seaboard, and England derive from cold, wet climates where it is important to let as much sunlight into the street as possible, so that sunlight and heat can reach both the houses and the street.

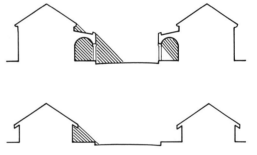

Piled snow and packed ice might convince the winter-weary northerner that a single-loaded street is best, with buildings only on the north side. Such a scheme would combine the advantages of a shadow-free street and a south-facing wall that could store and reradiate or reflect heat into the street. A modification of this idea, but with more development advantages, would place lower buildings on the south and higher ones on the north to catch as much winter sun as possible.

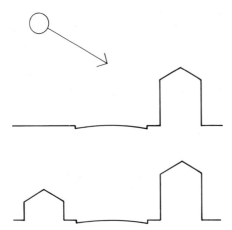

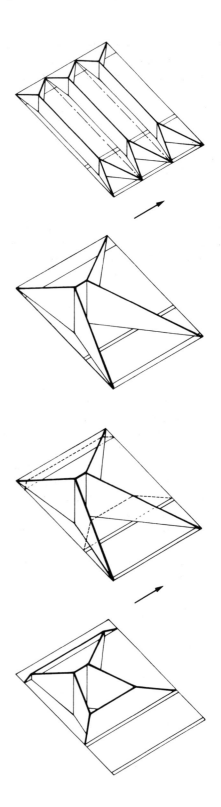

On the other hand, in warm climates, such as in Los Angeles, selective shadowing of the street becomes an acceptable practice. The envelope becomes larger and changes shape when it is allowed to extend beyond the site's boundaries to property lines across the street. These changes are related to orientation and to the size of the sites.

As seen in the accompanying four drawings, when the envelopes over 50-ft. lots are extended across the street and alley, a minimal increase in volume results. But if three lots are assembled into a single site, the same extensions across street and alley have a marked influence on the envelope.

The Influence of Block Orientation

Block orientation affects envelope size and
shape and, thereby, the buildings that form
our urban spaces. Nowhere is this more
clear than at street corners.

An East-West Block
Consider first the example of corner lots on
blocks running long in the east-west direction. A section through the north-south
street would show the envelope adapting
to morning and afternoon cutoff times. The
morning sun would extend the envelope
across the street to the west; afternoon sun
would extend the opposing envelope to the
east. The two envelopes would intersect in
mid-street. The corner envelopes would not
only be larger than those inside the block
but they would have different shapes.

Land assemblage along the east-west block
increases the heights of envelopes. However, the vertical faces of envelopes over
corner sites remain fixed and symmetrical
once they meet the cutoff slope as it extends across the street. The scale of the
street is henceforth fixed unless the rules of
access are changed.

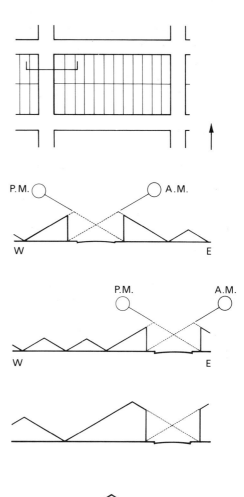

A North-South Block

Next consider the corner lots on blocks running long in the north-south direction. Winter shadows extend the envelope across the street to the north, while summer shadows extend the opposing envelope to the south. Again, corner lots have larger and unique shapes. In addition, the size and shape of the envelopes would be differentiated by orientation because of solar asymmetry in this section. The south wall on the street will be slightly higher than the north wall because the seasonal north-south path of the sun affects the envelope asymmetrically.

Land assemblage along the north-south block affects envelope size as much as in the east-west block. And here too, vertical faces of corner envelopes rise to limits prescribed by cutoff times. As assemblage proceeds, the south wall remains at a fixed height, while the north wall gets higher.

Each assemblage of lots increases the asymmetry of street development. The north wall heightens until it intersects the envelope's south slope. Assemblage beyond that point does not change the envelope's height at the street. The street's aspect remains essentially unchanged, and its solar properties are assured, regardless of future land aggregation.

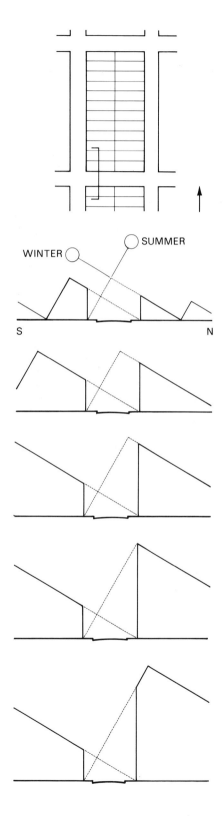

A More Detailed Look at Assemblage

The effects of assemblage can be more easily visualized if the whole 300 × 600-ft. city
block is seen in three dimensions. Blocks will
be shown with alleys and without; subdivisions will occur first with 100-ft. frontages,
then 200-ft., and finally 300-ft. frontages
along the street. Blocks are shown in two
orientations of the Jeffersonian grid.

Consider first the example of long north-
south blocks, with and without alleys.

Where a block has an alley, the solar envelope extends across the street in front and
across the alley in back. As we have already
seen, envelopes over corner lots are higher
and contain more volume because they can
extend across the street in two directions
instead of one.

As small lots are assembled along the entire
street, envelopes become larger and shift
polarity; where there is an alley, ridges that
ran east-west over 100-ft. frontage parcels
change and run north-south over 200-ft.
parcels.

This shift of the ridge orientation becomes
more pronounced as frontages increase to
300 ft. The same observation can be made
of envelopes over parcels that run the full
block depth without an alley.

If the envelope runs the entire length of the
block, its ridge will be continuous in the
north-south direction.

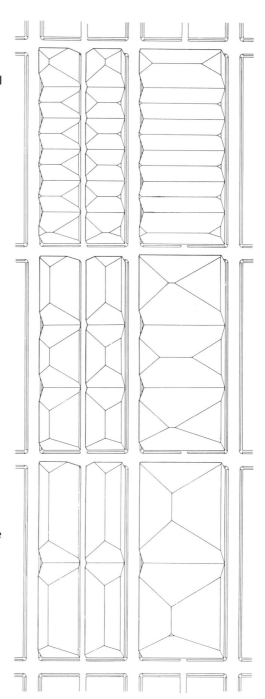

Land assemblage in east-west blocks produces similar changes of envelope size and shape, but significantly different envelope polarities.

The ridges over all 100-ft. parcels here run north-south instead of east-west as in the prior case; this is true in blocks with and without alleys.

On parcels with 200-ft. frontages and a rear alley, envelopes begin to peak. At 300 ft., the envelopes' ridges reorient to an east-west direction.

Where parcels run the entire depth of a block without an alley, envelope ridges over frontages of all sizes shown retain their north-south polarity. It would not be until the envelope ran the entire length of the block that the ridge would reorient toward an east-west polarity.

One significance of envelope polarity is related to south orientation and to its advantages for energy conversion by active or passive means. The advantage of south exposure lies with small land parcels in long north-south blocks but shifts to large land parcels in east-west blocks.

A strategy of seeking south exposure in new subdivisions or in urban rebuilding could, over a period of time, result in a differentiation of land-parcel size based on block orientation. The design significance of this will be discussed in later chapters.

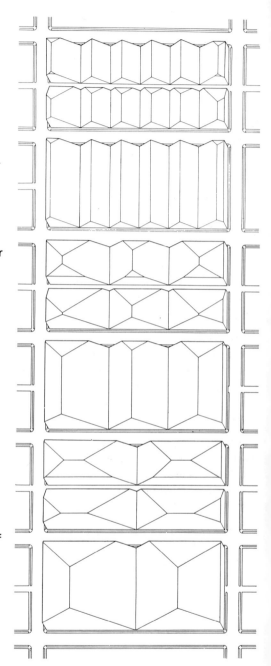

Hillsides

The slope of a site affects its solar envelope because the boundaries off which the envelope is generated are inclined and lie at different elevations. Consequently, the sun's slanting rays are foreshortened or elongated downhill as they cross the site and establish the envelope's limits. The direction of slope is also an important factor as previously discussed and as will be detailed in chapter 6.

Here, I will demonstrate envelope generation on a sloping site by using a technique from the descriptive geometry exemplar in chapter 4. As in the earlier exposition, vertical planes are used to depict graphically the sun's rays. Each plane is set to describe altitude and azimuth angles at a solar cutoff time. In this manner, the top edges of planes represent the solar envelope's upper, sloping boundaries.

Envelope Generation: A South Slope Application

This application involves three boundary conditions not demonstrated in the earlier exemplar: sloped property lines, a privacy fence, and an extension of the envelope to adjacent properties across the street. These conditions require some modifications of the procedure and several additional steps.

Step 1: Use the Winter Morning Cutoff Times

Rays (0900: $\alpha = 17.6°$; $\theta = 137°$) approach the site from the southeast and intersect the top of the privacy fence along the street and west boundaries. The volume thus defined does not cast off-site shadows beyond those of the fence at the same hour.

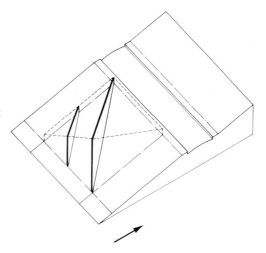

Step 2: Use the Winter Afternoon Cutoff Times

Rays (1500: $\alpha = 17.6°$; $\theta = 223°$) approach the site from the southwest and intersect the top of the privacy fence along the street and east boundary. The volume defined casts no shadows to the northeast beyond those of the fence at that hour.

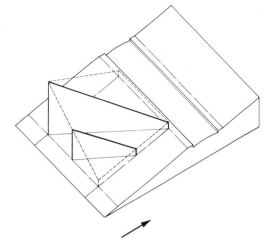

Step 3: Combine the Effects of the Morning and Afternoon Cutoff Times; Indicate Redundancy

The winter morning and afternoon rays both cross the site and intersect privacy fences on the west, north, and east boundaries. That portion of any descriptive plane that rises above an opposing, intersecting plane will cast shadows off the site at one or another of the cutoff times. Such portions are descriptively redundant and are shown above the dotted lines.

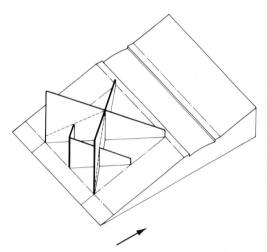

Step 4: Eliminate Redundancy; Delineate Envelope Ridge

When redundant portions are removed, the vertical planes slope toward the west, north, and east boundaries. No shadows will be cast beyond those of the privacy fences at either cutoff time. The dotted connection between highest intersections of planes suggests a north-south ridge.

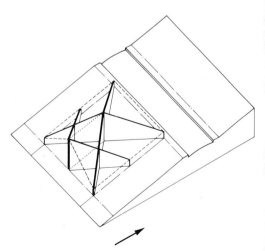

Step 5: Exhibit Site Envelope
The previous arrangement of planes can be simplified by replacing all but the two north hips with a high ridge and a south face that, in combination, define the upper limits of volume. This new construction defines the envelope's space and, on the sun machine, will cast shadows to the site's critical boundaries at cutoff times.

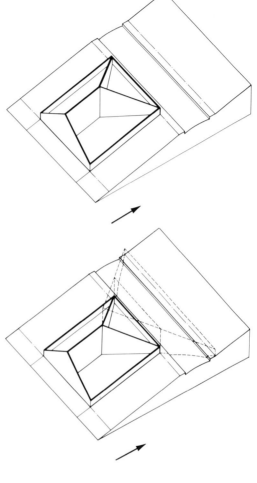

Step 6: Find Additional Volume Under New North Slope
If shadows can be cast across the street to the opposing neighbor's privacy fence, volume may be added to the envelope's north end. Winter will be the critical season because of low rays cast from the southeast and southwest. This new wedge of volume will rise above the first envelope and extend across the street at the same angle as the original north slope.

Step 7: Use Summer Morning and Afternoon Cutoff Times
When the north privacy fence is raised to these new limits, acceptable winter shadows will cross the street to the opposing neighbor. Portions of the plane above the dotted lines will, however, cast unacceptable summer shadows. Morning shadows will be cast on the neighbor to the west; afternoon shadows, on the neigbor to the east.

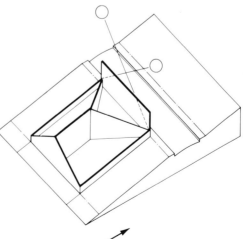

Step 8: Eliminate Redundancy; Find New Volume
When the redundant portions are removed, the shortened top edge of the north plane will cast winter shadows implying a smaller wedge of volume than was shown in step 6.

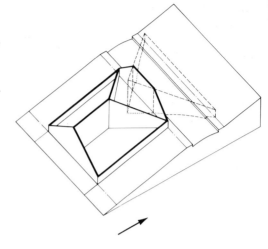

Step 9: Display Higher North Slope; Indicate New Ridge
The upper limits of this smaller wedge can be described with intersecting vertical planes. Their top edges describe a sloping triangle that is defined by both summer and winter cutoff times. Dotted lines suggest the connection to the original set of planes from step 5.

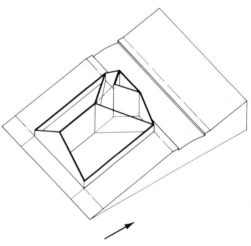

Step 10: Exhibit the Complete Solar Envelope
When that connection is made with a last vertical plane, the arrangement represents the completed solar envelope. When placed on a sun machine, this construction will cast shadows to all seasonally critical limits at the selected cutoff times. The volume cannot be larger nor of another shape without casting unwanted shadows.

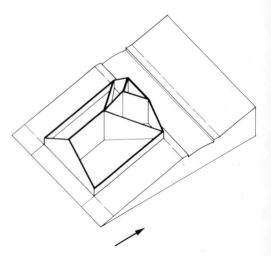

Adjacent Buildings

The last envelope application demonstrates
that an urban site will be influenced by the
buildings around it and by our attitudes
about solar access to their surfaces. For example, if adjacent buildings can perform
adequately with some shadowing of their
surfaces, the solar envelope can be designed with regard to their performance. In
this way, new and old buildings are interrelated and our perceptions of property limits
extend beyond site lines.

The interrelatedness of properties through
solar envelope zoning has implications for
energy conversion and environmental quality that will be discussed in detail in chapter
10. Here, I will simply demonstrate how the
envelope's size increases systematically with
the shadowing of surrounding buildings.
Step by step, volume is gained and, while
solar access is diminished, it is never completely lost.

Envelope Generation: An Urban Site Application

For this demonstration, I will take the size,
shape, and orientation of the first exemplar
site. The envelope to be transformed is then
the same as the one generated in that first
case.

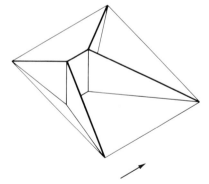

The strategy for obtaining each additional
increment of volume is to allow some shadowing of the surrounding walls in the
amount of 100 percent of all existing or future firewalls, and 30 percent of all existing
or future window walls. Roofs cannot be
shadowed.

I will assume that the east edge of the site touches a street. I will change the external conditions along the other edges of the site by adding firewalls. First one, then two, and finally three firewalls will be added to enclose the site. Then, I will extend the envelope across the street so that it touches a building on the opposite side.

Each of these steps adds volume to the envelope, but each step also diminishes solar access to the site itself and to its surroundings. Finally, only the street face of the envelope and the surfaces that slope up from the surrounding firewalls have exposure to the sun.

Step 1: Add North Firewall
A firewall is shown on the site's north boundary. Volume is added to the basic envelope by extending the ridge northward until it reaches the wall.

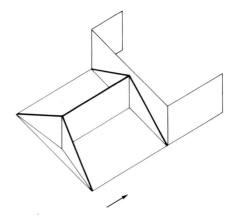

The modified envelope has three sloping faces on the south, east, and west. The fourth face is hidden by the firewall on the north.

Step 2: Add West Firewall
Two firewalls are shown, one on the north
and a second on the west boundary. More
volume is added to the envelope by moving
the ridge up and back toward the west
firewall.

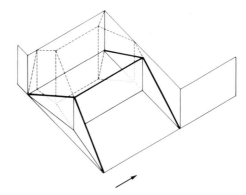

The resulting envelope remains exposed on
the south and east but is contained on the
north and west. Its exposed south and west
faces slope down to grade while two small
faces slope to the tops of firewalls on the
north and west.

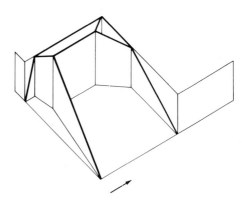

Step 3: Add South Firewall
Three firewalls are now shown: one on the
north, a second on the west, and a third on
the south. Still more volume is added to the
envelope by longitudinally extending the
ridge toward the south firewall.

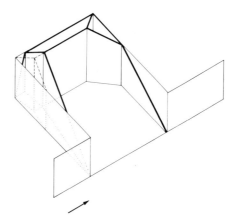

The resulting envelope is contained on three sides and exposed on the fourth side. Its faces slope to the tops of firewalls on the north, west, and south; the east face slopes to grade.

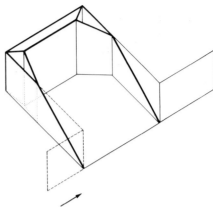

Step 4: Add Buildings Across the Street
A window wall is shown across the street to the east of the site. Unlike the firewalls, that could be completely shadowed; only 30 percent of the window wall is shadowed, according to the rules. Under these circumstances, volume is once more added by expanding the envelope eastward until its slope intersects the opposing wall about one-third of the distance from its case to its top. In this process, the envelope's ridge shifts from north-south to east-west, which increases its height.

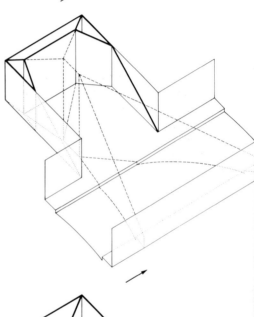

The resulting envelope has a vastly increased volume. It fans out across the street to include all of the firewalls at the site's boundaries and portions of the window walls on both sides of the street.

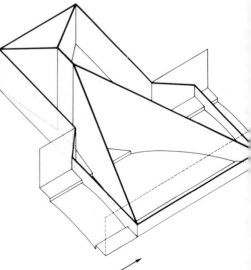

Step 5: Exhibit the Complete Solar Envelope
The developable volume must of course
stop at the property line. The extent of the
buildable volume is indicated by passing a
vertical plane through the fourth envelope
at the building line abutting the street.

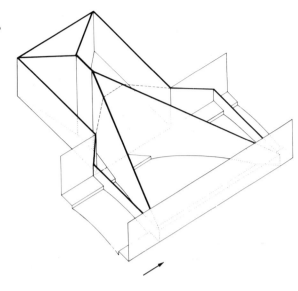

The final envelope assures solar access to
the rooftops of adjacent buildings and to 70
percent of the window wall across the
street. In addition, it has more volume under its sloping surfaces than do the presumably flat-roofed buildings surrounding it.
How this volume can be used and its implications for urban growth are matters that
will be discussed in chapter 10.

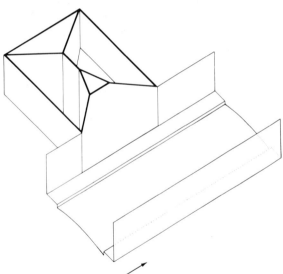

Attitudes Affect the Envelope's Size and Shape

A point made at the beginning of this chapter bears repeating, lest the solar envelope be perceived as a rigid constraint on development and design. In fact, the envelope's size and shape represent a balance among sometimes conflicting values.

Solar access is not an isolated issue. It must be seen in the context of market constraints, land uses, and environmental concerns.

The rules of generation represent choices. The examples of building site applications reflect one set of choices that, because they were taken, provided a particular set of rules for generating the envelope. Another set of rules will provide more or less volume.

Choices underlying the rules of generation must ultimately reflect society's values. People's attitudes will lead to different rules of generation under an array of circumstances.

The question of landscaping, and especially of trees, is inevitably raised in any discussion of solar zoning. This is especially true for housing where people become concerned that solar access zoning would exclude existing or planned landscaping. They begin to wonder what their neighborhoods would be like without trees.*

Solar access can be compatible with the desire for trees. Indeed, landscaping should be integrated into a good solar design. What is required is a recognition of the diversity and dynamic properties of plant materials. There must be strategies for using the sun as a source of light and heat that recognize the dynamic interaction of the sun, buildings, and trees.

---

*Some of the material in this chapter appears in a slightly modified form in R. D. Berry, R. L. Knowles, and D. T. Reza, *Solar Envelope Zoning Concepts: Hillside, Landscaping, and High Density Applications* (Golden, Colorado: Solar Energy Research Institute, 1981).

Envelope

One promising strategy raises the solar envelope to accommodate deciduous trees. The result is a lower envelope to regulate buildings and evergreen trees plus a higher envelope that regulates deciduous trees. The difference between the two envelopes is a function of where and when insolation is received.

The lower envelope, as previously described, functions all year to assure the solar access of surrounding properties with respect to a prescribed daily period and a set of boundary conditions.

The new, upper envelope is constructed with reference to solar needs that can vary seasonally. It is used to regulate deciduous trees that can provide positive seasonal variation for both on- and off-site needs.

The construction of this taller envelope is linked to a hypothetical reference, a minimum volume that is analogous to a building, specified in terms of where and when insolation is most useful. The solar performance of this reference is thus prescribed, but not the specific way solar energy will be used.

The reason for this is that design strategies for using the sun will very likely change in the future, along with emerging knowledge and hardware. Nevertheless, specific examples can help to establish the general correlation between the uses of solar energy and the kind of solar access required.

Premise of the Landscape Envelope: Different Access Needs

An example of current technology is a simple combination of rooftop collectors for hot water, and windows for light and winter heat. These devices have different access requirements. Rooftop access is required year-round for hot water, but the vertical walls of the house and the yard can be shadowed without impairing performance. When the vertical walls and the windows are used to store and transmit energy, whole-building access is required.

There is a temporal distinction in this example upon which a generalization can be based: Protection for the roof must be year-round; for the walls it can be seasonal. This is the premise on which the landscape envelope is based. Deciduous trees that lose their leaves in the fall and regain them in the spring can provide seasonally variable solar access that benefits an integrated approach to solar energy conversion.

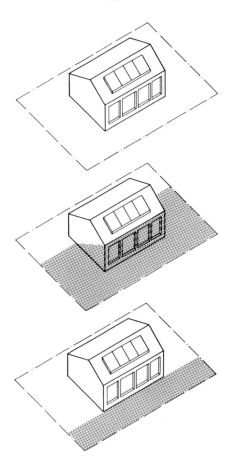

Architectural and Natural Elements Cast Different Shadows

In developing this integrated approach, the fact must be recognized that architectural and natural elements cast different kinds of shadows and hence their limits must be differently prescribed. The traditional privacy fence between properties must be recognized for solar access and design in two ways. First, the property owner who wants to enjoy the full protection of windows and vertical walls for daylight and for heat storage during certain periods of the day and year must set the house back out of the critical fence shadow. Second, the bulk of the neighbor's house must not extend above the solar plane that slopes upward from the fencetop at the cutoff time.

However these two conditions are met, by policy or design, deciduous trees represent an interesting exception because the density of their shadows varies seasonally. During the summer when shadows can be beneficial, the tree is in full leaf. In winter, when the sun's heat and light are most desirable, the tree branches are bare. A strategy based on this seasonal dynamic is most effective when trees are selected that allow the greatest seasonal density change.

Deciduous Trees Can Rise Above the Solar Envelope

This characteristic of some trees has been used historically to provide comfort. It can be recognized today in a solar zoning policy that allows the tree to extend above the building envelope to the higher limits of a landscape envelope. This more spacious boundary can be established to prevent year-round shadowing of the roof while allowing summer shadowing of the walls.

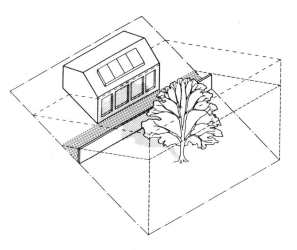

The limits of this landscape envelope, like those of the building envelope, are best determined by local zoning policy. They might vary widely from one city to another. Certainly there should be regional diversity. The following derivation is based on local conditions in Los Angeles where the privacy fence and the one-story bungalow are traditional. Other cities will, no doubt, need to work from different limits but the principles will generally apply.

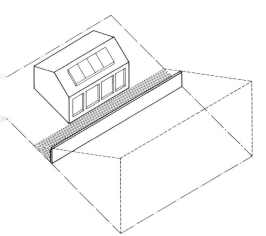

Higher Limits of the Landscape Envelope Based on a Solar-Use Reference

Development of the landscape envelope requires a multidirectional view of limits. Solar access to the southern sky may be sufficient for the present, but may not suffice in future. Effective design requires a more integrated approach. This includes assurance of solar access to the east and west and perhaps even to the northern sky, especially in higher latitudes where the summer sun shines for much of the day from either the northeast or northwest quadrants.

When a site runs long in the east-west direction, the long south boundary may provide sufficient solar exposure. But when the site runs north-south, most of the sun's rays are likely to cross the east boundary in the morning and west boundary in the afternoon. Privacy fences cast their shadows on one's own property as well as on the neighbor's. When a site runs long north-south, shadows from fences have their greatest daily impact along the east and west boundaries.

When the site runs long east-west, the shadow from a fence along the south boundary has greatest impact on a seasonal rather than a daily basis. The winter shadows are much larger than are the summer shadows. The north fence would impact on the neighbor's property but not on the site in question unless access were required in the early morning and late afternoon when the sun's rays come from the north.

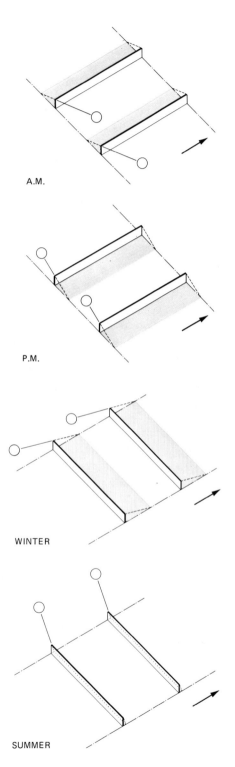

A.M.

P.M.

WINTER

SUMMER

A Hypothetical Box Provides a Solar-Use Reference
A hypothetical box, acting as a "solar-use reference" just inside these shadows, uses the full period of solar access. The minimum acceptable height for this reference volume is 12 ft., or one story.

In an east-west section, the volume is fully protected only if set back equally on both sides to the shadow's inner edge. The morning cutoff time establishes the east setback; the afternoon cutoff time establishes the west setback.

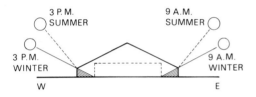

In a north-south section, the volume is fully protected only if set back to the shadow's inner edge on the south. The winter cutoff time establishes this south setback. There is no summer equivalent, since the selected cutoff times (9 A.M.–3 P.M.) for summer do not cast shadows from the north. (This condition varies with latitude.) Consequently, the reference volume intersects the solar envelope at 12 ft. Year-round solar access will be assured at this level and above, where such devices as water heaters are likely to be located. Below 12 ft., a different condition pertains. Where door and window openings are more likely to occur, the

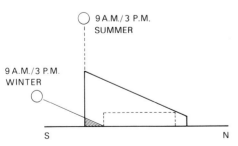

shade of deciduous trees in summer and exposure to the sun in winter may offer advantages. In other words, trees might not be constrained by the same rules that limit building heights.

A Second, Higher Envelope Is Constructed
This idea leads to a separate landscape envelope that rises above the building envelope by the height of the solar-use reference. This additional dimension allows moderate-size trees along the east and west boundaries, larger ones farther inside the site.

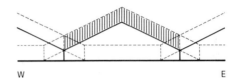

Trees can be quite high along the south, with smaller ones along the north where the neighbor's exposure must be protected.

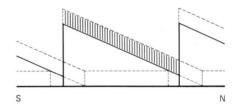

This strategy applies only to deciduous trees. Evergreens are contained by the same envelope that regulates building development.

Typical Sites

When the landscape envelope is applied to typical sites in the Jeffersonian grid, resulting tree sizes vary with orientation and lot size. More variation occurs in the north-south than in the east-west direction. As lots become smaller, trees become more difficult to accommodate.

Tree Heights Vary with Direction

In the east-west direction, trees appear symmetrically under the envelope. Referring to the diagram, property owner A is the affected party. Both B and C may plant deciduous trees that shadow A's walls in summer. A's roof remains in sunlight year-round. When B and C plant their trees, they have made the choice to shadow some of their own 12-ft. reference. But, of course, they are making that choice in full control of the actual roof height and the position of any rooftop devices. Property owner A is free to make the same set of choices.

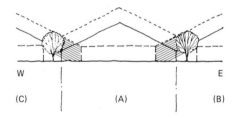

Tree sizes are different in the north-south section. Again, if A is the affected party, owner B is free to plant a much larger tree than is owner C to the south. B's only constraint lies in the limitation to the north, defined differentially by whether deciduous trees or evergreens are to be planted. During the six-hour period of assured access, as the envelope's shape suggests, B's shadows will not be cast south onto A's land. Owner C may only plant smaller, deciduous trees because winter shadows will always be cast onto A.

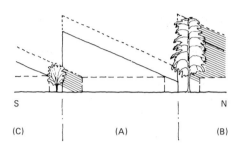

Above the tree-shadow envelope, owner A still has plenty of building volume and potential surface area for energy conversion. And like owner B, owner A may also choose to plant a large tree to the south.

The Effects of Variable Lot Size

The aforementioned examples were of adjacent, 100-ft.-frontage sites. But what happens when sites are larger or smaller; and what happens when their sizes are mixed?

When adjacent sites average in the 50-ft. frontage range or larger, the strategy just described remains operational. This conclusion is based on an assumed working dimension for the 12-ft. solar-use reference. Fifty percent of the lot's small dimension provides a minimum working surface for rooftop energy conversion. This dimension of 25 ft. on a 50-ft. site offers design choices for the owner that might include shadowing parts of the building's roof surface but not the collectors themselves.

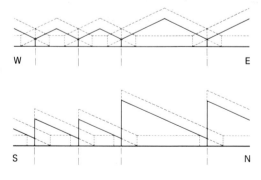

When sites exceed 50-ft. frontage, the roof plane increases. For example, a 100-ft. frontage provides 70 ft. for the plane or 70 percent of the site's minimum dimension.

At 50 ft. and above, frontages may vary with no serious obstacles to this strategy. Mixing frontages in new or "infill" development changes the envelope size, but the dimensions for solar uses remain sufficient.

When the frontage drops below 50 ft., an 8-ft. privacy fence casts shadows that take up proportionally more of the site. Either the fence must be lowered, or the strategy for energy conversion must be changed. When, for example, the site drops to 25 ft., the strategy described above is clearly no longer functional. Under such circumstances, the row house provides the best alternative. The setback for whole-building access is no longer practical and the party wall takes its place. The 12-ft. solar-use plane remains effective. Above it, the solar envelope provides for a gabled roof in the east-west section, a shed roof in the north-south section, but with no landscaping potential in the site's narrow dimension.

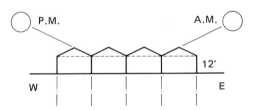

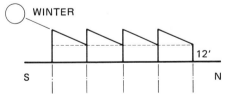

The houses can be made taller by lifting the solar-use plane, thus providing more building volume. But there results a significant change in the ratio between exposed surface and contained volume. In these taller houses, the potential for daylighting, cross-ventilation, and passive heating and cooling is reduced.

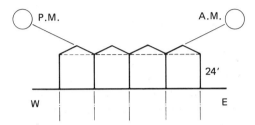

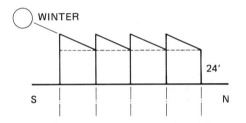

Climate must also be recognized in the choice of strategies. In general, a higher S/V may be preferable in mild climates. Designs would be more loosely packed, would expose more surface, and would probably provide more landscaping opportunities.

More extreme climates with greater thermal variation are more likely to require a lower S/V. Traditional houses obviously expose less surface and thus provide one answer to this need but with fewer landscaping possibilities.

Hillsides

The specific application of landscape envelopes to hillsides of different orientation
follows general principles that govern both
street and site planting.

South-Slope Exemplar

These principles can be explained by using
the example of a single slope (south) with
two different street orientations (up-down
and across the slope).

*Step 1: Extend the Solar Envelope Across
Streets*
The solar envelope must first be extended
over the street to provide a limit on evergreen street planting. Where the street runs
across the slope, this extension is in the solar plane of the envelope's north facet,
across the street, to the top of the uphill
neighbor's 8-ft. privacy fence.

The extension can be shown with the same
kind of arrangement of vertical planes used
earlier to demonstrate the solar envelope.

A simpler presentation of the arrangement
depicts the set of boundary faces rather
than the vertical planes that previously defined envelope hips and ridges. Here the
street envelope slopes like a shed roof, high
on the south and low on the north. It runs
continuously, rather than undulates as the
site envelopes do, because no property lines
cross over the street.

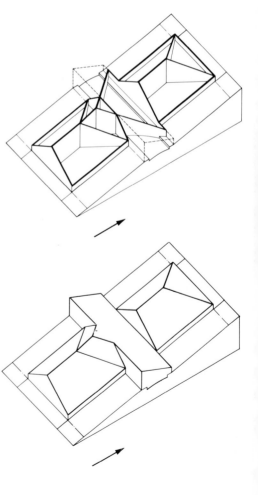

The resulting envelopes serve a dual function. Over the parcels, they act to limit the heights of buildings and evergreen trees. Over the street, the envelope acts only to limit evergreen street planting.

Where the street runs up-down the slope, the envelope extension is across the street in both directions. Unlike the first case where only the downhill envelope extends to the north across the street, this situation calls for an extension of both envelopes.

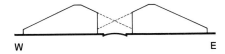

W   E

The extension can be shown, as before, with vertical planes. As the planes reach midstreet, they intersect to suggest a long, symmetrical ridge.

When the boundary faces of all envelopes are explicitly shown, the street envelope is clearly seen as a ridged construction rather than the shedroof of the first case.

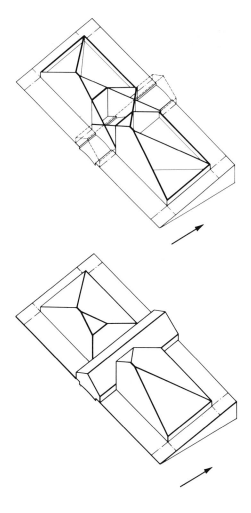

Step 2: Establish the Solar-Use Reference Inside the Envelope
To expand these envelopes for larger de-
ciduous trees, another step must be taken.
This second step involves casting shadows
from privacy fences. This establishes the setbacks for a hypothetical volume with assured solar access on all surfaces between
the cutoff times.

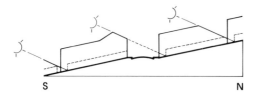

S   N

The function of this solar-use reference has
already been described. It is not an absolute
limit on development, but acts instead as a
reference on which insolation is assured.
Such a reference can act as an important
point of departure for integrated solar
design.

The reference is set back to the inside edge
of shadows from the privacy fence at cutoff
times. Consequently, its size and shape vary
proportionally with the size, shape, and surround of the site. In the example, setbacks
occur to shadow lines on the south, east,
and west. Since the sun does not cast shadows from the north between 9 A.M. and
3 P.M., setbacks on that edge result from
the envelope's height relative to the 12-ft.
reference. There is a setback from the north
edge of the uphill site, but none at the
north edge where the downhill site meets
the street.

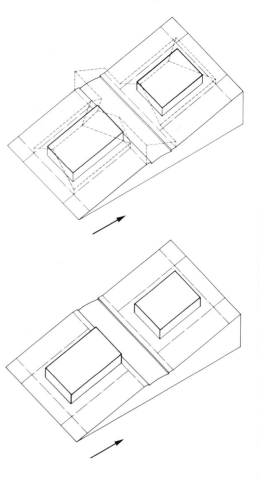

Step 3: Raise the Solar Envelopes for Deciduous Trees

The third step generates envelopes that regulate the height of deciduous trees. These second envelopes duplicate the shape of the earlier ones, but are 12 ft. higher.

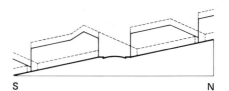

This final step can be visualized as a set of envelopes, one above the other. The lower envelope is shown as a set of boundary planes that regulate the heights of buildings and evergreen trees. The upper envelope is pictured as a set of 12-ft.-high planes extended vertically from the ridges and hips of the envelopes below. This higher envelope regulates deciduous trees that can provide summer shadow and winter sun below 12 ft., and all-year sun above 12 ft. on the solar-use reference. The procedure would be similar for the opposing street orientation.

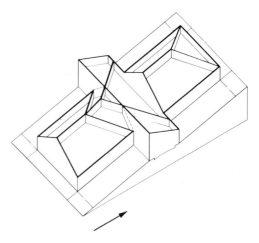

Streets Across the Slope

The explanation that follows will compare three slope orientations: south, north, and west. To make the comparison less confusing, site size and street orientation will be held constant. Sites will have 100-ft. frontage and 130-ft. depth.

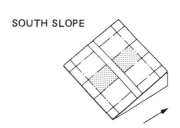

SOUTH SLOPE

This exposition will compare sections in the direction of slope, or up and down the hill, since most development and design problems arise in that direction rather than across the slope. Consequently, for this first discussion where streets cross the slope, sections will be cut through the street, from the downhill to the uphill side.

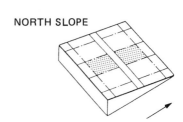

NORTH SLOPE

A general comparison of solar envelopes on the three slopes reveals some differences and a few similarities. First, regardless of slope orientation, envelopes are always different on opposing sides of the street. The street's orientation across the slope always results in envelope asymmetry.

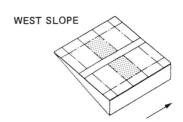

WEST SLOPE

Second, envelopes on north and south
slopes have similar shapes, including the
street envelope that is high on the south,
low on the north. This is in contrast to west
slopes where envelopes have quite different
shapes. This difference is perhaps most pronounced in the street envelope that is lower
on each side of the street than it is toward
the middle.

A comparison of sections reveals more precisely the differences of envelope size and
shape. Envelopes on south slopes are generally the largest; on north slopes, the smallest. West slopes, on average, produce
moderate-size envelopes with markedly
larger envelopes uphill than downhill from
the street. Envelopes to the south side of
the street exhibit a characteristic lump of
volume on both north and south slopes.

The sections show both the solar-use reference volume and the landscape envelope
that is generated from it. (Both are dotted.)

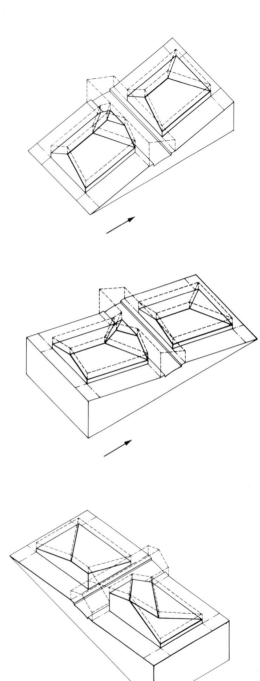

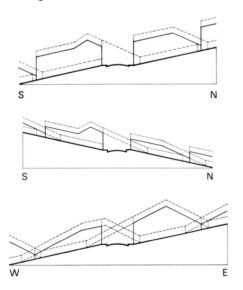

The discussion of these examples will focus on street planting. Because these trees would be in the public right-of-way, they might be planted either by the community or by the property owner, but, as a matter of policy, are kept low to provide rooftop access for all sites. In the north-south sections, street planting will be asymmetrically regulated by the higher of the two dotted lines. (The lower line represents a northward extension of the building envelope to the 8-ft. privacy fence across the street.) In the east-west sections, street planting will be symmetrical. It will be regulated by the higher set of crossing lines, one representing morning rays, the other, afternoon rays of the sun.

Street Planting
When deciduous street trees are shown in the north-south sections, their heights are seen to be asymmetrical across the street, but the same on both north and south slopes. This similarity results from a level road bed, the edges of which act similarly as references for casting shadows. In this example, trees are twice as high on the south as on the north side of the street. Their heights are regulated by winter shadows that must not impact on the roof-plane of the reference volume. Summer shadows will extend north from the taller trees to shadow the southern half of the street.

There is a different shadow rhythm on west and east slopes. Morning shadows are elongated downhill to the west; afternoon shadows are foreshortened uphill to the east. Morning shadows establish the height of trees along the downhill side of the street. Afternoon shadows set the same height on the uphill side.

A.M.

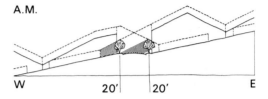

P.M.

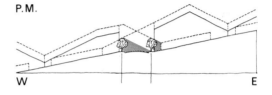

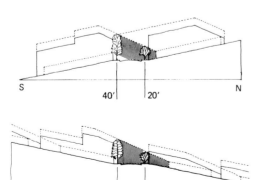

On-Site Planting

Certain choices are presented to the property owner when deciduous trees are planted on the site itself rather than along the street, in the public right-of-way. For example, if the owner is willing to design the relationship between trees and building, much larger-scaled landscaping can be achieved.

Taller, on-site trees can be located so as not to interfere with rooftop access on south slopes. Deciduous trees, 60-ft. tall, can be planted that shadow the street's south half in summer; and, with bare branches, they shadow the entire street in winter. Across the street to the north, 50-ft. trees can be planted on-site if the owner locates devices carefully at the 12-ft. level or anywhere higher in the building envelope.

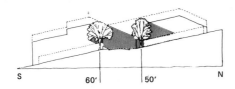

Taller on-site trees may also be planted on north slopes, but the options are somewhat more limited, especially on the downhill site. South of the street, larger trees can be planted as they could be in the last example, with no diminishment of rooftop access. North of the street, however, a smaller tree casts winter shadows over the entire length of a 12-ft.-high surface. The owner must decide more carefully among several options. If tall trees and rooftop access at 12 ft. are desired, the precise path of the moving shadows must be determined. A

more rigorous study of the situation will very likely show that options still exist if the moving shadow is studied in all dimensions. Also, the owner can choose a more transparent tree that casts less winter shadow, thus allowing nearly total access. The summer is no problem because the tree's shadow would fall short of the reference roof.

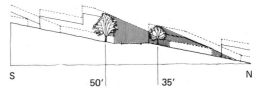

A difference must be recognized between morning and afternoon shadows on west slopes. This is less true on the uphill than on the downhill site.

A.M.

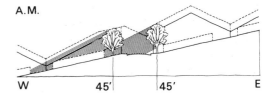

Uphill, the morning shadows have no impact on the solar reference. Afternoon shadows do impact on its 12-ft.-high roofplane. The owner can either locate devices higher in the envelope, or toward the south side of the site.

P.M.

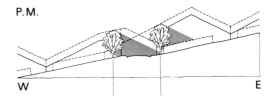

On the downhill site, morning shadows have a definite impact which might still be overcome by a combination of the strategies listed.

Street and On-Site Planting
Diversified combinations may be achieved
when trees are planted both in the public
right-of-way and on the adjacent private
property. The variety of trees can be broad-
ened. Their size, shape, density, and leafing
cycle can be systematically varied.

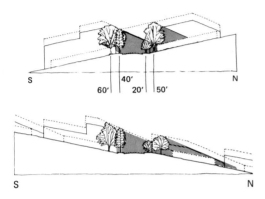

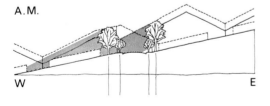

Street trees planted in the public right-of-
way would tend to be smaller than the
largest trees on private property. This
difference results from the more stringent
controls on street trees where there can be
no decision to shadow a rooftop. On private
land, the choice is the owner's to make as
long as the neighbor's solar access is not
violated.

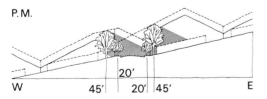

When landscaping strategies include combinations of street and on-site planting, an
important difference must be recognized
between the solar envelope's impact on
public street trees and private property
trees.

The envelope is continuous over the street's
length. Consequently, trees of a constant
size can be planted. Sides of the street may
have different sizes and shapes, but the
rows can be uniform.

On-site planting must rhythmically rise and
fall with the solar envelope as it undulates
to meet property lines. The creative exploration of planting strategies within such a
framework can lead to an extraordinarily
rich landscape.

Streets Up and Down the Slope

As with the discussion of streets across the slope, this exposition will only consider sections in the direction of slope. Since the street in this case parallels the slope, it will not appear in the drawings. Instead, the sections are taken through adjacent sites as they rise above one another on south, north, and west slopes. This procedure is followed, as in the last case, to point out issues of hillside development that are more pronounced up and down than across the slope.

As in the last case, there are some striking similarities between north and south slopes, and differences occur between those two slopes and the west slope.

SOUTH SLOPE

NORTH SLOPE

WEST SLOPE

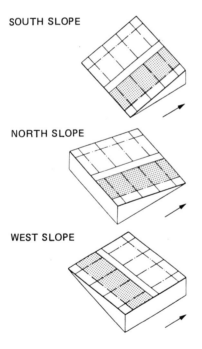

On north and south slopes the envelopes are similar, but much higher on the south slope. When envelopes are compared on opposing sides of the street, they mirror each other's size and shape. The shape of the landscape envelope over the north-south street is symmetrical and tent-like.

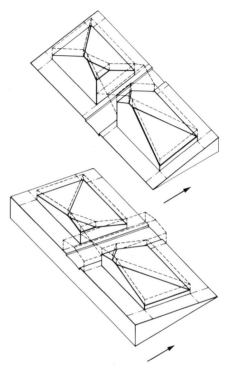

Opposing envelopes on the west slope have dissimilar shapes. They face each other in a north-south direction across the street and, along with the street envelope, are characteristically asymmetrical.

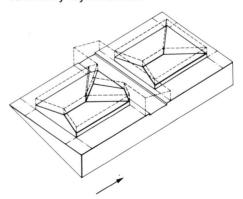

As in the previous case, a general comparison reveals extreme differences of envelope size between south and north slopes.

South slopes not only have the largest envelopes, but the contrast between their uphill and downhill sides is pronounced. The section shows that the solar-use reference extends nearly the entire width of the site, thus providing the owner with greater flexibility in choosing solar design strategies.

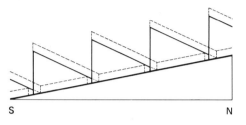

S   N

North slopes provide the least volume under the envelope and less contrast between the uphill and downhill sides. The solar-use reference extends over barely one-half of the site's width, thus limiting the owner's solar design options.

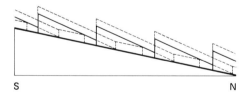

S   N

The west-slope envelopes are actually smaller in this section than are those on north slopes. They lack a high peak along the site boundary. Instead of rising continuously from one edge, they must drop at both boundaries.

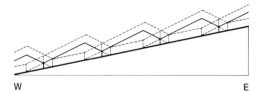

W   E

The size distinction between trees in the public right-of-way and on private land exists in these cases as it did in the last, except that the street does not appear in the sections. And the same difference exists between regulation of street trees by public policy and the freer choice of the property owner.

What is plain in these sections that did not appear in drawings of the last examples is a more intimate relationship between neighbors. This relationship clearly has a great deal to do with privacy and view, two issues that will be discussed later. Here, the concentration will be on the shadow impact of one neighbor on another, as well as on impacts within a property. The procedure for discussing shadow impact will be to consider three adjacent property owners: A, B, and C. Owner A will always be the impacted party; the trees of neighbors B and C will shadow A's land.

On south slopes, for example, property owner A might find very high trees uphill on B's land to the north and much smaller trees downhill on C's land to the south. In neither case would there be a shadow impact on A's property above the 12-ft. reference height. Clearly, however, both B and C must exercise some design skill to be able to achieve those high trees along each one's southern boundary.

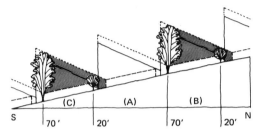

On north slopes, the picture is generally the same except that the solar envelopes lie closer to the site. There is less building volume and trees must be smaller. Owner A will be impacted from the south by C's trees, but only to the prescribed degree.

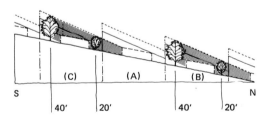

The vertical south wall of the solar-use reference will be shadowed by leafless trees in winter, while rooftop access is assured above 12 ft. year-round. And, as on the south slope, property owner B may plant a sizable tree without impacting on A. Owner B must exercise choice to have the option of a larger tree that acts integrally for an effective solar design.

A last interesting point in contrasting south and north slopes: while large trees can only be planted on a property's south side, that side is downhill on south slopes and uphill on north slopes. This fact probably has more relevance to privacy and to view than it does to solar access.

On west slopes, the time of day establishes whether owner A will be impacted by B or by C. In the morning, A is impacted from uphill by B's smaller tree. In the afternoon, the impact on A is from C's larger tree downhill. In each case, the shadows are only on the vertical walls and not on the roof of the solar-use reference.

In the morning, however, both B and C impact on their own 12-ft.-high roofs. That impact varies seasonally. The whole roof is shadowed in the winter when trees are bare; only about half is shadowed in summer when trees are in leaf and the sun is higher in the sky. In the afternoon, the shadow impact of B and C upon themselves is negligible at all seasons.

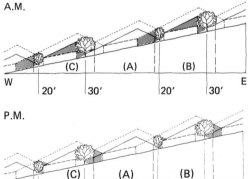

In conclusion, the preceding discussion of landscape differences based on orientation has only touched on general plant characteristics of size and shape. Obviously, much work can be done to extend the differentiation of plant material to include more detailed structural properties, including growth rate and leafing cycles.

In addition to trees, plants of smaller size, including ground cover, may be selected to fill out a more complete picture. The result can be combinations of plants and buildings that are differentiated in response to slope orientation.

If solar design is to attain its purpose of using the sun to improve the quality of life, the several means to that end must be understood and evaluated, separately at first and then together.

Particular instances of natural adaptation can never be observed in isolation. Systems in nature are complex and seem always to be moving along several paths simultaneously. And so it is with built arrangements. They act in complex ways to provide for our needs. To help us handle that complexity we need a framework for design, a construct.

The construct for solar design used in this book is a synthesis of three basic modes of building adaptation. These become the means to the end of enhanced quality of life.

The significance of a concept of three building adaptations is that it provides the designer with both a broad design palette and a large, solid platform from which to challenge modern development. This challenge must be on two levels. First, there is the issue that today's development is too costly to maintain. Second, modern development breaks the ancient natural relationship between what things look like and how they perform.

In nature, these two points are apparently resolved by complex interactions among three basic modes of adaptation. These modes have counterparts that are static and dynamic expressions of the same functions.

The static expressions are location, form, and energy conversion. Different communities of plants and animals will consistently locate, form, and convert energy for characteristic growth and development.

The dynamic counterparts for these three modes are sometimes more apparent. A change in location is *migration*. A change of form is *transformation*. The rate of energy conversion is the *metabolic rate*. These modes are usually found in complex combinations that, taken together, rhythmically structure nature.*

Ancient human settlements employed all of these modes at one time or another and in various combinations. In what we are inclined to label "primitive architecture," adaptation of shelter to the elements could not depend on high rates of energy conversion. Consequently, location and form were the most likely means employed to respond to climate and use.

*For an earlier application of natural adaptive modes to building, see Ralph L. Knowles, *Energy and Form* (Cambridge, Massachusetts: MIT Press, 1974), pp. 10–15, 71.

Modern equivalents can be found in all basic adaptive modes, but clearly metabolism leads all the rest. Today we rely too much on metabolic means, the mechanical or chemical conversion of energy, to temper the environment. In the process, we have neglected the expressive potential of older, traditional means. We have almost abandoned the adaptive modes of location and form in favor of metabolic modes; the current energy problem is in part a consequence of this dependence.

Solar design challenges the proposition that present modes of energy conversion have made the ancient and traditional modes obsolete or inoperative. The hitherto unrecognized benefit for us is that these older, abandoned means hold the potential not only for energy efficiency but for an enhanced quality of life. The information we have discarded we may now need to reclaim.

I challenge recent design practice to encourage a reexamination of traditional modes of adaptation as a possible solution to the apparent conflict between energy conservation and the quality of life. The challenge will be delineated with an exposition of research on location, form, and metabolism as integrated modes of adaptation for new settlement and for urban redevelopment.

Location

People have often migrated as an adaptation to environmental stress and have sometimes carried their shelters with them. Most shelters, however, are fixed in place. Their location is the first adaptation to the environment. The three components of location are orientation, juxtaposition, and relation to the general surround.

Orientation

Buildings can be oriented to mitigate the effect of natural variation. One of the clearest examples of this ancient mode can be seen at Acoma pueblo, near Albuquerque, New Mexico. The buildings of this thousand-year-old settlement are aligned in rows that run east and west; they consequently have broad exposures to the north and south. The terraces of each house are oriented to catch the south sun.

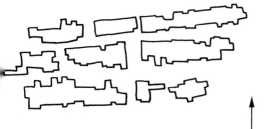

The significance of orientation can, in part, be demonstrated by experimentally re-orienting the same house so that its terraces face north. The result is a winter reduction in the area seen by the sun, without a comparable summer reduction. The advantages of seasonal mitigation realized on the south terraces would be in good part lost by re-orienting the building without changing any other of its properties.

A modern application of this principle may be demonstrated by comparing two orientations of a large slab-like building form. If the broad faces are exposed to east and west, the overall summer gain is much greater than if the broad faces are exposed to the north and south. The effect in the second case is to reduce the difference between winter and summer energy gains on the combined faces of the form. If, for the moment, other issues of internal performance are set aside, the effect of the large south exposure is to even out demands on mechanical support systems.

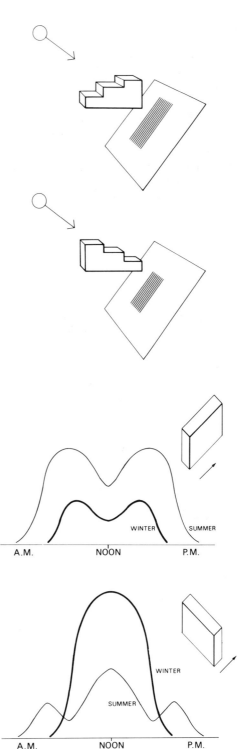

Juxtaposition

The juxtaposition of buildings can be planned so as to mitigate the effects of natural variation. Acoma is a good example of juxtaposition as well as orientation. The rows of Acoman houses are spaced to avoid winter shadows on terraces. Close inspection will find no significant exceptions to this rule; a remarkable finding, considering that people have continuously lived, built, and rebuilt in this settlement for ten centuries.

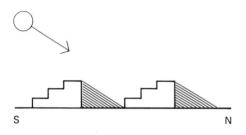

An application of juxtaposition will result in different lot sizes and shapes, corresponding to variations of slope and orientation. The physical arrangement would vary with the site, the criterion being maximization of insolation.

Relation to Surround

The relation between a planned unit development and its surround can sometimes require a locational adaptation. Acoma again provides a useful historical example.

Acoma is sited atop a high plateau that severely limits development space. The result is a conflict with right of solar access. The Acomans resolved this conflict with the closest possible spacing between rows of houses, while still providing winter sun to each dwelling. Right of access could obviously have been achieved by free-standing rows of south-facing houses; the limiting edge of the plateau tightened the constraints and produced an inevitable spacing.

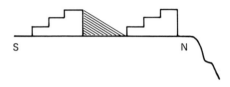

An application of this principle will yield different spacing between new subdivision and existing strip development. Where a major commercial street runs east-west, residential development on the south will be located much closer to large buildings than on the north, where long shadows can interfere with a house's solar performance. Some sort of buffer zone will thus be required on the north; such a zone might contain an array of service functions.

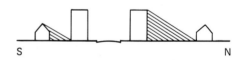

Form

Ancient people adaptively transformed their shelters in a rhythmic way. Tent flaps opened and closed in response to natural variations. More recently, wooden shutters, glass windows, curtains, and drapes have all been used to adapt our buildings to natural variation.

These are all minor transformations; a technology capable of much more fundamental changes in a building's form can be imagined. Also, the sequence of development can be planned, so that over time, transformation toward a better environmental fit can be realized for sets of interrelated buildings. Such planned transformations are a real possibility, but for this discussion I want to focus on the historical fact that most buildings have a fixed basic form.

Form can be viewed as a second mode of adaptation to environmental variation. The three components of form are size, shape, and structure.

Size

A building's size affects the relationship between exposed surface and contained volume. This ratio (S/V) determines susceptibility to what is commonly called "skin phenomenon." An idea of it can be obtained by comparing two cubes of different size. A unit cube with one face on the ground plane exposes five faces ($S/V = 5.0$). If the cube's edges are doubled, the five exposed faces have an increased total surface area of 20, while the volume has increased to 8 ($S/V = 2.5$).

This phenomenon results in a reduced susceptibility of large buildings to external variations. Their inside space responds more slowly to what happens outside their skins than does the space inside smaller buildings. A corollary is that a large building is less susceptible to environmental stress than the same volume distributed among several smaller buildings.

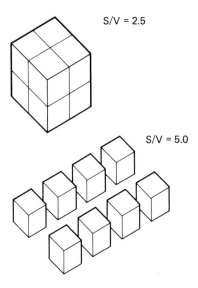

S/V = 2.5

S/V = 5.0

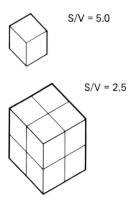

S/V = 5.0

S/V = 2.5

Shape

The shape of a building can respond to natural variations in two distinct ways: First, shape affects the relationship between exposed surface and contained volume and can therefore, along with size, be adapted to generalized stress. This can be seen by comparing cross-sections of the same volume in different configurations. Shape does not influence S/V as much as size, but it is nonetheless an important consideration when designing for minimum energy demand.

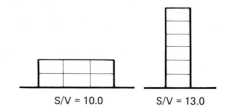

S/V = 10.0   S/V = 13.0

Second, shape determines the effect of directional forces. Take the example of six identical volumes arranged to have seasonally different solar impacts. Stacked vertically and exposed to the south, the volumes will experience greater winter than summer gain. Just the reverse is true for the same volume stacked horizontally on the ground.

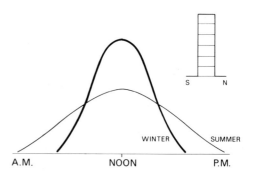

The significance of shape as an adaptive mode can be easily seen by making a simple analysis of Acoma pueblo. The shape of Acoma selectively exposes more surface to the south, less to the north. The effect of this directional surface exposure is to capture more south sun and reduce heat losses on the north. A somewhat more detailed look at this arrangement reveals an interesting correlation between the distribution of building function and the vertical differentiation of S/V.

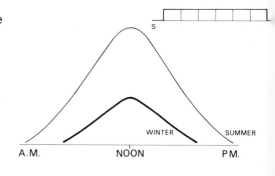

The ground floor was used for food storage. It contains the most volume and exposes the least surface area relative to that volume. Inside temperatures are consequently less affected by outside extremes, resulting in steady temperatures. Storing food at the ground level also avoided the drudgery of carrying heavy harvest loads farther up into the house.

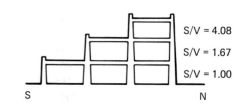

S/V = 4.08
S/V = 1.67
S/V = 1.00

The second story was used for sleeping. It contains less volume and exposes relatively more surface area (the S/V is more than 50 percent greater than at the ground floor). Inside temperatures are more variable than at the first floor, but for sleeping this may be less important than being up off the ground and having more openings to fresh air.

Finally, the third story was used for cooking and eating. It contains the least volume and exposes relatively the most surface (the S/V is four times that of the ground floor). Inside temperatures are still more susceptible to external variation at this level, but the cooking fires add heat during the cold winter months and good ventilation helps during the hot summer. Also, the fire smoke would rise from this floor and thus escape the eyes and noses of those on the terraces and in the rooms below.

Such integrated performance is the result of adaptation over long periods of time, during which the building's form accumulates symbolic importance. (It might be mentioned in this regard that the Acomans' traditional passage to the spirit world is made in three steps.)

Structure

The properties and disposition of materials comprising a building's structure can be used adaptively in response to an array of environmental components. For example, construction materials act selectively to mitigate both seasonal and daily temperature variations. This selectivity distinguishes between the thermal performance of vertical and horizontal structural components.

The low winter sun strikes most directly the vertical masonry bearing walls that have a high heat transmission coefficent and heat storage capacity. The high summer sun strikes directly down onto horizontal surfaces comprised of timber, reeds, and

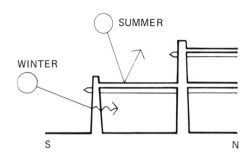

grasses covered with clay; these roof terraces have a lower heat transmission coefficient and heat storage capacity.

The result is a mitigation of seasonal internal temperature variation, because winter sun is stored and transmitted over time into the building while summer sun is kept out. There is also a daily effect, because heat stored in the walls during the day is released throughout the night into the building, a very effective way of handling the extraordinary daily temperature variation of the high desert.

A final point should be made about Acoma's load-bearing walls. Their great thickness at the bottom provides more thermal stability for the storage spaces on the ground floor. As the walls rise, their thickness and hence their thermal mass decreases, but different living functions on the second and on the third floor do not require such a thermal steady state as does the storage of vital food supplies.

In most buildings, even today, materials are generally organized in the plane of the enclosing envelope. In such an arrangement, materials tend to act as a sort of filter. They modify the environment by virtue of their thermal and weathering properties. The resulting aspect is generally flat, as in the load-bearing walls of Acoma and even in the curtain-wall buildings of the modern era.

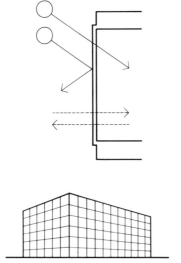

However, there are alternative ways to arrange the structural materials of a building. They might, for example, be organized normal to the plane of the building's envelope. Arranged in that way, they might shade, shadow, and shelter, as well as filter. Instead of flat, the resulting surface aspect might be either textural or even spatial.

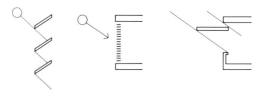

The material of the building can be organized inside as well as outside in response to external stress. How the building is compartmentalized determines to a great extent its inertial properties as well as its spatial character. This is very clear at Acoma, where the increased compartmentalization of larger spaces at the ground floor helps provide more thermal stability. The upper floors are smaller and, of course, more exposed and therefore experience more thermal variation inside.

Most modern buildings seem to fall into one of only a few basic modes of compartmentalization, which, if properly understood, can be used adaptively in response to external variation. Some, for example, are organized with their small spaces on the perimeter and their large spaces inside. Temperature variation would be quite high in the small spaces because they act in direct and immediate response to outside conditions. The large spaces inside have greater thermal inertia; they are protected by a blanket of small spaces and are consequently slower to respond to outside forces, reacting instead to variations of occupancy.

Other buildings are organized with their large spaces near the perimeter and their small spaces inside. A plot of temperature variation would show that the large spaces act in direct but delayed response to out-side conditions because of their greater thermal inertia. The small spaces inside are sheltered from external stress but are usu-ally not desirable for occupancy, in part be-cause they respond too quickly to buildups of body heat and stale air.

The characteristics of different-sized spaces in combination with their occupancy levels can be used adaptively in response to dif-ferent orientations. In low-occupancy build-ings, small spaces might be placed on the north as a barrier to heat loss, while large spaces on the south act to gain winter sun. In high-occupancy buildings, large assem-blages of people might be put in large north-facing spaces to temper otherwise cool rooms. Such adaptive uses of form and occupancy will reduce much of the load on heating and air-conditioning systems, as well as provide an overt expression of per-formance in our buildings.

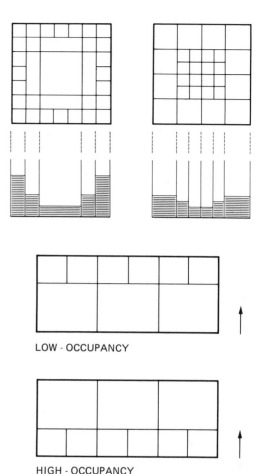

LOW - OCCUPANCY

HIGH - OCCUPANCY

Metabolism

Metabolism is the third basic adaptation to environment. The term, as used here, refers to the sum of all chemical and mechanical processes that provide energy for environ-mental regulation within buildings. As sim-ple combustion, this mode of adaptation has always been with us. Only in its most re-cent complex mechanical forms have we be-come particularly dependent on it, almost to the exclusion of other adaptive modes.

With few exceptions (such as the radiant heating systems of ancient Rome), occu-pancy and open fires remained the only metabolic means until the eleventh century. From the earliest times, people huddled close together in central spaces to share body heat around an open fire.

The technological advance from central fires under a hole in the roof to mantled chimneys built into the walls of individual rooms brought both health and social changes. In *A Distant Mirror*, historian Barbara Tuchman writes that this eleventh-century change in Europe brought lords and ladies out of the common hall, where all had once eaten together and gathered for warmth, and separated owners from their retainers. No other invention brought more progress in comfort and refinement, although at the cost of a widened social gulf.*

Separate fireplaces may also have contributed to improved general health. Close physical proximity increases the likelihood of passing infectious diseases, so that a decentralized heating system would probably have had some mitigating effect on epidemics during that period.

Not until the nineteenth century did central heating and mechanical ventilation begin to develop in its modern forms. Architects Robert Brucemann and Donald Prowler have recently documented this rapid development of mechanical-system design, primarily in the hospitals and the public buildings of England and France.† In the United States, however, the most important applications of central heating and mechanical ventilation did not occur until the second half of the nineteenth century, when the commercial high-rise buildings of Chicago were built.

---

*Barbara W. Tuchman, *A Distant Mirror* (New York: Knopf, 1979), p. 11.

†Robert Brucemann and Donald Prowler, "19th Century Mechanical Systems," *Journal of Architectural Education*, February 1977, pp. 11–15.

Through the efforts of architects who worked in this genre, centralized heating was then applied to houses. A typical example of an early transfer can be seen in the Glessner house, designed by H. H. Richardson and built in Chicago in 1886–1887. The basic design is sensitive to site and climate. The ancient tools of location and form were developed by Richardson, along with a decentralized system of individualized fireplaces. Then, almost as an afterthought, Richardson provided space for modern ducts and registers that could be connected to a central furnace at a later time. The connection was, of course, eventually made.

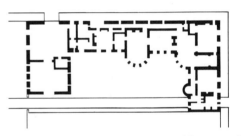

Based on a drawing (106) in The Architecture of H. H. Richardson and His Times *by Henry-Russell Hitchcock (Cambridge, Mass.: The MIT Press, 1966).*

Richardson began with an architecturally well-adapted house that combined thick masonry walls on the north side with window walls around the south-facing garden; only then did he add central heating. If central heating had been further developed than it was, Richardson might have based his entire design on it, instead of relying on architectural means, but the point is hardly worth arguing. We have now achieved almost total reliance on chemical and mechanical systems without Richardson's help.

With increasing applications of centralized heating, and especially with the development of mechanical cooling after World War II, the ancient techniques that Richardson's generation inherited have fallen into disuse. Today, virtually all building design is based on the presupposition of centralized heating and cooling systems. No real integration of the ancient and the modern has yet occurred. The traditional architectural modes of location and form have given way to the newer chemical and mechanical modes.

The fact is that our schools have now educated several generations of architects who depend exclusively on nonarchitectural means of environmental adaptation. The problems of this approach are now emerging, partly as an energy-consumption dilemma, but perhaps, more to my point, problems of architectural expression have appeared. A paucity of vocabulary has emerged as a professional and artistic dilemma: If all environmental problems can be handled by chemical and mechanical means, who needs the architect?

This is a situation where one dilemma may at least partly answer a second. The energy-consumption dilemma can, in some degree, be answered by the means needed to enrich the architect's vocabulary and to make the architect professionally and artistically more complete. The means include the integrated uses of location, form, and metabolism. Location and form have already been discussed in some detail. Metabolism will now be discussed as a function of occupancy, on- and off-site chemical conversion, and control.

Metabolism by Occupancy

People give off heat that results from the chemical processing of food. When that heat is controlled to temper a building's spaces, it becomes a metabolic component of adaptation.

The heat from large concentrations of people can be transported to serve other parts of the building. A common energy-conserving technique sends heat from occupied public spaces on one side of the building to a colder side with lower occupancy. Other techniques transfer the heat buildup in large occupied inside spaces to colder outside spaces.

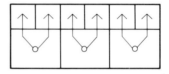

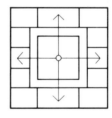

A less-mechanized, but in some cases just as effective, use of body heat involves moving the people in a building rather than transporting their body heat. The case is included here not because there may be immediate and wide application but because it contains an interesting principle for further development. The simplest demonstration of the possibilities may be made by considering a large, simple building with windows all around; it may be an unheated assembly building exposed on all sides, the sort we all remember from our camping days.

The designer's task is to schedule the location of large assemblies within the building to equalize thermal conditions throughout the space. The task involves moving people to use their body heat as a source of energy for conditioning the whole building.

The designer would then congregate large groups in the north during winter. In the morning, when solar energy is being received from the southeast, people will be moved to the northwestern corner; in the afternoon, when the sun shines from the southwest, groups will be concentrated in the northeastern corner. Summer will bring about a southward migration in this arrangement. On a summer morning, concentrations will occur in the southwest, while afternoon assemblies might occur in the southeast.

WINTER

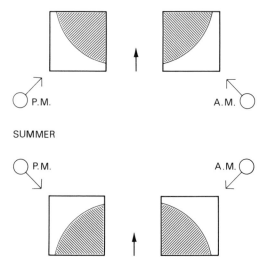

SUMMER

If the task requires the designer to shift small instead of large groups of people, chances are that the direction of migration will have been reversed to gain solar exposure and comfort for the small group. Certainly this would be the case in winter and perhaps even on a summer morning, when ambient air temperatures are low. The first task was to condition the space by shifting body heat to those portions of the building that were not receiving solar energy. The second task was to provide comfort within a large space for a few people, requiring that they move toward and not away from the sun.

This notion of migration to attain comfort appears in the architectural literature of ancient Rome. Vitruvius, in his treatise on architecture, describes the best arrangement for various living activities in terms of migration. Dining, for example, is described as best occurring in different spaces of the house at different times of the year in order to take maximum advantage of the migrating sun. More recently, many Victorian houses contained rooms designated as autumn or summer parlors, and morning or afternoon porches.

In our own times, the freedom to schedule congregations of people may not always exist. But where it does, migration becomes part of an effective adaptation by balancing solar energy and human metabolic energy in a rhythmic way.

On- and Off-Site Chemical Processes

Metabolic energy for building adaptation is provided by both on- and off-site chemical processes using quite different levels of technology.

Off-site processes generally involve combustion to produce electricity that is carried through low-efficiency transmission lines to be used by relatively efficient on-site machines. Such processes generally deliver one unit of energy for use on the site for every three units required to manufacture and transport the energy. The technology of such systems is costly and highly centralized. The centralization of control is essential to deal with the problems attending peak-load demand. The peak loading of electrical systems tends to occur in the summer, when cooling requirements are heaviest.

On-site processes generally involve combustion to heat space and water directly, without converting to electricity first. There are no high transmission losses in power lines because such fuels as gas and oil are transported by a relatively efficient means and are then burned on site. On-site combustion tends to be inefficient. But from initial combustion to final use, on-site conversion systems perform more efficiently than off-site ones. The technology of conversion and control is less centralized and therefore less costly at a regional scale. Problems of peak loading tend to occur in winter, rather than in summer, because heating loads are high during the cold months.

Metabolic Control

Control over the chemical and mechanical processes of energy conversion has both objective and subjective aspects. The evaluation of different control modes can be made in the objective terms of cost, but the evaluation would be incomplete without taking into account how people feel about their interface with the system—their ability to make choices about the system performance.

Centralized control within a building probably has a lower first cost, but is less responsive to individual users. The lower first cost derives from simple controls that "blanket"

spaces with similar levels of heating, cooling, and lighting. However, to centralize control means "to take it out of my hands and put it into somebody else's." That "somebody else" is not going to experience the world through my mind and body and therefore cannot possibly respond to my specific needs in a variety of changing environmental conditions. In buildings where control is centralized, and where people cannot take individual action on their own behalf by opening and closing windows or raising and lowering light levels, complaints tend to focus on the system. Resentment accumulates around a featureless foe.

Decentralized control may or may not have a higher first cost. Presuming that a higher first cost will derive from more complex controls that recognize local differences, the long-term costs of maintenance become more subject to user attitudes. A conservation ethic, for example, can vastly reduce operating costs. Control shifts from a faceless entity to one's own hands: "The choices are mine." Windows can be opened or closed, lights can be turned up or down, and individually controlled fans can provide the amount of air movement desired under variable conditions. The system is thus under my control and I am free to exercise my ancient right—to complain about the weather!

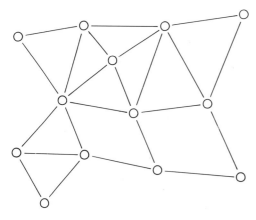

The Design Sequence

The three basic modes of adaptation have been independently analyzed for a better understanding of their nature and application. The actual design of a building should integrate them all in a sequence based on the limits of their usefulness. The sequence should begin with location, then form, and end with metabolism.

This design sequence is meant to be anticipatory. It exposes options to reduce environmental stress by specific siting and building means before introducing more energy-intensive mechanical means to handle the remainder of the load.

Location should be investigated first. Prior conditions such as public policies and site restrictions are likely to limit the designer's options regarding location. For example, requirements for setbacks and access may combine with site size and shape to exclude any possibility for proper orientation to the sun. This fact should influence the designer's subsequent decisions about building form and metabolism.

Form should be investigated as a second adaptive mode in the design sequence. Good location can usually be enhanced with building form, and bad location can sometimes be corrected with careful attention to building size, shape, and structure. Form

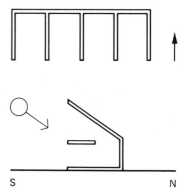

S   N

then becomes a logical extension of location as an adaptive mode. The integration of the two modes should produce an irreduceable result, a unified whole expression of performance.

Advantage can be taken of a south orientation in small- and moderate-sized buildings by opening them up to the sun and by using materials that usefully store winter insolation. The benefits derived from proper juxtaposition can be extended by using forms that capture the incident energy when it is needed.

Form can sometimes correct poor locational situations. Where the long dimensions of a site face east and west, south exposure may be gained by breaking the building into smaller parts, separated by courts that allow penetration of winter sun.

Where a site is so constrained that parts of a planned unit begin to shadow each other, the individual buildings may be organized so the upper portions exposed to sunlight contain the major living spaces, while the lower, shaded portions contain service functions.

Metabolism should be investigated as the last adaptive mode in this design sequence. If the designer has found reasonable options for location and form, little work may remain for the metabolic systems. If, on the other hand, the designer has properly explored the potential for location and form and found few options, then, and only then, the major environmental load may have to be borne by metabolic means. This may be the case with some urban infill structures, which offer limited location and form options.

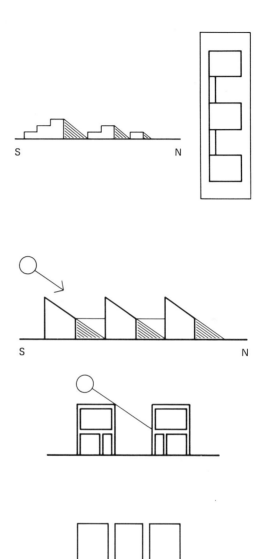

Our current problems related to energy and quality of life are partially the result of reduced choices that left metabolic means as the only apparent solution for comfort. But metabolic costs are continuous over the life of a building; everything should be done to minimize such a long-term investment in maintenance cost by relying more on location and form early in the design process.

Environmental Complexity

The natural environment of a building is a complex structure of forces that act from different directions at various durations. Usually the complexity can be reduced to only a few forces that act with strong directionality, but even this more simplified picture may require the designer to establish a hierarchy in the adaptive uses of location, form, and metabolism.

Sometimes complex sets of environmental forces act congruently so that, for example, desirable sun and wind may come from the same direction. In this fortunate circumstance, the building may be oriented to catch both sun and wind on its broad south face and the building may thus be open on that side.

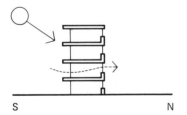

S   N

On the other hand, directional forces more usually act incongruently, making choices necessary. The sun and wind may come from different directions. The designer must then choose among adaptive modes: Which mode will be matched with each directional force?

The designer's choices will, of course, be influenced by other factors; where choices exist, values must be set. For example, the sun may be recognized through a primary locational adaptation in which the whole building becomes oriented to the south. Adaptation to a west wind would then be handled with a secondary form mode in which the building's surface structure scoops in the wind for natural ventilation. Conversely, if the designer chooses to place more value on cross ventilation, the primary locational mode may orient the whole building to face east and west.

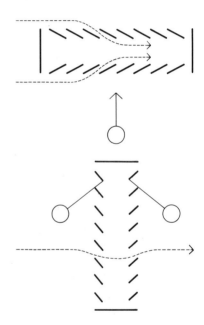

Failure to control the sun on broad east and west faces results in high metabolic costs. In this case, control is a matter of arranging the building's surface structure to exclude the sun when it would result in overheating. The designer can exercise choice in selecting location or form strategies for control, holding as many options as possible open as the design process advances. Where location and form adaptations are insufficient, metabolic means can be used to fill the gap.

Natural Intervals and Adaptive Modes

A general correlation can be drawn between the interval of natural variation and its appropriate mode of adaptation. Location and form are more applicable to long intervals; metabolic adaptations are more suitable to short intervals. This then becomes the foundation for a design strategy based on time, or rhythm. A mismatch of interval and adaptive mode results in a penalty for energy or quality of life or both.

The correlation between the interval of natural cycles and design strategies reflects the relative permanence and flexibility of alternatives. The seasonal path of the sun results in an annual cycle of heat and light that lends itself to control by location, or orientation and siting. Form can be used to control certain aspects of both the seasonal and daily effects of the sun. Metabolic intervention may be appropriate for controlling daily effects not controllable by location and form alone.

The fact that the annual and daily cycles of the sun are predictable brings them into the province of the designer. The designer's sensitivity to rhythm can be critical in choosing among alternative design strategies.

Consider the hypothetical example of a design for a resort hotel with on-site requirements for parking and for recreation. The site is restricted on the east and west and therefore the pool and parking lot are presumed to lie on the north and south of the building. By now it should be clear to the reader that the relative location of those facilities should be determined by seasonal

variation. With the exception of a few hours of summer days, the north side of the hotel will always be in shadow. The shadows will extend farther in winter; this can be very important to a southern resort where swimming continues all year. Obviously, the design solution is to put the pool to the south of the hotel and the parking to the north.

Someone may raise the issue of the sunbather who gets too much sun and not enough fun. But the answer to this is not to deny solar access to the pool; an umbrella is a far more appropriate response because it allows the sunbather to exercise choice.

Of course, the pool could be located to the north of the hotel and the sunbathers could be provided with sunlamps and heaters if they wanted heat or light. But the penalties in energy and life quality are significant.

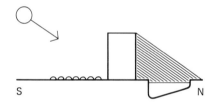

S   N

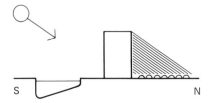

S   N

The resort hotel has a special need for solar access, but its needs are not really so different from most buildings. Like the resort hotel, the south exposure is an advantage for most buildings in the northern hemisphere, regardless of their specific shapes.

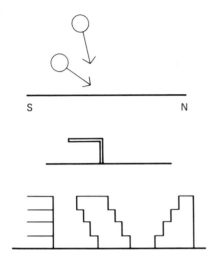

Form is critically related to both yearly and daily intervals of variation. The example of Acoma pueblo has already been discussed in some detail, but modern applications of its design strategies can certainly be made.

Acoma uses shape to mitigate seasonal variation. It exposes more surface to the south than to the north; south-facing vertical walls catch and transmit solar heat in winter; and horizontal terraces catch, but resist, summer radiation. The shape responds more to seasonal than daily variation, but the structure handles daily variations within seasons. The vertical masonry walls heat up more slowly on summer days and they are exposed to fewer hours of solar radiation than in winter. The heat they do receive in summer is stored and released during the night, when temperatures drop. This gradual release of thermal energy helps to mitigate daily temperature variations.

Theoretically, thicker walls might extend the thermal time lag from days into months, storing summer heat for use in winter. But that would present extreme structural problems; imagine the thickness of door and window jambs! In any case, it seems more appropriate to start each day with a new cycle of energy as long as the sun regularly provides it. Where it does not, thicker, or even partially buried, structures may help.

Structure can also mitigate daily variations. Both the thermal properties and the disposition of materials can act in combination to control higher ambient afternoon temperatures and the west sunlight that lead to overheating.

The interval of natural variation for which a metabolic response is most appropriate may be no longer than a day or perhaps even shorter. On-site combustion is fast and can handle hourly changes in the thermal environment. Electricity supplied to the site can also respond to short-term variations in the thermal and luminous environment.

The designer must keep in mind that metabolic energies are costly when used to overcome large natural variations and to sustain stable conditions. These long intervals are best handled by architectural manipulations of location and form. Metabolic systems can then be allowed to do what they do best—respond quickly to uncertain changes in the environment.

8   The Implementation of Solar Design

The transformation of the solar design construct of location, form, and metabolism into buildings is the final step in turning idea into reality. In some ways, this is the least understood step because it depends on cognitive processes that are themselves only vaguely understood. Even so, most designers would acknowledge that the step is made more easily and surely if it includes alternatives to meet unforseen obstacles in the designer's path. The components, then, of implementation are clear design objectives and a cluster of known alternative paths for achieving them.

Implementing solar design means to conceive and plan the improvement of the quality of life by relating specifically to the sun. In the present work, this means the employment of location, form, and metabolism within the solar envelope.

The answer to the question of whether the solar envelope increases the architect's design options for improving the quality of life is not entirely automatic. The question will have been answered positively if the envelope holds open the options of location, form, and metabolism as architectural tools for providing client comfort, choice, well-being, and joy by relating to the sun.

To address the question, I will be referring to the previously drawn correlation between the interval of solar variation and the appropriate mode of adaptation. In this chapter I will develop this concept as a basis for implementing solar design.

Location Sets Rhythm

Some sort of spatial reference is needed to measure the magnitude and direction of natural variation. When the solar envelope acts as that reference, its orientation can accentuate one natural rhythm over another.

A building that nearly fills the envelope's volume will therefore have imprinted on its faces some approximation of the envelope's basic rhythm. To modify that rhythm, the designer must break the building free of the envelope and change orientation. One way or another, by manipulating space, the designer changes time.

The building's location determines its basic rhythm. If some form component of the building is then used adaptively, the resulting architectural expression will be dominated by rhythmic variation. Finally, there may need to be a metabolic adaptation to the residual variation that could not be previously handled by location or form.

The general adaptive sequence here occurs in three cause-and-effect groups; the designer uses the first to set the second and the second to set the third. Location sets rhythm, rhythm sets form, and form sets metabolism. Of course, design is not a linear process, but this sequence is useful as a strategy for design development and design evaluation.

Presuming that development pressures will tend to force one to fill the largest available volume, orientation of the envelope's main bulk will fundamentally affect the entire adaptive sequence. To illustrate this, I will next discuss location, form, and metabolism as modes of adaptation within the solar envelope.

The following examples use time constraints of 7 A.M. and 5 P.M. in summer, 9 A.M. and 3 P.M. in winter, and the 34° north latitude of Los Angeles. The examples are within a subdivision grid oriented on the cardinal points.

Before we discuss the actual designs, however, we need to know more about solar variations as measured on the envelope itself. It is these variations that instruct design strategies.

Long North-South Envelope; The Rhythmic Diagram

The solar envelope for a lot oriented long in the north-south direction will have major faces exposed to the east and west and will lack the substantial south exposure so useful for energy conversion. Design strategies must recognize an east-west directional variation across the short dimension of the envelope and, if possible, make up the lack of south exposure in some way.

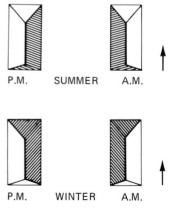

| P.M. | SUMMER | A.M. |

| P.M. | WINTER | A.M. |

The Diagram Indicates a Daily Envelope Rhythm

Analyses of the solar envelope can be made using simple diagrams that represent the main directions of rhythmic variations between envelope faces. This method is useful for describing rhythmic variations on buildings as well as sites and, thus, can indicate principle design variations.

When applied to the envelope, the diagram shows that each face has a distinct rhythm or set of rhythms of thermal and luminous variation. If the rhythmic states are represented by separate points connected to show adjacent envelope faces, the main direction of rhythmic variation will appear as a directed line in the diagram.

In the case of the long north-south envelope, the diagram will contain a double-headed east-west arrow, indicating that the dominant solar rhythm is across the north-south ridge. Diagonal lines shown without arrowheads represent subdominant variations across the envelope's diagonal, or hip, edges.

These edges separate small north-south faces, with major seasonal variation, from large east-west faces, with major daily variations. While the envelope's dominant rhythm is daily, these minor rhythms should be recognized as being more complex, with both daily and seasonal components.

The Diagram Indicates East-West Design Variations

Design within the envelope must take into account the several rhythmic variations signalled by the diagram. The diagonal indicators are most likely to occur at building corners. The major design variations, however, must occur in the short dimension between the envelope's large east and west faces.

Any building contained by the envelope must be designed so as to take into account the differences between east spaces that receive solar energy in the morning and west spaces that receive it in the afternoon. These differences dominate and must be solved by the designer.

The cross section in the direction of the diagram's arrow is most characteristic of the building as a form adaptation. It should be expressive of the building's nature. If that section is not solved, the building has no chance of performing as an adaptive whole. The designer must recognize that east and west exposures tend always to accentuate, rather than to mitigate, seasonal variations by receiving generally higher summer than winter gains on both elevations. This usually results in higher maintenance costs in modern buildings.

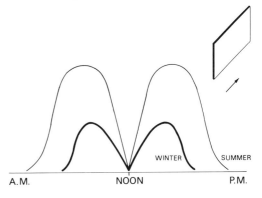

Long East-West Envelope

A seasonal tempo dominates the long east-west envelope. The dominant solar variations will be measured between the large north and south faces. Design strategies must therefore encompass a north-south directional variation between winter and summer across the envelope's short dimension and should take particular advantage of the south exposure for energy conversion.

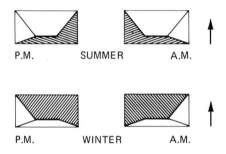

The Diagram Indicates a Seasonal Envelope Rhythm

The diagram of rhythmic variation will contain a single north-south arrow. Diagonal lines in this diagram, as with the first, indicate more complex rhythmic relationships along the hip of the envelope or the juncture of large north-south faces and seasonal variations from east-west faces and daily variations.

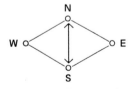

The Diagram Indicates North-South Design Variations

Major design variations must occur in the north-south direction, indicated by the arrow. Any building designed within the envelope must be constrained by the boundary condition between spaces that face south to the main winter sun and those that face north to small amounts of summer sun. The designer need be less concerned about morning and afternoon irradiation in this orientation, as the east-west faces are small.

The design strategy here must be built around a recognition of significantly greater winter than summer insolation (measured on the combined north and south faces), with major differences due to the south exposure. This recognition will yield advantages not usually obtained in most modern designs. These advantages will be of special significance in housing and smaller commercial buildings, which have high S/V ratios; the advantages are generally lost in large deep buildings of low S/V.

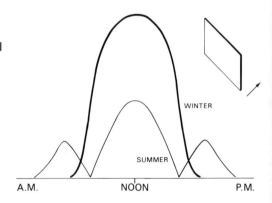

Rhythm Sets Form

What has been discussed so far is the way
the envelope's orientation sets the basic
rhythm to which the designer must adapt;
location sets rhythm. Now I would like to
demonstrate how, by design, rhythm can
set the building's form. To do this I will exhibit designs for 2,500-sq.-ft. houses for two
differently oriented 7,500-sq.-ft. lots. The
intent is to test the feasibility of using form
as a design adaptation within the envelope.
The conditions of solar access are assumed
to be quite generous to the neighbor. The
envelope thus constrains the design sites
rather severely; much more severely in the
first case than in the second, as it turns out,
because of the higher ridge and greater
basic volume of the long east-west envelope used over the second house.

Long North-South Building

The first house design is on a long north-
south lot. A diagram of rhythmic variations
on the envelope faces indicates an east-
west (daily) tempo. Under such a constraining envelope, the designer employs form in
a way that reduces solar impact from the
west and gains south exposure.

Parts of the house are relocated and juxta-
posed to gain that south exposure. The
house is broken apart into its various components, then separated by open courts.
One section is for parking, another living
and food preparation, and a third and
fourth for sleeping and general purposes.
The courts provide a series of south exposures for admission of winter sun into major
spaces.

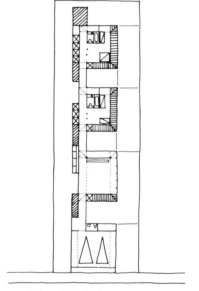

Designer, Alfons Oberhofer.

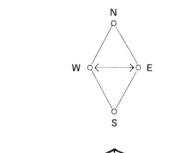

The south face of each element is opened to the winter sun and closed to the summer sun and contains a flat-plate solar collector. The major spaces are arranged on the south of each element. The east face is provided with overhangs that protect from the summer sun and allow the lower winter rays to penetrate the house. Behind the north face, with no overhangs, are the smaller and service spaces of each element. The west face of the house is made into a long corridor, containing storage, service, and the spine of the house. This arrangement does a lot of the work of insulating the house's main living spaces from the hot west sun.

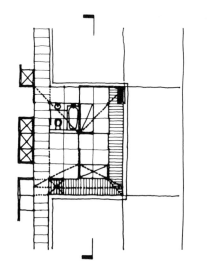

The overall form of the final design resembles that of a European train car, with rooms connected by an aisle containing circulation and services running the full length of one side. The afternoon sun is closed out on the west, while the south and east sun are admitted to the court and can shine on the exposed faces of the building.

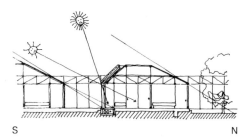

S   N

The arrangement hardly suggests a developer's popular model. The yard is not in one piece, because of the large setbacks under the sloping envelope faces. There are several interesting ideas demonstrated, however, and many options will come to the designer's mind, including techniques for going partly below grade and for sharing boundary conditions with the neighbor. This possibility is developed by allowing minimal shadowing of a neighbor in the second design.

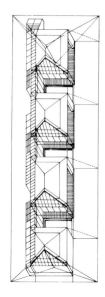

Long East-West Building

The second design is on a long east-west lot. The orientation has advantages that increase design options: first, the envelope ridge is higher; second, the potential volume is greater; and third, the major exposure for which the solar envelope assures access is to the south.

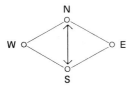

One design result is a one-and-a-half-story house, much more compact than the design on the preceding site. Parking is separated from the house and moved toward the street. The house itself is sited at the rear of the lot, providing a large yard.

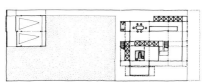

Designer, Alfons Oberhofer.

Major spaces are arranged on the south and east of both the first and second floors, while service spaces are placed on the north and the west. The building's south face allows deep penetration of winter sun, and shallow penetration of summer sun, into the main living spaces.

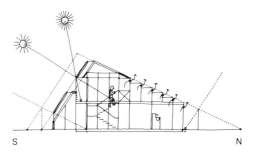

The large south face also provides areas for flat-plate solar collectors. The east face is provided with some overhang to keep out the summer morning sun. The north face is more or less completely closed to prevent heat loss but with provision for natural ventilation and some light. The west face over small and service spaces is sheathed with materials that insulate from the summer afternoon sun.

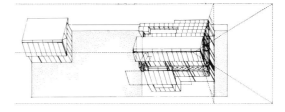

A generally more usable house and certainly more design choice is thus achieved more easily on this site than on the first, while at the same time causing minimal shadow impact on the neighbor.

Square Building

Clearly, form is influenced by site orientation in both of the foregoing design examples. Shape and structure are both adaptive to dominant rhythms set by orientation. In each house there is a directional adaptation to rhythm that differentiates the building's form more strongly in one direction than another.

The responsive nature of houses on more nearly square sites is, as might be expected, not as obvious. Where a site's edges are nearly equal, the final shape may be less clearly directional and the structure less specifically related to one tempo or another, presuming the house presses against the volumetric limits of the envelope.

Form Sets Metabolism

Before proceeding with metabolism, the last mode of adaptation, let us quickly review the last two, location and form, as they have been applied in the two house designs under the solar envelope.

Location of the two houses is specifically set by their site orientation. This is generally true of siting, but the situation is exaggerated under the solar envelope. The envelope's orientation usually establishes the building's exposure to the sun and determines the rhythm of that exposure. Size, shape, and structure provide the design vocabulary.

The effective size of the building might be varied for adaptive purposes by compacting the building's volume or by spreading it out among several smaller pieces. The S/V ratio would be smaller in the first case than in the second, and therefore the building would be less vulnerable to natural variation.

Shape and structure take their cue from the rhythm of solar impact. The building's shape tends to respond to seasonal variation by opening up to the south when possible.

The building's structure responds to daily and seasonal variations by compartmentalizing space, using materials with different thermal properties. In houses, smaller spaces might be arranged on the north and west, larger spaces on the south and east. The enclosing materials might have generally higher insulating properties on the north and west than on the south and east, although the ability to modify the day and night thermal properties of a wall can have many advantages from a metabolic viewpoint.

Metabolism is Directional

Thermal and luminous variations that are unacceptable inside a building and cannot be mitigated by either location or form must finally be handled by metabolic means. Building metabolism depends on rhythmic energy transactions that provide a steady state. Two properties of these transactions are worth noting. First, they are directional within the building. Second, they deplete energy resources over the lifetime of the building.

Consider directionality first. Anyone who has worked next to the window wall of a modern building is familiar with overheating in the morning along the east wall and underheating on the west, with just the reverse during the afternoon.

Short of redesigning the whole building, there are two possible solutions to this problem. One is to ship energy to cool the east and perhaps even heat the west in the morning, then reverse it in the afternoon. The alternative, as we have seen in the preceding chapter, is to move people from one side of the building to another as conditions change. In other words, one solution is to move energy; the other is to move people.

In a general way, a diagram of rhythmic variations on the envelope's faces can also be applied to describe consequent energy transactions within the building. The diagram's east-west arrow, which originally signaled daily variations on the envelope's

faces, may now anticipate the sorts of mechanical or occupant responses described in the office building. If the transactions were seasonal, they would be signaled by a north-south arrow in the diagram.

Energy Depletion

Metabolism is a mode of adaptation that usually depletes energy resources continuously over the building's lifetime. Location and form are modes that do not.

There are exceptions, of course, such as migration, but metabolic systems are primarily electrical or mechanical systems that use fossil fuels directly or indirectly, or they are active solar systems. Active solar systems use solar energy as fuel, just as any other mechanical systems do; but the solar fuel is inexhaustible.

Except for its fuel, however, an active solar system is like any other mechanical system; it is installed on or added to a building to provide comfort where location and form do not.

Location and form may be considered passive design strategies. They rely directly on the sun to provide comfort and choice, and are primary architectural modes of adaptation. They cannot be added to a building or installed on one; they *are* the building.

I find the terms active and passive to be inadequate descriptors in an emerging picture of adaptation that may ultimately include biological as well as mechanical means of converting energy. My preference for the terms location, form, and metabolism lies in their greater descriptiveness of integrated processes.

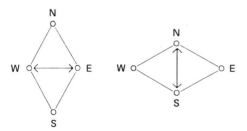

Two Metabolic Modes: Flat-Plate Solar Collectors, and Migration

The foregoing house designs include two metabolic means: flat-plate solar collectors and occupancy. Flat-plate collectors are used on the roof and walls of both houses. In the first house they are kept high enough to allow a view (from underneath) into the courts, as well as penetration of winter sun to heat the masonry floors of the main living spaces on the south. Collector surface area adequate for space and water heating derives from this courtyard arrangement.

No special breakup of the second house's volume is required to increase south exposure. The long side of the lot faces south, and because solar access is thus assured, there are plenty of design options that will provide adequate collector surface. Furthermore, there is provision for adding ground-level collectors in the future.

The second component of metabolism considered in these preliminary house designs is internal daily or seasonal migration. People might move along east-west or north-south paths, depending on the particular house's basic orientation to the sun.

Houses might be specifically arranged with spatial continuities to facilitate such migrations. If occupants could easily move toward comfortable and away from uncomfortable conditions, toward the sun or away from it, they might choose mobility as an adaptive mode and may, to a certain extent, even choreograph their lives in recognition of natural daily and seasonal tempos.

How the house is arranged inside might become expressive of a quite special way of life, with emphasis on nature's rhythms. The spatial scale or structure of the house might be designed with reference to a temporal scale or rhythm. The result might be a rich orchestration of sensory experiences. Migration would very likely occur in the east-west direction at a daily tempo in the first of the foregoing houses, while in the second house it might occur in the north-south direction at a seasonal tempo. The diagrams of rhythmic variation described earlier can be applied to the building to represent the direction of migration most useful for comfort, choice, and a general sense of well-being.

Winter migrations through the first house might be toward the east in the morning and toward the west in the afternoon to catch the sun; summer migrations might be in just the reverse direction to avoid the sun. While this might be the general condition for the house as a whole and even for the courtyards, separate migrations in each part of the house might occur seasonally toward the south glass and into the courtyards depending on where conditions are most suitable.

The most significant migration through the second house would probably tend toward the north and south, with secondary migrations in the east and west directions. The primary migration is, of course, in response to the seasonally variable penetration of sunlight through the south wall. Depending on whether the sun felt good or not, a choice might be made to move toward the south glass or to shift back into the house's more sheltered deep spaces. In the second house there is also some provision for a daily east-west migration. Dining, for example, might be shifted between west and east, so that people may eat at either end of the house at different times of day and season. Facilities for eating would, of course, have to be sufficiently flexible, informal, or portable.

What I am describing may be viewed by many designers as a way that a few people may choose to live, but not as an essential component of adaptation. Obviously, it may not always be appropriate. I am describing it to offer a choice, an option, or one more way that adaptation might take place. Nor is it completely devoid of artistic potential for the house as an expression, or even a celebration, of life's natural tempos.

Migration as an adaptive mode is particularly dependent on one's direct sensory involvement with the surround and response to immediate conditions. As such, it might be facilitated by the house's arrangement and the permanence of that arrangement. Spatial continuities might be thought of as more than circulation; they may provide paths of rhythmic migration, a special and reassuring way to see the building through time.

Energy Properties of the Envelope

We can think of the solar envelope as a sort of container with energy-related properties that may not always be transferred directly to buildings within but that should be one of the starting points for the designer. Two of these properties are a south facing surface (S_{south}) and surface-to-volume ratio (S/V).

If these properties are appropriate to the desired building performance, the building may conform almost exactly to the envelope's physical dimensions, assuming that the building volume pushes against the limits of the envelope. Should the envelope supply the wrong properties, the building must depart from the envelope's boundaries to attain a different and more desirable set.

There is a penalty in departing from the envelope: a loss in volume. Consequently, there is a clear advantage to land-planning and development procedures that produce envelopes with advantageous energy properties that may easily be transferred to buildings without great loss of volume.

The Metabolic Implications of Orientation and Size

A more detailed look at the solar envelope reveals that its energy properties change significantly with the orientation and size of the site. Consider orientation first.

The amount of S_{south} on the solar envelope is critical for energy conversion. For most of the United States, a simple rule for south exposures can be followed: the more, the better. This is, no doubt, too simple a rule to cover the more complex design problems, but the designer would not go far astray by starting from it in the evaluation of design options, especially for housing. For this purpose, the designer must also consider the size and orientation of the site.

The absolute amount of S_{south} varies with size, although the south face will increase at a slower rate than volume if the site increases proportionately in all directions. Doubling the edge dimensions of the envelope will increase S_{south} by the square, while volume will increase by the cube. The result is a net loss of S_{south} per unit volume.

Beyond a certain envelope size, the ratio between south face and volume (S_{south}/V) asymptotically approaches zero. If development within a large envelope requires more south exposure, volume must be systematically cut away from the envelope. South exposure is gained, but volume is lost.

A different sort of relationship between volume and south exposure develops when the envelope's orientation is changed. For example, given the same site shape, and proportions of 1:3, a site oriented long on an east-west axis will generate 40 percent more volume and 400 percent more south face over the north-south orientation. This net gain of S_{south}/V can have many advantages for solar design.

a building in a severe northern climate would be designed for minimum S/V, while a building in the mild, warm south would be designed for maximum S/V. The daily and seasonal variations also influence the desired S/V. For example, passive design works especially well where daily variations are great and seasonal variations minimal.

Thus, it is important for the designer to keep in mind the correlation between envelope size and S/V. As we have already seen, doubling the plan dimensions of a site will halve the S/V ratio of its solar envelope. A phenomenon that is perhaps less expected is a change of S/V with orientation. The same-sized site will have a smaller S/V when it is oriented longer in the east-west than in the north-south direction. The reason is the relatively larger volume under the envelope in that orientation.

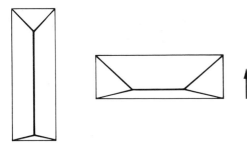

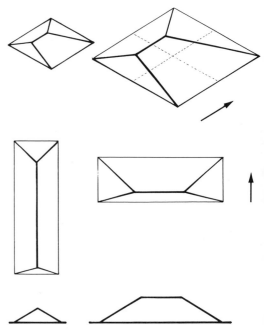

Consider next the overall S/V ratio of the envelope. The overall S/V is important because it is an indicator of susceptibility to environmental stress. Small buildings expose more surface for the volume they contain; they are thus more susceptible to external variation. Large buildings contain relatively more volume for the surface they expose and are thus less susceptible to external variation.

The effect of external variation on the performance of a building varies with the location and program of the building. In some climates, a large S/V ratio is beneficial; in other climates a low S/V is preferable. In general, the greater the external variation, the smaller the S/V should be. For example,

So long as the larger volume can be produc-
tively used, there seem to be twin advantages to building within a long east-west
envelope over its north-south relative. They
may have the same footprint, but the long
east-west envelope produces a greater S_{south}
combined with a smaller overall S/V. In relatively small buildings, especially for housing,
education, and commercial uses, such considerations should have an effect upon
design.

The Metabolic Implications of Assemblage

Land assemblage within the urban grid can
drastically alter the S_{south} and S/V of solar
envelopes. The way this happens is largely
dependent on the direction of assemblage.
The direction of assemblage, in turn, is generally dictated by block orientation.

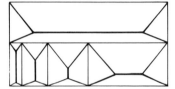

S_{south} increases dramatically with land assemblage, but only when blocks are oriented long in the east-west direction. The
ridges of small-frontage lots run north-
south. The south face of individual envelopes will be quite small, but, with assemblage, the ridge direction will shift and the
south face will grow.

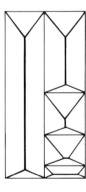

When the blocks are oriented long in the
north-south direction, the story is quite different. The overall envelope's south face
does not dramatically increase with land assemblage; beyond assemblage of two or
three lots, there is no increase of S_{south}.
When the ridge of a small-frontage lot runs
east-west, S_{south} for any individual envelope
is relatively large, but in this case, with assemblage, S_{south} does not increase.

A comparison of S_{south} as a result of assemblage in these two directions demonstrates the shift in advantage. These effects of assemblage on south exposure suggest some interesting policy, as well as design, implications.

Conventional wisdom suggests that land assemblage is always useful because it increases design and development options. On the other hand, solar exposure might suggest that land assemblage is not always advantageous. Where the block runs east-west, land assemblage has insolational advantage; where the block runs north-south, it does not.

Land assemblage is more important in regard to south exposure than in regard to S/V. An example of how envelope volume increases with land assemblage is useful here. An envelope over a 100-ft.-frontage site has more than twice the volume of two envelopes over adjacent 50-ft. lots, because of the additional wedge of volume added between opposing faces of the two adjacent envelopes when they are assembled. This wedge is partly responsible for adding volume faster if assemblage takes place in the east-west direction.

Comparing assemblage in two directions demonstrates that small-frontage lots have more developable volume in a north-south than in an east-west block. But that advantage shifts quickly to larger sites in an east-west block.

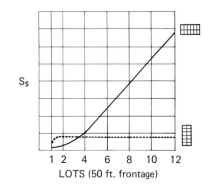

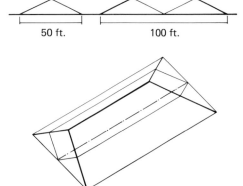

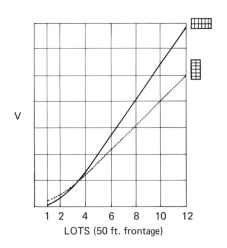

If the direction of assemblage affects the rate of volumetric increase, it also affects the rate of decrease in S/V. Of course, envelopes over small sites have dramatically higher S/V ratios than envelopes over large sites. But perhaps just as significant is the fact that small sites have a higher S/V when blocks are oriented east-west; large sites have the advantage when blocks are oriented in the north-south direction.

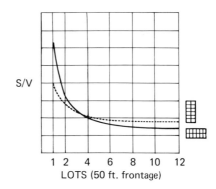

S/V

LOTS (50 ft. frontage)

Under the space and time conditions for the examples in this book (34° north latitude; 7 A.M. to 5 P.M. in summer, 9 A.M. to 3 P.M. in winter), this difference in direction seems to disappear when assemblage produces lots of about 150- to 200-ft. frontage. At that scale, the envelope characteristics of S_{south} and S/V are the same for the two orientations. At smaller and larger sizes, the two different orientations become unequal in both characteristics.

The information relating orientation and assemblage to S_{south} and S/V may be used as a new basis for laying out subdivisions. More important, during our present stage of urban rebuilding, it will be useful to recognize these differences of existing block orientations when zoning policies are being written.

Renovation and retrofitting of existing, older buildings may be a good solution under one set of orientation conditions, while land assemblage and a change of land use may be appropriate with a different orientation. Policies might be developed to discourage a change of land use in the first instance and to encourage it in the second.

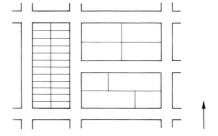

There is an interesting textural implication of orientation viewed in this way. The grain of transformational growth in our cities will, once solar access is taken seriously, become directly related to street orientation.

The Solar Envelope
Viewed from the Sun

It is instructive to view the solar envelope from the position of the sun, looking down upon and moving around the earth. For this, we can use a series of computer-generated images to picture what one would see, hour by hour.* The solar envelope, of course, will have four sloping surfaces lying at angles that change as the day progresses and two vertical faces (shown here without grids) where the envelope meets a street and alley.

There are several key points to note as these images turn and change. The sun's line of sight is parallel to different faces at the beginning and end of each sequence, the cutoff times. At 9 A.M. in the winter, the north- and west-sloping faces first lie parallel to your line of sight. As time passes, the envelope's north-sloping face comes into view and remains visible until 3 P.M., when it and the east-sloping face lie parallel to your line of sight.

The fact that the north slope is insolated through the winter solstice is of critical design importance. With the knowledge that even the north slope has an assured access to the winter sun, the designer can broaden strategies for heating and lighting spaces.

---

*The images were generated by Charles S. Dwyer at the Computer Center, University of Southern California.

I must return to the south face for my last point about this dynamic view of the envelope. The south face, along with the west at 7 A.M. and the east at 5 P.M., lies parallel to your line of sight. What is remarkable about this summer passage is its relative quickness. The summer solstice takes the sun through approximately the same bearing angle from 11 A.M. to 1 P.M. as the winter solstice takes from 9 A.M. to 3 P.M. In other words, the summer sun passes through the same ground-plane angle in only two hours that the winter sun passes through in six. When this exposure differential is added to the fact that the summer's higher sun produces a much smaller angle of incidence on the south face, the historical use of a south exposure takes on new meaning for future applications.

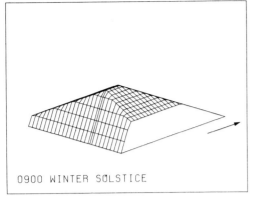

0900 WINTER SØLSTICE

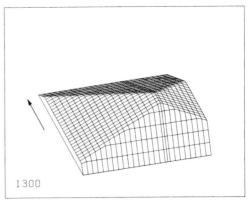

1300

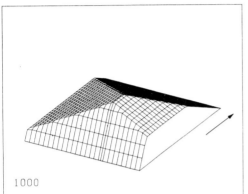

1000

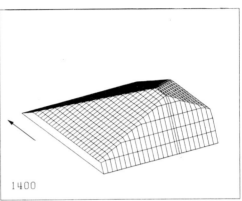

1400

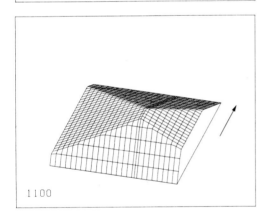

1100

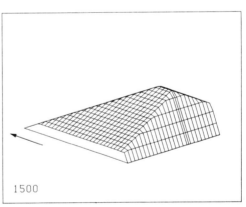

1500

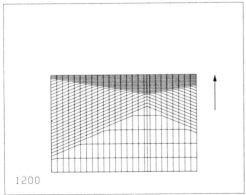

1200

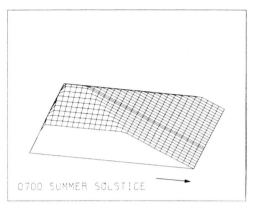

0700 SUMMER SOLSTICE

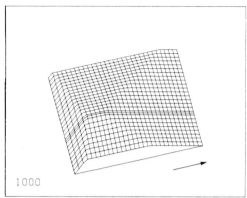

1000

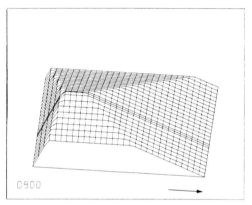

0800

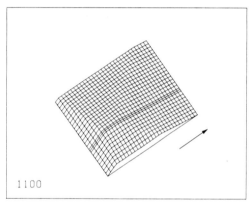

1100

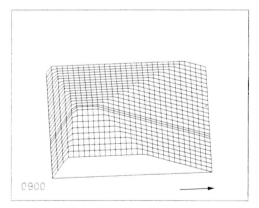

0900

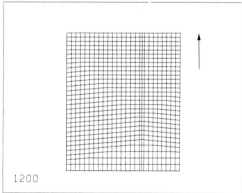

1200

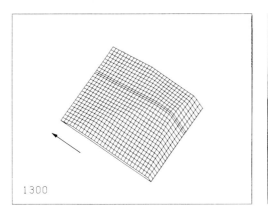

1300

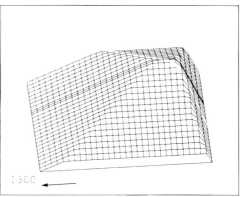

1500

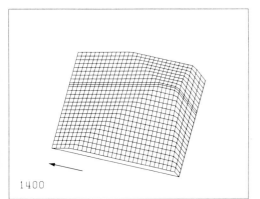

1400

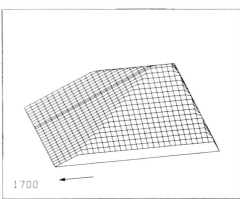

1700

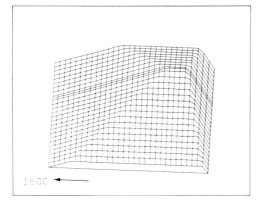

1600

9 Architectural Design Projects

Overview

The basic proposition underlying the projects described in this chapter is that comfort, choice, well-being, and joy are enhanced when the designer's palette includes direct access to the sun. The concepts comprising this statement are critical and have been carefully chosen. The designer's palette includes the integrated uses of location, form, and metabolism as rhythmical adaptations to the sun. Direct access to the sun is an ethical and legal right assured by the solar envelope.

I am tempted to extend this thinking to include the argument that solar envelopes ensure good design by suggesting a formal relationship to the sun and by assuring its qualitative and energic powers. But, of course, the design freedom within the envelope offers the potential for poor, as well as good, design. The envelope does, however, present a formal model and set of values that can, if used wisely, enhance design potential.

In this chapter I will present design work that reflects a desire to use and control sunlight, as well as an exploration of the envelope's formal potential. As such, it demonstrates the forms and values of good solar design while assuring the neighbors' rights to do the same.

As a framework for design, the solar envelope presents both problems and opportunities. At first encounter it seems severely constraining; but with practice a variety of ways emerge to resolve these limitations of size and shape. Some of these ways depend upon a recognition of the exact spatial limits of the envelope. Hence in this chapter I will give diverse examples of envelopes, ranging from simple envelopes that conform to a building site to those that are raised to accommodate privacy fences, or those that are allowed to cross streets.

Within the envelopes, certain architectural characteristics will appear with great consistency, despite the variety of sites and projects. These reflect location and form as modes of adaptation, and include daylighting, courtyards, roof terraces, and other sun control devices, such as sunscreens. These internal elements follow and accentuate the rhythmic characteristics of the sun's movement, so that time becomes a dimension of architectural form. That is to say, the envelope shows us how to recognize and use rhythm as a design strategy.

Courtyards

Courts appear because the twin requirements of height and daylighting need to be reconciled. The envelope restricts the height of the building, broadening its plan dimensions and causing the designer to carve out spaces to introduce sunlight and heat to deep interiors. Single-story designs can easily be toplighted through clerestories and skylights, but multistory designs more often must rely on courts that vary in size, shape, and orientation. These design strategies recall the courtyard buildings of the last century, where the courts offered pleasant qualities of privacy, light, and air to their users.

The court is architecturally significant in two related ways. First, it provides interior spaces with outdoor views and access; and, second, it heightens the sense of solar rhythm.

The first consideration is straightforward and results from the desire for contact with the natural world. For example, in the mild climate of Los Angeles, courtyards can provide open sky and wind, trees and flowers, fountains and the sounds of birds inside the building.

In colder climates, some of the same design strategies for gaining light and heat may apply, but the courtyard may be covered to temper the air and mitigate the additional S/V ratio such design implies.

The second consideration, that of accentuated solar rhythms, derives from having access to sunlight within the building. Aside from this main point, there is a perceptual irony in the incongruity of visual cues between the outside of the building and the inside of the court. For example, when the north side of the building is dark in winter shadow, the north side of the court is sunlit. The south side of the building is sunlit, but the south side of the court is shadowed. A similar phenomenon occurs on a daily basis with the east and west sides of the court and building. While these observations are somewhat peripheral to a discussion of solar rhythms inside the court, they become important when we consider legibility and orientation.

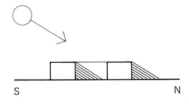

S   N

Solar rhythms vary with the court's shape and orientation. An oblong orientation of the court accentuates either a daily or a seasonal rhythm as read by the shadow's edge as it moves across the floor. For example, a rectangular court that is long in the north-south direction will accentuate the sun's daily migration across the sky at all seasons. This results from the shadow's direction of most evident change. The shadow's long edge sweeps from west to east as the sun moves overhead from east to west. Each morning of the year, a lighted area appears near the west wall. As it advances eastward, it holds a straight front, paralleling the court. By late morning, all that remains of the shadow is a thin line against the court's east wall. Past noon, a similar line appears along the west side. But this one, instead of receding, expands behind an area of diminishing light that is finally consumed near the east wall.

With some variation, this phenomenon occurs every day of the year. Of course more of the southern court is dark in winter, but the longer shadow edge sets the dominant movement. Since shadows parallel the court walls, their longer edges sweep this court daily.

The main direction of change shifts in a rectangular court that is longer in the east-west direction. As the winter sun hovers low in the southern sky, the shadow's long edge lingers near the court's north wall all day long. The court stays mostly darkened. In sharp contrast, sunshine floods the court floor on a summer day. Only a thin shadow clings to the court's south wall. At either season, daily variation of shadow size and shape are minimal. Seasonal changes are much more pronounced in this second court than they were in the first.

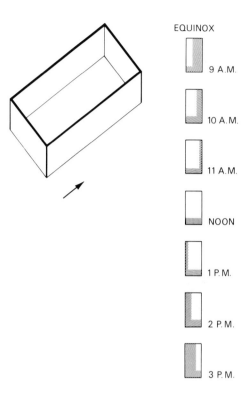

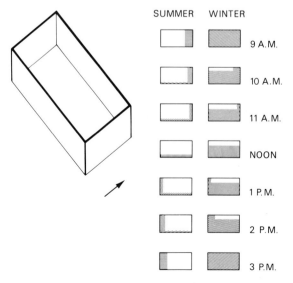

Terraces

Terraces appear where the sloping sides of the envelope intersect the rectilinear geometry of a building. Since the envelope's shape is based on sun angles, slopes vary with orientation. The effects can be both structural and spatial.

Column spacing and beam size can be affected by the envelope's slope. This is especially true when there is a need to develop as much volume within the envelope as possible. Generally speaking, column spacing increases as slope decreases. The use of structure to contain space and control light within a sloping envelope will very likely require a willingness to explore new structural possibilities beyond what is conventionally employed at present.

The terrace spaces may be enclosed and added to the perimeter of the building. They may, in some climates and building types, be left open for planting, recreation, or outdoor circulation. Their best use requires an understanding of how they change as the sun moves.

Like the courtyards, terraces accentuate the rhythmic characteristics of the sun's movement. A terraced pyramid that fills a solar envelope can be used to describe, first topographically and then rhythmically, differences of terrace size and shape based on orientation.

Under an envelope (9 A.M.–3 P.M., winter; 7 A.M.–5 P.M., summer), terraces facing south are narrower than the others; but if surfaces are read by shadows rather than by the topography of edges, terraces appear to change. They become alternately broad and narrow. If the pyramid's form were read in the shadows alone, a complete description would require the passage of one entire year.

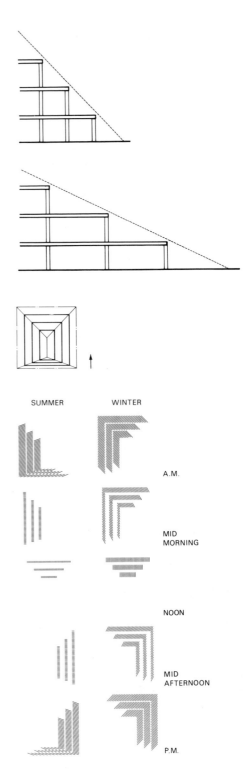

SUMMER   WINTER

A.M.

MID
MORNING

NOON

MID
AFTERNOON

P.M.

Sunscreens

Once solar access to a building is assured, there must be architectural strategies for controlling radiation, admitting it directly or indirectly as desired for heat and light, or rejecting it. Sunscreens are such architectural strategies and, as a component of building form, must respond to rhythmic variations of sunlight entering spaces.

A cubical form, open on two opposite sides, can act to describe how the sun enters architectural spaces and how its penetration varies with time. As before, a comparison between an east-west and a north-south exposure will clarify the effect of orientation and provide a basis for varying a building's facades. Such a comparison will show the seasonal advantages of a south exposure.

Throughout a summer day, very little direct sunlight penetrates a space open to the north and south. The sun's rays come mostly from overhead and from either directly east or west where roof and walls act to exclude it. This advantage is lost when the space is turned to face east and west. Morning and afternoon rays can penetrate the openings directly unless sunscreens are provided. Control is especially critical on the west where the sun enters on a hot summer afternoon. Of course, landscaping can also be used to screen the sun, as has been described in chapter 5.

Over the shorter winter day, little sunlight penetrates a space open to the east and west. The sun's rays come mostly from low in the southern sky where the south-facing wall excludes it. When the space is turned to open north and south, the winter sun's light and heat can penetrate the whole space throughout the day. While this condition may be generally favorable, and demonstrates again the advantage of south orientation, it can lead to periodic over-

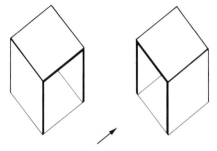

SUMMER　　　WINTER

9 A.M.
10 A.M.
11 A.M.
NOON
1 P.M.
2 P.M.
3 P.M.

heating in some climates, for which adjustable sunscreens or landscaping may be required.

Where sunscreens are fixed, they can become major, multifunctional architectural features. Because they result in articulation of the building facade, sunscreens also add diversity and richness to a building's appearance, as well as differentiation useful to orientation.

The structural relationships of vertical walls and horizontal terraces to a sloping reference provides an array of possibilities for introducing natural light deep into a building. Each affects the building's scale differently.

For example, the sunscreen can form a vertical wall, thus departing from the slope of the envelope, which then results in a terrace outside the wall. On the south, this terrace may be skylighted close to the wall for a deep penetration of natural light, with the sunscreen not only controlling the amount and duration of light but its direction according to its intended use. In this way, for example, the sunscreen could direct the light up to the ceiling for ambient daylight or down to the floor for heat storage.

A second approach to sunscreens conforms more closely to the slope of the envelope and encloses more of the terrace for a kind of second-order space that can have many uses, including private offices, sun control, storage, and outside terraces.

A third approach to screening the sun employs skylights that interfere with the view, but contain additional space within the building instead of leaving it outside on the roof terraces, where it may be difficult to use for some functions and in some climates. This example also conforms to the slope of the envelope and is suggested by it.

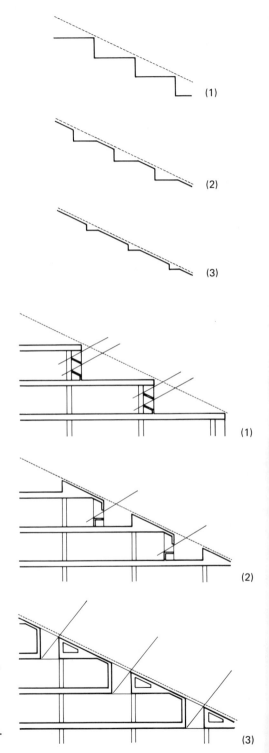

Different exposures produce a variety of sun control techniques based on daily and seasonal intervals. Where terraces face east and west, higher afternoon temperatures can produce significant variations of treatment. Where terraces face north and south, recognition of high summer and low winter sun can produce dramatic asymmetries in the treatment of building facades. The south facade will seek to admit the heat of the winter sun and reject the heat of the summer sun, while using as much natural light as possible in all seasons.

The following projects explore how such architectural features as courtyards, terraces, sunscreens, and landscape can broaden the designer's palette and enhance our buildings. As design problems, the projects reflect varying degrees of complexity, and, as solutions, varying degrees of refinement. But a vocabulary of solar design, demonstrating location and form as primary adaptations, and the formal investigation of the solar envelope are present in all.

The projects are the designs of third- and fourth-year architecture students at the University of Southern California. I have chosen student work as illustrations because examples of real projects demonstrating the concepts of solar design I have discussed, within the limits of a solar envelope, are only now starting to emerge.

Future efforts may modify or even reverse my conclusions, but, so far, I am encouraged by the quality of design emerging from the discipline of the envelope. The examples in this chapter have been selected to present design ideas relevant to mid-density commercial and housing applications. I hope to demonstrate that there is an enhanced potential for good design within the constraints of solar zoning. Further, I hope to draw professional architects and planners into an even more intensive search for aesthetic meaning within this novel design framework.

Small Commercial Building: Corner Site

To introduce the exposition of design issues within the solar envelope, I have selected three different corner sites and applied a multiuse building program to them. In discussing these cases, I will compare their main organizational differences under the envelope. Corner sites provide a variety of orientations to the street and to the sun that are less likely to occur on sites inside the block. The program of diversified needs is typical of many small buildings and separates this first discussion from that of the housing projects to follow later in the chapter. The final examples illustrate the courtyards, roof terraces, and sunscreens discussed in the preceding section.

The program is for a District Government Center that contains a branch library, a small auditorium, office space suitable for use as district field offices for a variety of governmental units, and parking, either on or below grade. The controlled uses of sunlight and heat are emphasized in the library and offices.

Sites

Three sites are shown on different street corners within the Jeffersonian grid. Each site averages between 200 ft. and 250 ft. along one street and 150 ft. along the intersecting street. The longer dimension in each case results from assembling several 50-ft. lots from an original plat. The developable volume on each site is defined by an envelope that touches grade at the rear and side of each site and that crosses the intersecting streets in two directions, thus producing large vertical faces on the streets. Envelopes are generated for cutoff times of 7 A.M. and 5 P.M. in summer, and 9 A.M. and 3 P.M. in winter.

Large extensions of the envelope over street corners result in a major shift of envelope ridge orientation. The northeast corner is a case where the envelope ridge changes from east-west (over the original 50-ft. lots) to north-south over the assembled land parcel. One major design result of this shift is that the higher into the envelope the building extends, the more the design is constrained to face east and west. Lower in the envelope, of course, the options for orientation are greater.

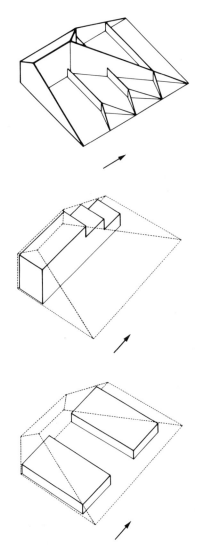

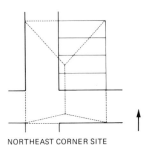

NORTHEAST CORNER SITE

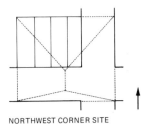

NORTHWEST CORNER SITE

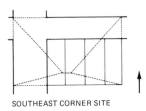

SOUTHEAST CORNER SITE

Building Designs

The envelope over the northeast corner site combines high vertical faces on the south and west with sloping faces on the north and east.

The major exposure on this site is to the east and west. The plan, which is characteristic, includes a court on the east and elevators and stairs on the west. This arrangement works best for two reasons. First, the main entry is from the west, and is convenient to elevators and stairs that serve the higher envelope volume where offices are stacked. Second, the court is positioned to face east rather than west to avoid the afternoon heat of summer. The court is also as close to the main entry as possible without consuming the envelope's main bulk.

Protection from the western sun is critical on this site. Protecting the main entry is also a problem, which is solved by recessing the first floor at the street. The doors are set back out of the sun's rays. This arrangement leads to different possibilities for sunlighting the entry space both from large inside spaces in the morning and from the street in the afternoon.

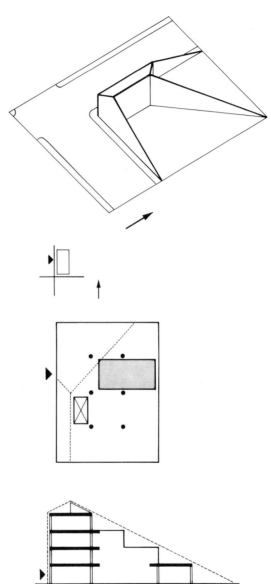

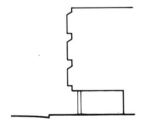

W   E

The envelope over the northwest corner site combines high vertical faces on the south and east with sloping faces on the north and west. The high ridge runs east-west, just the opposite of the first site.

The major exposure on this second site is to the north and south. A typical plan locates the elevators and stairs near the front entry where the envelope's main bulk faces south. The library is placed on the north under the envelope's main slope.

This organization avoids the major west exposure that characterizes the first site. Seasonal, rather than daily, rhythms of light and heat are accentuated. The main entrance lobby and offices above are easily shadowed in summer and, if desired, sunlighted in winter. The library's sloping roof enjoys year-round insolation at the latitude of Los Angeles, allowing the designer to admit solar light and heat as desired.

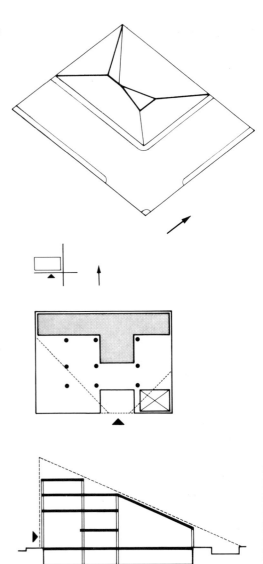

S   N

The envelope over the southeast corner site also provides a north-south exposure. This third example combines vertical faces on the street sides with a nearly vertical face on the south and a more gentle slope on the west. The high ridge, as on the second site, runs east-west.

Here, too, the polarity of organization accentuates seasonal rhythms. Adaptations of shape and structure must respond to winter and summer variations of light and heat.

A major difference between this third site and the second is that entry is from the north instead of from the south. The library is pressed south to avoid confusion with circulation. Elevators and stairs are located midway between the entrance and the library, on a direct circulation path that must also connect vertically to the envelope's main bulk where most of the offices are stacked.

Winter sunlight enters the south-facing library on this site. Winter shadows also darken the front entrance on the north. The first condition requires sunscreens to control both solar heat and light; the second can be alleviated by notching the building, catching sunlight to brighten east- and west-facing surfaces that flank the entry court.

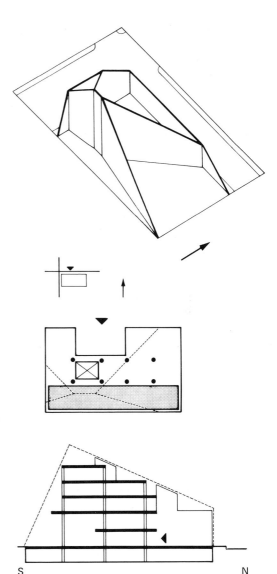

S   N

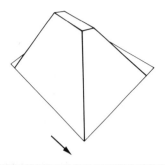

A comparison of design images shows a variety of shapes and structures that reflect the solar envelopes and the typical organizations for each site.

A view of the northeast corner envelope clearly shows the ridge and major east-west exposure. Seen from the same view, a design for this site arranges building elements around an open court. Daylight and south orientation are provided inside the building. Offices open onto sunlit roof terraces.

The court faces east to the morning sun and can be seen through the main entrance. Its contrasting qualities, light when seen from the dark entry in morning and dark when the entry is in afternoon sun, act to focus attention and to provide a control reference for all circulation. Terraces step down around the court so that it is differently enclosed and lighted on each of its four sides.

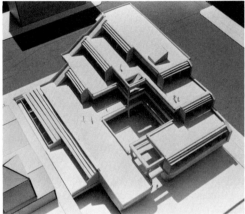

View from northeast; noon, summer.
Designer, Daniel Wright.

A view of the northwest corner envelope shows its large, south face toward the street.

The main lobby is on the south, as are most of the offices. Sunscreens are comprised mostly of horizontal elements that act effectively on the south. Around the building's corner on the west, the sunscreens change size and shape and actually become small rooms that extend outward from the main offices. These rooms are enclosed by surfaces that exclude the west sun and admit north light. Each one provides its own kind and quality of space.

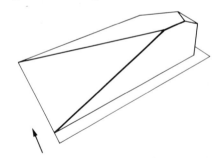

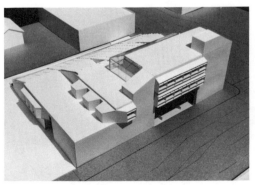

View from southwest; noon, summer.
Designer, Nora Sarkissian.

The library occupies the north slope of the solar envelope. Its skylighted roof has both vertical and horizontal components. In other words, such a surface has some properties of both a wall and a roof. This combination allows for the controlled introduction of north light through a system of louvers or baffles.

A view of the southeast corner envelope shows its steeply sloping south face at the rear instead of the front of the site.

This last design for a corner site confronts the special need to face in two directions, north to the street and south to the sun. The other two sites were entered under the envelope's main bulk where elevators and stairs could easily serve the space above. The resulting designs made an easier transition from one side to the other. Here, there is an organizational split, evident in the two halves of the building form.

View from west; noon, summer. Designer, Nora Sarkissian.

Like the earlier designs, this one exhibits different geometries for admitting controlled sunlight. Each building face has a characteristic structure to control the sun. At corners where different elements meet, transitions of size and shape occur. The overall result in all designs is a variety of form that reveals itself as the light turns on shapes and details of surface.

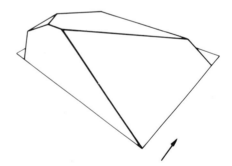

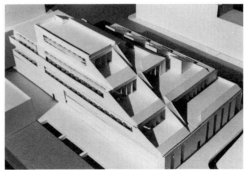

View from southeast; noon, winter. Designer, Tony Labayog.

Multifamily Housing: 100-ft. and 150-ft. Frontage

Housing forms generally derive less from the envelope and more from other program requirements than a project such as the District Government Center. This is due to the relatively small size of residential spaces and their great need for light and fresh air. The S/V ratio increases dramatically over the projects shown in the preceding section.

The selected examples shift the focus of my exposition somewhat from the envelope's impact on functional organization to qualities of architectural space. This reflects good design practice, independent of solar zoning. The envelope assures solar access to neighbors, but it is the skillful designer who must assure solar access and environmental quality to development within a solar envelope. The point is worth stressing because as experience grows in handling the envelope, primary emphasis can shift to traditional design values. Assurance of solar access, however, allows a dynamic interpretation of architectural space as read in the rhythmic changes of sunlight and shadow.

Shadows may be read as the two-dimensional evidence of three-dimensional volumes, with dynamic properties distinct from those of the surround. To describe these properties, the earlier graphic analysis of shadow variations on floors and terraces will now be replaced with drawings depicting rhythmic changes of volume.

If shadows can be read on the walls, as well as on the floor, of an oblong court, the space defined is more clearly seen. This shadowed volume is generally larger in winter than in summer, regardless of the court's orientation. But there are some specific trade-offs the designer must consider.

For example, if the designer wants a sunlit court in winter, the best orientation is long in the north-south direction. But a long

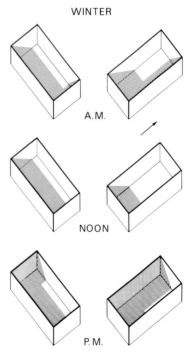

WINTER

A.M.

NOON

P.M.

193

Multifamily Housing: 100-ft. and 150-ft. Frontage

east-west orientation provides the greater expanse of south-facing wall through which winter light and radiant heat may deeply penetrate rooms facing the court.

The designer may value summer shadows and seek to increase their influence, especially for a summer afternoon. Here again, the best orientation varies with purpose. A long north-south direction provides the most summer afternoon shadow in the court itself, but the surrounding rooms benefit from the opposing orientation, where they can face either north or south into the court. Clearly, the designer must choose among quite different sets of conditions.

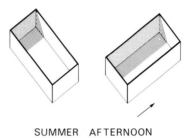

SUMMER AFTERNOON

The earlier example of a cubical form, open on opposite sides, can serve again to demonstrate what happens inside the rooms of a dwelling. As the sun enters from either open side, the room is subdivided. One part lacks sunshine. The other is filled with it; objects and people are lighted and heated directly by the sun's rays.

Between these two adjacent volumes, there is a dividing boundary that turns at different rates and in different directions, rhythmically changing the size and shape of each space by day and season.

The point was made earlier that a southern exposure naturally controls sunlight, admitting it in winter and rejecting it in summer, whereas control on the east and west is less differentiated by season. A look at the recurrent, internal subdivisions of light and dark can lead to decisions about building form and interior arrangements.

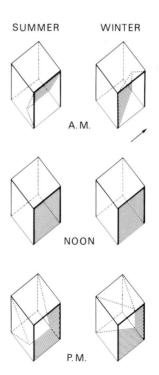

SUMMER   WINTER

A.M.

NOON

P.M.

In rooms that open to the east and west, the dark portion expands daily behind an eastward, rotating boundary. Past noon, the lighted part advances in the same direction. There are seasonal differences in the size and shape of both dark and light segments. Since together they must total the room's volume, one expands while the other contracts to a tiny fragment before disappearing completely. The direction of this change is constant throughout the year.

When the room is turned to open north and south, the direction and rhythm of change varies. The most evident direction of boundary movement is north and south. In summer, the lighted segment is tall and thin and lies close to the southern opening. As winter approaches, the light expands north-ward into the room, confining the dark to small, wedge-shaped spaces against the walls and ceiling. As summer returns, the dark wedges expand to fill the room again.

These cycles provide us with a dynamic spatial system for organizing our buildings. The designer must, in such a context, consider *when* as well as *where* events occur. The experience of color and texture, space and light, heat and the absence of it, all require an awareness of natural recurrence.

The application of a dynamic spatial system can lead to strategies for selecting building materials, furniture layouts, paint and fabric colors, and even the placement of paintings and sculpture to extend their influence and to delight us anew each time we pass. However, my purpose here is simply to reinforce a few of the more conventional adaptations of location and form that appear in many buildings throughout history and that are emphasized in the following discussion.

Two form adaptations, particularly, follow from the previous analysis. The first calls for sloping the roof down on the west to exclude the hot summer afternoon sun. The morning sun is allowed to penetrate all year. The low winter rays still pass under the eaves in the afternoon.

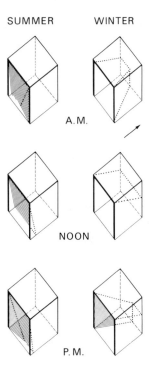

SUMMER   WINTER

A.M.

NOON

P.M.

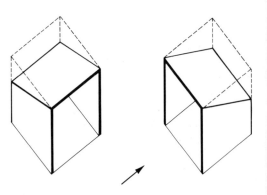

195

Multifamily Housing: 100-ft. and 150-ft. Frontage

The second adaptation requires the roof to slope down on the north, following the sun's winter rays. The southern opening is undiminished, while the north exposure is reduced.

The removed segments both contain space with undesirable properties of light and heat. Sloping to the west eliminates a portion of space that is prone to summer overheating. Sloping to the north gets rid of a fragment with no winter sunshine in it at all; what remains is fully insolated for most of a winter day.

Both strategies appear in the following designs. The second is used particularly to reduce the critical north-south spacing while assuring solar access to more housing units on a site.

The designs respond not only to architectural questions of environmental quality but to real market constraints. The sites are all in a part of Los Angeles originally platted for densities averaging just under six dwelling units per acre. Recent market changes require higher densities of four to six times those of existing, neighborhood housing; also, smaller unit types fall in the size range of from 800 to 1,200 sq. ft.

Because these designs favor a south exposure, they suffer some loss of envelope volume, depending on site orientation. Nonetheless, they achieve densities of about 30 dwelling units per acre on north- and south-facing sites, while on east- and west-facing sites of the same size, densities reach 45 dwelling units per acre.

The designs all provide off-street parking either below or on grade, in addition to meeting prescribed density ranges. The construction is typical of such housing in Los Angeles and meets all Uniform Building Code requirements for space, access, and safety.

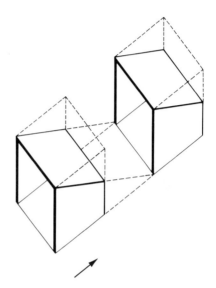

Sites

Sites are at midblock, rather than corner locations, and face in several directions. Two different sizes are used. The smaller sites have 100-ft. frontages, are comprised of two 50-ft. lots in the original plat, and average 13,000 sq. ft. The larger sites have an area of almost 20,000 sq. ft. with 150-ft. frontages. As with the District Government Center, solar envelopes are generated for cutoff times of 7 A.M. and 5 P.M. summer, 9 A.M. and 3 P.M. winter.

There are two significant differences in the solar envelope rules for these housing studies that derive from the existing, surrounding environment: A six-foot privacy fence is integrated with the solar envelope and the envelope is set back from the street.

The first modification is responsive to local zoning, which provides for a 6-ft. privacy fence at the property line. Many such fences exist in Los Angeles neighborhoods. Typically, shed and outbuildings are built up to the fence but do not rise above six feet at the property line. To match this existing condition, the envelope is raised six feet above the ground on all sides, allowing shadowing of the neighbor's fence and significantly increasing developable volume.

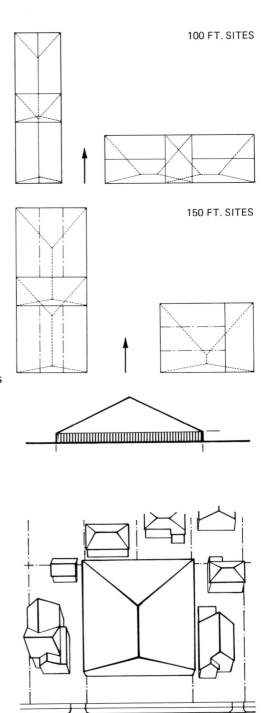

100 FT. SITES

150 FT. SITES

197

Multifamily Housing: 100-ft. and 150-ft. Frontage

The second modification of the envelope derives from existing zoning provisions for setbacks. Although local zoning only demands 15-ft. setbacks, the envelope was generated on the basis of 30-ft. setbacks to respect the existing quality of the street, including front yards and trees. Both the 6-ft. fence and 30-ft. setback influence the quality of shadowing and privacy from older surrounding houses.

The shapes of envelopes over sites that face either north or south to the street do not vary significantly, regardless of 100- or 150-ft. frontages. However, on east-facing and west-facing sites, the larger frontage shifts the envelope's polarity 90° from that of the original platting. While the modular envelopes run long east-west, their assembly changes the final envelope's polarity to north-south. The seasonal rhythm of the small envelopes is then replaced by a daily rhythm.

Building Designs

The envelopes over 100-ft.-frontage sites that face north or south have ridges normal to the street. The southern envelope is allowed to shadow the street to the north and therefore has a longer ridge than the northern envelope.

A typical plan for either envelope gains south exposure by locating buildings parallel to the street. The dominant rhythm on north- and south-facing sites is diurnal. To get south exposure for a seasonal rhythm, buildings must be oriented opposite to the envelope's ridge. Major living spaces can then be exposed to the south, with service spaces to the north.

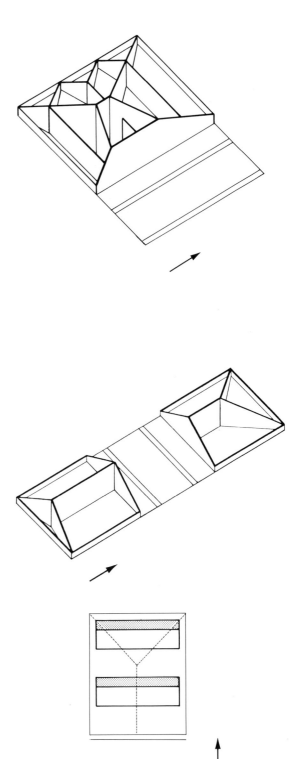

Such an arrangement requires the kind of form adaptation already described in which volume is sacrificed to expose more building surface. This loss always occurs where south exposure is valued and where more than one row of units is required.

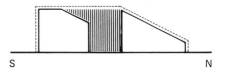

A view of the south-facing envelope shows the north-south ridge and the slope over the rear of the site. A characteristic design, seen from the same angle, gains south exposure by removing envelope volume. The result is as if there were two smaller building envelopes, sloping to the north and spaced to gain solar access to both south faces. The density is 30 dwelling units per acre.

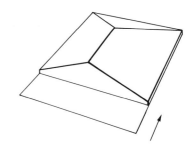

The south opens to the sun; spaces are larger, higher, and deeper, and the building's structure is more complex.

On first inspection, this design would seem to shadow itself. The southern row appears to limit sunshine to the north. But, as seen on the heliodon, the arrangement provides exposure to winter sunshine for virtually the entire day.

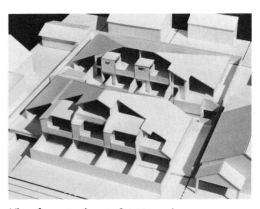

View from southeast; 9 A.M., equinox. Designer, Rich Knarr.

The precise shape of rooftops is such that the sun at cutoff times angles across the sloping roof hips of the southern row. What is "seen" by the sun is the major portion of the south face of the second row of units. If both rows were longer, this would not be the case. But the 100-ft. frontage allows sunlight to come in from the side over the east and west site boundaries, as well as over the site's south boundary. This is important to keep in mind: Access across a south boundary is necessary but not sufficient, especially where the site runs deep in the north-south direction.

199

Multifamily Housing: 100-ft. and 150-ft. Frontage

The design's north side is much simpler than its south side. Spaces are smaller, lower, and shallower under the north eaves. Like the facets of large, opaque crystals, the roof planes reflect changing light. Because the rows of units are low on the north and reflect sun from their slopes, the characteristically long, deep shadows of winter are reduced in the space between units and have less effect on neighbors.

The envelopes over 100-ft.-frontage, east- and west-facing sites are taller and have more volume than do those in the opposing direction. They have large, steep south faces. Their street sides are vertical and mirror each other.

On a west-facing site (as on the east) south exposure is typically attained by locating two rows of units perpendicular to the street. Since the envelope's rhythm is seasonal, buildings can parallel the envelope's ridge. The dominant rhythm of both the envelope and contained buildings is the same.

If only one row is used, units can rise to fill the envelope's high bulk. But if two rows are required, the southern units must be carefully adapted to gain both the greatest height and solar access for the northern row.

View from northeast; 9 A.M., winter. Designer, Rich Knarr.

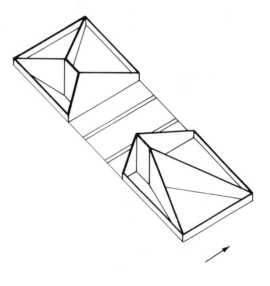

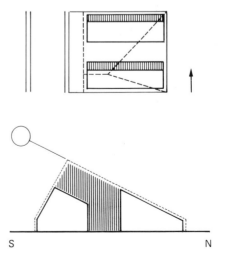

S   N

A view of the east-facing envelope shows the high south ridge and the long slope down to the site's north edge.

A design seen from the same direction gains south exposure for a northern row of units by admitting low winter rays between tower-like shapes on the south. In this way, much of the envelope's large bulk can be used to achieve a density of 45 dwelling units per acre, fifteen more than on the other site.

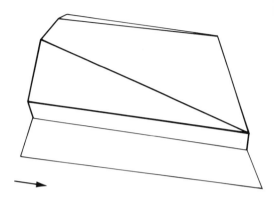

View from east; 9 A.M., winter.
Designer, Thomas Chessum.

201

Multifamily Housing: 100-ft. and 150-ft. Frontage

Since the envelope already has a seasonal rhythm, there is nothing to be gained by reorienting units. Form is the important adaptive mode here; its skillful use allows south exposure with minimum loss of volume. The results can be richly varied and quite asymmetrical in the north-south direction; by carefully arranging units, the southern row can be higher than the northern row and, of course, the unit types vary between the two rows.

A detail of the housing on east- and west-facing lots is worth a closer look. Under the northernmost edge of the envelope, clerestories and skylights can be used to introduce south light and heat into the northern reaches of the house. Gardens may even grow on the north with south-facing walls that catch the winter sun.

The size, shape, and structure of units is varied to mitigate daily and seasonal variation. Clerestories are diagonally cut in two directions to avoid shadowing within the site.

The planning of interior spaces is also responsive to solar access concerns. Because the upper parts of units naturally receive greater access to sun when rows are close together at this density, major living spaces are located above minor ones; living and bedrooms are on top, kitchens and dining rooms below. Thus a kind of vertical migration evolves within the building based on solar access.

Sites of 150-ft. frontage provide some design options that the 100-ft. sites cannot offer, simply because there is more room on the site and more volume within the envelope. The results typically involve adaptations of location and form different from those seen on the smaller sites.

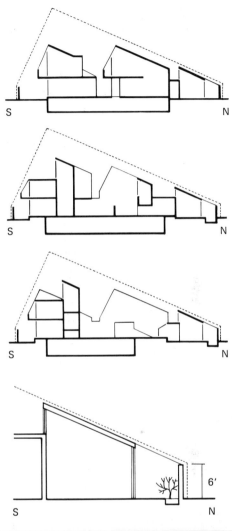

*View from southeast; 3 P.M., winter.
Designer, Thomas Chessum.*

For example, the additional width on a north-facing site provides a very long, high envelope ridge. Instead of facing all units to the south, this design fills the envelope's high ridge, thus exposing broad building faces to the east and west. While sun control problems are thus increased, more units can be added for a density of 43 dwelling units per acre rather than the 30 units on a 100-ft. site with the same ridge orientation.

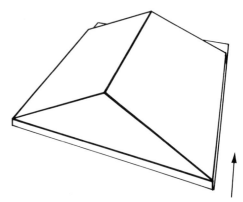

View from southeast; 9 A.M., winter.
Designer, Paula Waller.

203

Multifamily Housing: 100-ft. and 150-ft. Frontage

A second example of how increased frontage can broaden design options is seen on a 150-ft. east-facing site, where the ridge changes polarity and volume increases dramatically. To use this volume effectively requires a more complex service linkage between dwelling units with different heights and orientations. Different solar rhythms representing different qualities of life, or different life-styles, result.

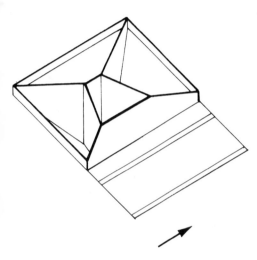
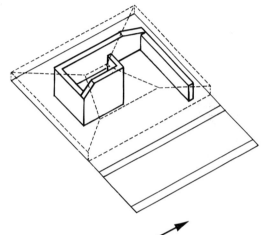

A typical plan displays internal variety and complexity of shape. Unlike the smaller frontages, this site requires design decisions relating east and west exposures to service and living spaces, as well as north and south, and the combinations need to mesh for structural and service continuity.

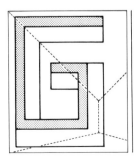

This characteristic design achieves a density of 54 dwelling units per acre. The major exposure of units is either to the south or east into the main court. Roofs slope down to the north and to the west, following the strategies of form already described. Units are located with sufficient space between them to avoid shadowing the major living spaces. Each perimeter unit has a small private garden that catches winter sunshine on walls and terraces. Even those gardens along the north catch winter rays and reflect them from south-facing walls.

View from northeast; noon, equinox. Designer, Nora Sarkissian.

Heliodon studies of this design reveal courtyards with patterns of light and shadow that change dramatically over time. The fact that some units open mainly to the south and some to the east provides a richly varied set of interior conditions as well.

Throughout a winter morning, the south-facing units become lighter as the sun approaches its zenith. The east-facing units become darker, but take advantage of sun entering a low wing that opens south into a private garden. As these units lose east light, they gain south light and so have winter sunshine penetrating all through the day.

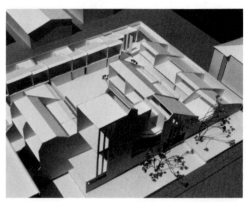

View from southeast.

Because the winter sun is low in the sky, long shadows are cast inward, mainly from the vertical edges of openings. Their boundaries rotate through rooms, generating triangular shapes of changing light and dark. Reflectance from surfaces induces a general luminescence in the rooms. The source of intense light seems omnidirectional. This condition remains fairly constant throughout the day in spaces opening to the south, but in those opening to the east, the sun's movement generates strong differences from morning to midday to afternoon.

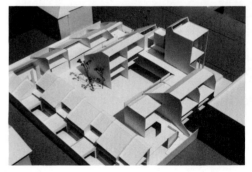

View from southwest.

The daily changes inside east-west facing spaces are just as pronounced in summer and, as pointed out before, call for adaptations of shape or structure to mitigate the afternoon sun especially. In south spaces, the summer sun does not penetrate very far and there is virtually no change throughout the day. The light quality is soft and, rather than seeming to come from everywhere, the light seems to have no source at all. There is little reflectance from surfaces.

Summer shadows are cast more from the horizontal tops of openings and from eaves than is the case in winter. Consequently, long shadow boundaries sweep sideways through spaces, defining rectangular shapes rather than the triangles that radiate from corners in winter.

These heliodon observations indicate that, because the design adapts to the sun, spatial transformations occur in a way that is made predictable through particular choices of location and form. An awareness of this possibility can lead designers to more imaginative adaptations that enrich our built environment. Design strategies sensitive to diverse natural rhythms can multiply our visual cues and intensify our awareness of space and time.

Multifamily Housing: 100-ft. Frontage, Hillsides

Hillsides are inherently more varied than flat sites because of their multiple orientations to sun, view, and street. Sometimes all three lie in the same direction; at other times they lie in opposing directions. When access to all three is valued, the designer is confronted with special challenges that, if met, result in greater diversity of architectural forms.

Slope orientation determines not only the total amount of insolation that a slope receives; it also determines the interval of variation. For example, north slopes accentuate seasonal variation; east and west slopes accentuate daily variation. Hence, designs must adapt to conditions that are initially biased toward one rhythmical variation or another, independent of property lines and street layout.

Hillside housing is unique because of its greater potential for view. Indeed, scenic views are a major attraction and often determine market value. But a view to the distance is often compromised by a view into the neighbor's private domain.

The uphill neighbor who looks down on you and the downhill neighbor on whom you look represent traditional design concerns that were less evident in the projects shown in the preceding sections, but become very important when designing for the side of a slope.

The following designs seek to provide as much amenity for potential residents as possible within the moderate density range of 25–35 dwelling units per acre. This is easier in some orientations than others, where the solar envelope imposes severe constraints on design and development potential.

The higher number is easily met and even exceeded on south slopes. There, envelopes provide more volume than needed, with plenty of opportunity for private outdoor space. The principle challenge on south slopes is to take architectural advantage of the inherent capability of southern exposures to mitigate seasonal variation.

North slopes present a more difficult test. Obviously, if they become too steep, the winter sun does not reach them at all. On the sites chosen for this discussion, the density range is met or not, largely according to street orientation. Lower envelopes impose severe limitations on design freedom and developable volume. Land coverage must increase and roof terraces must be fully utilized if the density range is to be met. Under these circumstances, the most difficult problem is how to capture the sun's winter rays.

West slopes do not as severely constrain development, but they provide their own special problem: How to close out the hot afternoon sun, while ensuring a downhill view and south exposure.

Landscaping, particularly with deciduous trees, is an important addition to these designs. Trees appear on the hillside designs first because that is the time they were studied, not because they are more appropriate here than in the earlier flatland designs. Deciduous trees extend above the building envelope in accordance with the rules of generation laid out in chapter 5. Their additional height allows summer shadowing, especially of east and west exposures. It also allows sunlight and heat through the bare branches in winter. Evergreens are required to stay within the original building envelope.

Trees present the designer with a set of special challenges. The effects of growth and seasonal change are not easy to reproduce; on the other hand, exciting opportunities lie in recognizing the interrelatedness of solar rhythms and tree-growth cycles. The energy-related potential of seasonal changes has already been discussed in chapter 5; there are other qualitative changes that pertain to neighborhoods as well as to single sites.

Trees provide the most noticeable enhancement of streets in the following designs. The consistent application of envelope rules develops particular street identities. The size and shape of trees vary with slope and orientation and thus define spaces differently from one location to another. Time

modifies this aspect. Heliodon studies show rhythmic changes of tree-lined spaces indicative of what happens in natural time.

For example, trees along the south edge of a street provide cool, flickering shade for people walking below their branches in summer. The same trees in winter admit a warming lacework of sunlight that contours the street and dissolves the faces and clothing of passersby.

Trees in the designs also segment the street into spaces that are semipublic and public. The street itself belongs to all, but between the trees and the facades of adjoining buildings there is a less active place, smaller and more contained. This space serves as the least public place before stepping onto the site. Heliodon studies of these spaces show moving shadows on buildings; these shadow cycles are full of implications for people's comfort. In addition, the privacy such a space affords is greater in summer than in winter, when bare branches offer less protection.

These designs represent only a beginning in the study of trees and landscaping. Much more research is needed to determine the effect of leafing cycles and other factors on the amount of insolation that penetrates bare branches and on design qualities of space, privacy and view. The effect of orientation needs to be studied, as does the microclimatic role of landscaping with trees that change by day and season.

My purpose here is only to suggest a design potential for ecological adaptation of buildings and trees that are differentiated by orientation of slope. North-slope communities should look and act differently from south-slope communities. East and west should be different still, thus adding richness and legibility to the landscape and reinforcing the natural structure of the hills.

Sites

The four sites chosen for this discussion are representative of slope orientations (north, south, and west), street directions (with and across the grade), and lot orientations to the street (north, south, east, and west). Most of the study sites occur on streets with orientations approximating the Jeffersonian grid. The exceptions are noted as they occur. The average area is 14,000 sq. ft. with frontages of approximately 100 ft. Slopes are from 15 to 20 percent. Above that gradient, the specified density range cannot be met at 34° north latitude.

In order to increase volume and development potential on critical slopes, the solar envelopes are generated by simple rules that vary in minor ways from the preceding examples. This manipulation also raises some new design issues. Instead of seasonally differentiating cutoff times, as in the preceding designs, the hours of assured access are 9 A.M. to 3 P.M. all year. One effect of this change can be seen by comparing the two versions of an envelope for a south-sloping hillside. The greater period of solar access results in less volume. The new cutoff times increase volume, but raise additional design issues. The envelope's south face becomes nearly vertical; on south slopes, if followed architecturally, this can produce an unacceptable vertical wall above the neighbor. (It may be advisable to retain a sloping envelope above the property line. This avoids legal difficulties arising from potentially different building heights at shared ownership lines.)

A second change in the envelope rules also increases developable volume. The height of the envelope is experimentally raised by using an 8-ft. privacy fence, instead of the previous 6-ft. privacy fence, as the basis for envelope generation. While this change also adds volume, it, too, has consequences that must be recognized by the designer.

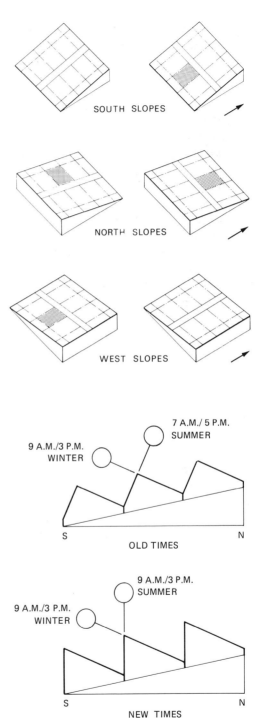

SOUTH SLOPES

NORTH SLOPES

WEST SLOPES

9 A.M./3 P.M. WINTER

7 A.M./5 P.M. SUMMER

S — N

OLD TIMES

9 A.M./3 P.M. WINTER

9 A.M./3 P.M. SUMMER

S — N

NEW TIMES

A third change is that no setback has been provided at the street. The envelope is generated to cast shadows up and down the street to the northwest in the morning and to the northeast in the afternoon. The result is a lump of additional volume on the envelope's north end. The generation of the envelope becomes slightly more complex but, as can be seen by comparing these to the previous flatland examples, the result is additional development potential. And, as with the other rule changes, design problems emerge in the trade-off. Whether such decisions as setbacks should be determined by the designer, as in these cases, or by public policy, as in the previous projects, will require testing in real communities where values can become clear over time.

The last rule for envelope generation is an entirely new condition. Trees are now an added design element in these projects. Deciduous trees may extend 12 ft. above the solar envelope in public rights-of-way and on private sites. This higher landscape envelope assures that trees do not cast shadows to heights greater than 20 ft. at the property line of adjacent sites.

Finally, before proceeding with the designs, it is useful to lay out and to compare envelopes generated for all combinations of slope and street orientation. The result is a framework for diversity that clearly enhances design choice beyond conventional development practice. The translation of rhythmic time into forms distinguished by slope and orientation offers a unique sense of place amid architectural diversity.

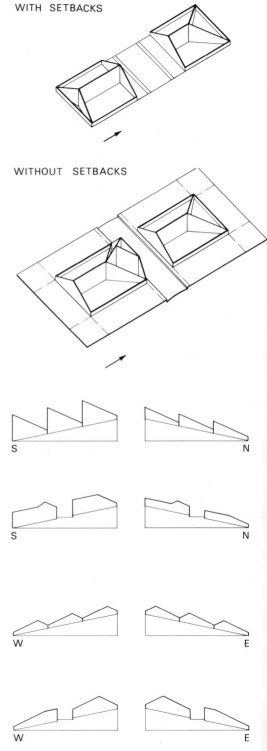

WITH SETBACKS

WITHOUT SETBACKS

Building Design

South Slopes

The envelopes over land parcels lying uphill from each other, across a street, generally demonstrate significant differences from each other. The uphill envelope, with its street frontage to the south, is very much like the envelopes seen earlier. The downhill envelope, with its street frontage to the north, gains additional volume because of the envelope rules for hillsides.

A second pair of south-facing sites is separated by a street running north-south between them, so that each envelope, if seen from the same view, is a mirror image of the other. The envelopes are high on the street and south edges, low on the back and north edges. The envelopes are characterized by a long, high, south face that orients toward the downhill view, as well as toward the sun. Access to the street must take its incline into account.

The site to be discussed is downhill from a street that runs across the slope. Street access is from the uphill side, the opposite side from sun and view.

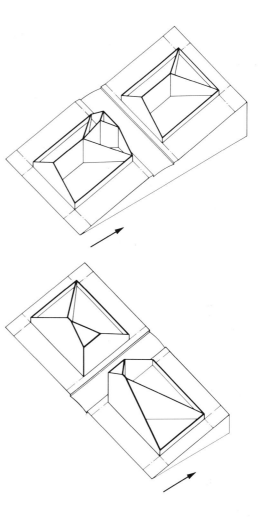

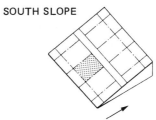

SOUTH SLOPE

The solar envelope limits the height of both buildings and evergreen trees on the site. The envelope is symmetrical in the east-west direction, but a higher volume occurs on the north because shadows may cross the street. Shadows from the envelope move daily along the street from the west in the morning to the east in the afternoon. Seasonally, they cross north over the street in winter, then return south in summer. An extension of this basic envelope northward, across the street, provides a limit on the height of evergreens along the street. The street envelope therefore extends the site's north-south asymmetry.

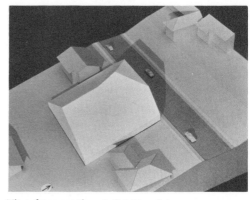

View from southeast; 9 A.M., winter.
Site envelope.

The addition of 12 ft. to the height of both envelopes provides more volume for deciduous trees. The central ridge provides the greatest height for site trees; the south side allows the tallest street trees. Trees on the street's north half must be smaller to minimize shadowing. Clearly, a species without abundant branches has an advantage in winter.

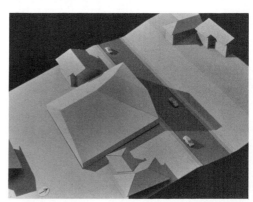

3 P.M., winter.

This design, taking advantage of the potential of large trees on the site, and of maximum building volume, employs a central landscaped court. Parking is provided at the top of the site below the front units. Vertical circulation and view are gained by flanking the court with units that cascade downhill, creating roof terraces that allow occupants to enjoy both the view and the southern exposure.

3 P.M., winter.
Site and street envelope.

9 A.M., winter.
Landscape envelopes for site and street.

3 P.M., winter.
Landscape envelope for site plus street trees.

9 A.M., winter.
Designer, James Rodriguez.

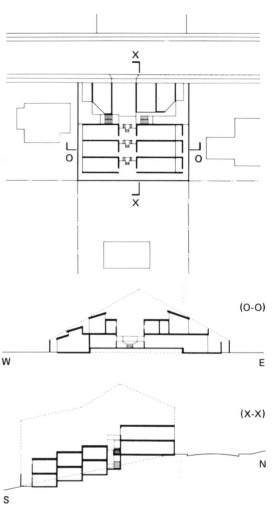

View from southwest; 3 P.M., summer.
Designer, James Rodriguez.

The design makes good use of the envelope's shape by employing high units on the north, toward the street, and lower units on the south. In this manner, there is an advantage in accentuating the site's south inclination. Units to the north are raised even higher than the grade slope, thus improving solar access.

The problem of street scale resulting from these taller units is alleviated by the large entry court. The court provides additional amenity by allowing a pedestrian to enjoy a downhill view between the buildings.

The density achieved by this scheme is 35 dwelling units per acre, which proves to be typical of south-slope designs under the solar envelope.

A second design on the same site uses a reverse strategy. Instead of a central garden court, the space is filled under the high central envelope ridge. This arrangement provides more southern exposure through stepping clerestories and carefully oriented skylights, but it sacrifices the advantages of a central open space. The two strategies result in the same number of dwelling units.

View from southeast; 3 P.M., summer.
Designer, Mark Scheurer.

North Slopes

The general configuration of north-slope envelopes is similar to those already described on south slopes, but they contain far less volume; potential densities are drastically cut. This is especially true on a downhill parcel that faces up toward the street.

As on south slopes, sites located either side of a north-south street are mirror images of each other. Both sites have more developable volume under the solar envelope than the downhill site just described; the additional volume is the result of a long south edge, where the envelope's height is greatest.

The first of two different north sites is west of a street that runs up and down the slope. Automobile and pedestrian access must occur at different grades across the site. Sun, view, and street lie in three different directions.

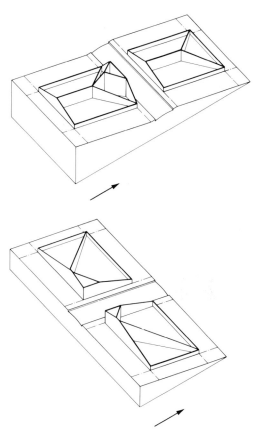

NORTH SLOPE

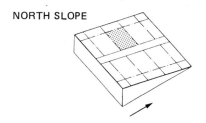

The solar envelope is not symmetrical on either the north-south or east-west axis. Partly, this results from the different directions of sun and street; partly, it results because the site slopes down in two directions, north and east. A small lump of volume appears at the street end as it would where the street runs across, rather than up, the slope.

Shadows from the envelope cross the street daily from west in the morning to east in the afternoon. Shadows are foreshortened in the morning and elongated in the afternoon, because of the site's northeast tilt.

The street envelope has a longitudinal ridge that, if the street and slope ran exactly with the cardinal points, would be completely symmetrical.

View from southeast; 9 A.M., winter.
Site envelope.

9 A.M., winter.
Site and street envelopes.

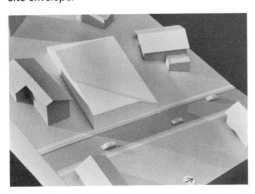

3 P.M., winter.

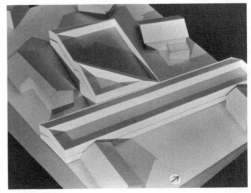

9 A.M., winter.
Landscape envelopes for site and street.

The additional envelope height for deciduous trees provides for nearly symmetrical street planting and for on-site trees that can rise above building heights anywhere on the site.

The northeast inclination of this site tends to reduce afternoon insolation. The winter disadvantage of this situation for downhill sites can be mitigated with tree species that have a spare branch structure. There is a summer advantage, however, that is enhanced if the tree also has abundant leafage, especially along the street's eastern half where shadows can protect west facades.

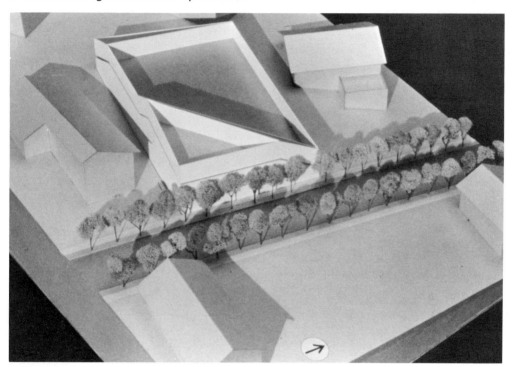

9 A.M., winter.
Landscape envelope for site plus street trees.

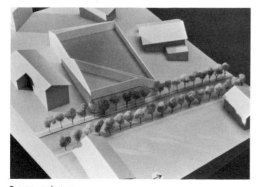

3 P.M., winter.

A design with its southern exposure uphill and its view downhill works by arranging two rows of units perpendicular to the street.

The plan shows a one-way traffic loop with parking under each unit. The section reveals the difficulties in gaining solar access from uphill and a view downhill while also maintaining privacy between units.

The design presses hard against the south wall to gain space and solar access where the envelope's height is greatest. Above eight feet, the wall may be used for thermal mass, but windows will be sacrificed. The designer has chosen to slope back from the south wall above eight feet and to employ windows. Both light and thermal capacity may be used to advantage above eight feet, because the existing house to the south does not shadow the wall and future construction will be constrained by the north slope of an envelope on that property. Downhill, in the second row of units, the designer has used south-facing skylights and clerestories and has closed the unit's south wall to ensure privacy from the terraces above.

9 A.M., winter.
Designer, Fred Lamey.

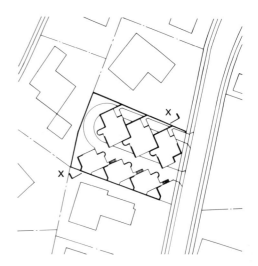

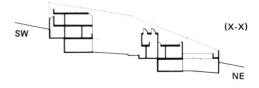

View from northeast; 11 A.M., summer.

View from east; 1 P.M., summer.

An alternate design on the site achieves the same density of 26 dwelling units per acre with a single row of narrow, deep units. Parking is entered from the site's lower edge only.

This design opens the development to direct sunlight by stepping back from the property line. A combination of opaque and transparent walls step toward and away from the property line.

The section shows openings to the south and through the roof that control light and heat. A combination of flat and sloping roofs allows exposure in several directions. Some rooms face south and uphill, others face north and downhill, but all have some south exposure through clerestories and skylights. Views downhill to the north are achieved from terraces without the internal privacy problems of the other scheme.

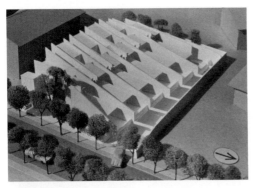

View from northeast; 9 A.M., equinox. Designer, Carol Bracco.

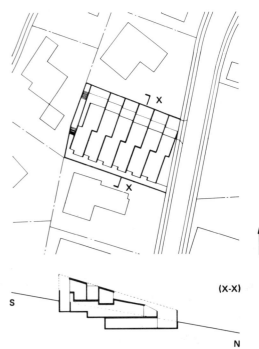

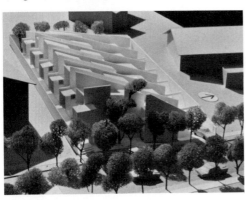

View from southeast; 3 P.M., summer.

The second of two north sites is downhill from a street that runs across the slope. Street access is from uphill, the same side as the sun but in the opposite direction from the view.

The solar envelope over this site is far more constraining than over the other north-sloping site. It meets an 8-ft. privacy fence on the north, east, and west; and the street grid is 20° off the cardinal points—a shift that significantly reduces envelope volume, as discussed in chapter 3. The result of this combination of site constraints is the lowest density of all the hillside sites: 20 dwelling units per acre.

One design for this site gains access to the winter sun by systematically lowering some of the roof areas. This strategy for gaining the most sunlight and losing the least volume involves the combination of low, flat roofs and high, sloping roofs that follow the envelope's upper boundary. Clerestories catch the sun all year long because, even on winter solstice, the envelope's north slope receives direct sunlight between 9 A.M. and 3 P.M.

NORTH SLOPE

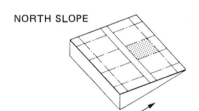

View from southeast; 3 P.M., summer.
Site envelope plus street trees.

3 P.M., summer.
Designer, Hashem Mikail.

The design employs a north-south entry court that not only allows the low winter sun to penetrate deep into the complex during midday but also provides a downhill view from the street. Courtyards face to the southeast and southwest, where the winter sun can be most easily caught in the morning and afternoon.

Access to the street is on the south, or uphill, side. Residents drive their cars down a ramp to the back of the lot and park under the housing, using stairs for passage up to the terrace levels.

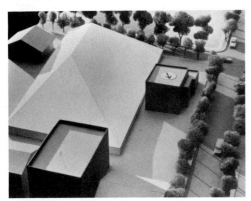

View from northeast; 9 A.M., winter.
Site envelope plus street trees.

9 A.M., winter.
Designer, Hashem Mikail.

The downhill view to the north is provided by broad sections of roof that serve as private outdoor spaces. Privacy between this site and the neighbor is not a major problem. The low buildings under the envelope don't allow an easy view onto the next property, beyond that resulting from the topography of the hill.

A second design on the same site uses a different strategy for capturing the sun from the south. Two rows of units run long in the east-west direction with an entryway between. This design has sloping roofs that cannot be used as outdoor space. It achieves 20 dwelling units per acre, as did the other scheme, but without the roof terraces to provide more open space per unit.

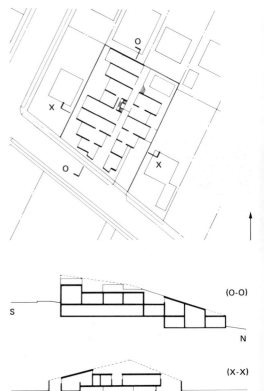

View from southeast; 3 P.M., summer.
Designer, Effrain Oliveres.

View from northwest; 9 A.M., winter.

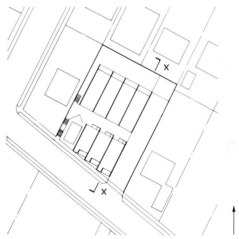

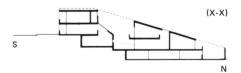

West Slopes

Solar envelopes for west slopes generally contain a moderate amount of volume compared with those on the south and north. They are highest along the site's south edge. When the street runs across the slope, uphill sites provide more volume than downhill sites. Shadows can move westward across the street, rather than being stopped at the neighbor's privacy fence.

A second pair of west-facing sites is separated by an east-west street running uphill. Their ridges are perpendicular to the street, but somewhat uphill of center. The north-facing site has additional volume because shadows may be cast northward across the street.

The site to be discussed is south of a street that runs up the slope. Street access is from the site's north frontage, the view is downhill and westward, and solar access is from the south, thus presenting some unique design problems.

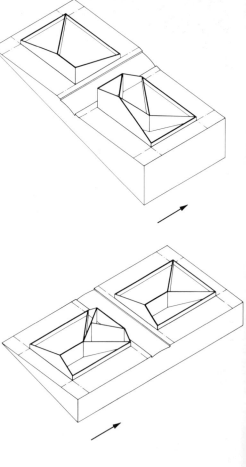

WEST SLOPE

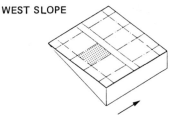

Shadows from the site move daily along the street. They are elongated downhill and westward in the morning; afternoon shadows are foreshortened uphill and eastward. The hourly difference of shadow impact on houses across the street is especially pronounced on a winter day. This impact is minimized by aysmmetrical planting, but a careful selection of species can obviously help the situation.

The first design for this site employs a typical strategy that sacrifices volume, but gains southern exposure and thus direct solar access. High internal spaces capture the sun and allow penetration into deep spaces. The north is more closed to prevent heat loss and to ensure privacy from the street and between the rows of units.

View from southeast; 9 A.M., winter.
Site envelope plus street trees.

3 P.M., winter.

9 A.M., summer.
Designer, Rodrigo Brana.

The main automobile entry is on the site's downhill edge. People enter along the same edge, where there is a stair that leads down to the parking. Deciduous trees at that edge provide privacy and protection from the summer afternoon sun.

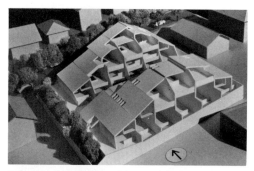

View from southwest; 11 A.M., winter.

View from northwest; 1 P.M., equinox.

Residents approach dwelling units by using a central access way that connects to a service area and through to the major living spaces that face south. Each unit has a private deck facing south and west to the view. Interior spaces open to the south and close to the hot western sun under a long, continuous west roof.

A second design on the same site has less southern exposure but more dwelling units. Whereas the first achieves a density of 32 dwelling units per acre, this scheme achieves 35, the same density as on south slopes.

Entry is gained directly from the street with units stacked side-by-side in north-south rows. Exposure to the south must be achieved through the roof and through the east and west exposures, which is a more difficult control problem.

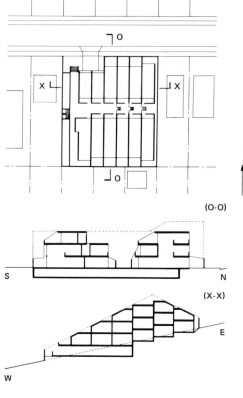

1 P.M., equinox.
Designer, Michael Morey.

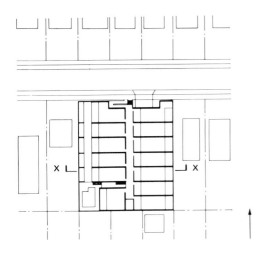

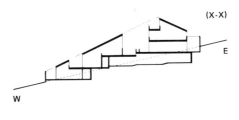

Considerations for Adjacent Properties

An important aspect of design within the solar envelope lies in the relationship between buildings on adjacent sites. This relationship is not unique to hillsides but is accentuated by sloping land.

The previous designs have all been shown on isolated parcels surrounded by existing houses. This is likely to remain the situation during the transition from conventional to solar zoning. But as projects within the solar envelope accumulate, and as urban densities increase, development will take on a different aspect. The next chapter looks more closely at urban design applications of the solar envelope, but I would like to conclude this chapter by mentioning some of the problems that are likely to arise from continued development.

The design conflict arising from the need to resolve a site's orientation to both sun and street has been thoroughly discussed. This conflict is intensified as higher densities are sought. But it is probably with the addition of hillside views that the problems of adjacent sites come most sharply into focus. Where sites face each other across a property line, rather than across the street, privacy becomes particularly difficult to maintain while assuring view and solar access.

The difficulties with south slopes can be seen immediately. While the most volume can be achieved, the greatest problems of privacy can also occur. Typical of the solutions to that problem are landscaped open spaces that provide some separation between neighbors.

Assuring privacy is less difficult on west slopes, and even less so on north slopes. Lower envelopes avoid the extreme height differential that occurs on the south. North slopes present the least problem. Service

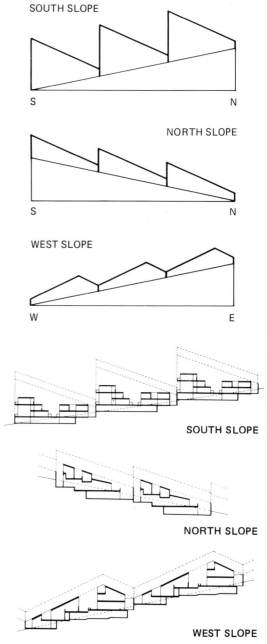

SOUTH SLOPE

S   N

NORTH SLOPE

S   N

WEST SLOPE

W   E

SOUTH SLOPE

NORTH SLOPE

WEST SLOPE

and access are likely to occur along one edge, especially along the north edge where the volume loss is minimal; the result is a buffer space between neighbors.

Design Choice

So much variety results from the different hillside sites that each designer's natural inclination to make a unique scheme is easily satisfied. The solar envelope, building programs, and design values themselves generate immense variety. However, on a given site, there is still room for different approaches to such issues as orientation to sun, street, and view.

Even where the envelope is as restrictive as it is on north slopes, design choice is available. Different entrance strategies on the same site can produce quite different design solutions. Each of the examples on a north slope produces the same density, 26 dwelling units per acre.

When different slopes are seen together, the framework for design choice appears ecological to the degree that it varies in accordance with environment. Solar envelopes change with slope and, as natural communities meet, an edge results. It is at such edges, over the top of a hill or across a hollow, that the variety of conditions becomes most evident and the environment is most enriched.

The solar envelope is so constituted, so systematically arranged, as to suggest an organic fit with its surroundings. In fact, one way to view the envelope is as a set of boundaries defining a place with special recurring properties of light and heat—very much as the biologist would define a "niche" that supports a distinguishable plant or animal community. And, from a design viewpoint, the analogy may be useful to a degree, especially in a project that is large enough to take on some properties of a community.

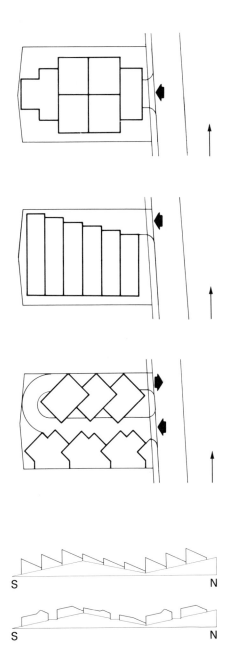

A critical test of the solar envelope and the proposition that it will not inhibit, but enhance, design quality comes at the scale of urban design. It is at urban scale that the envelope's potential as a flexible regulator of growth can be realized. It is at urban scale that the interrelationships between old and new development and between solar envelopes become major form-givers. And it is at urban scale that the rhythm embodied by the envelope informs the tempo of urban growth.

Whereas the preceding chapter dealt with single-building applications of the envelope and the exploration of location and form as architectural adaptations to natural rhythms, this chapter will deal with the urban qualities that result when envelope zoning is applied to a district, neighborhood, or very large architectural project. Here the concern is with multiple and adjacent projects and thus with sites, buildings, and land uses in combination. The solar envelope emerges as an important planning tool, informing the form and sequence of urban change. Rhythm emerges as an urban design strategy.

Levels of Urban Regulation

A prudent course for guiding high-quality urban growth must balance development with solar access needs, as discussed in chapter 2. Achievement of such policy objectives, however, requires more than one level of planning regulation in order to meet different existing and emerging urban conditions. There are at least three levels at which the solar envelope can be used to regulate growth.* They represent increasingly complex and comprehensive levels of planning control, with trade-offs between development and solar access consistent with public values. I shall explore the urban design issues intrinsic to each by describing their application in three different urban contexts.

*These three levels of planning control have previously been called Order, Structure, and System, and were described as frameworks for community development requiring different levels of control related to potential diversity. See Ralph L. Knowles, *Energy and Form* (Cambridge, Massachusetts: MIT Press, 1974), pp. 115–133.

The First Level of Regulation

The first, or minimum, level of regulation occurs when the specified boundaries are uniform as, for example, with a privacy fence. When the boundaries are fixed, the envelope is principally controlled by decisions about the period of solar access. After that, envelopes vary only with the size and shape of sites. If subdivisions are regular, the envelopes will have similar shapes and sizes.

This level of regulation is typically applied to such situations as an area of uniform housing sites, each with its own solar envelope. If streets may be shadowed, envelopes share the same boundary with opposing sites as they do with those adjacent on all sides. Envelopes may be generated independently of each other.

The relative simplicity of this arrangement can be seen in a point-line set describing adjacencies between envelopes. The points represent envelopes for each site, the lines

a shared boundary. If the boundaries are all uniform, there is no variety of conditions each envelope meets. If the subdivisions are uniform, the only change in the number of shared boundaries occurs at the corners of the blocks.

The urban design project demonstrating this level of control over solar access is in a residential area of Wilshire Boulevard, where the surrounding buildings are mostly two-story houses. The rules for solar access involve a translation of whole-site access that integrates a privacy fence into the envelope to increase volume and attain more realistic densities. In this approach, all properties receive equal amounts of sunlight

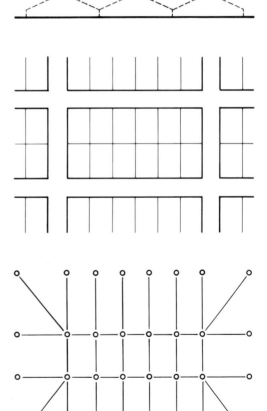

above the privacy fences. There is no question of prior right. Future development can count on the same conditions of solar access to the entire site.

The result is a number of independently designed projects that together have urban design implications because of their proximity to each other. Street qualities can be generally controlled by initially setting envelope constraints, but, once prescribed, the envelope automatically regulates each increment of development independently. When and where future construction takes place is of no consequence. The conditions of adjacency are constant.

The Second Level of Regulation

The second, or moderate, level of regulation occurs when more complexity requires higher levels of control. The envelope's boundary conditions vary along the perimeter. The relative complexity of the envelope is mainly controlled by decisions about how the envelope shall meet its surroundings. Implicit is a directionality to growth that results from the scaling of new to old development. Each new phase of development changes the surround and thus the context within which the envelope is generated. An idea of self-regulating control is thus introduced that was lacking in the simpler replication characterizing the Wilshire approach to solar access.

The greater sophistication of this second level of regulation makes it appropriate for application to more complex urban situations. A typical example might be an older part of a city containing a variety of sites, existing buildings, and land uses. The spatial conditions, and perhaps even the duration of solar access or cutoff times, may vary across the different boundaries of a site. As the number of adjacent conditions grows, an envelope's boundaries become more complex.

A point-line set of this application illustrates the greater complexity. The regular aspect of the first network is replaced; there are fewer points, but each meets more conditions. This complexity reflects both the greater variability of the envelopes and of the site situations to which this second level of regulation applies. Some points have obviously higher contact diversity than others, reflecting the flexibility of this moderate level of regulation.

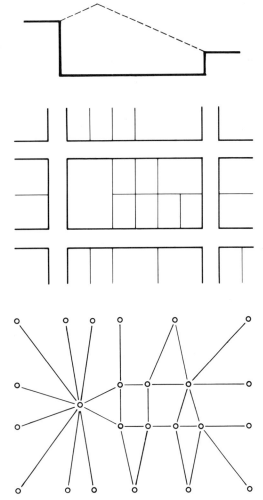

The project illustrating this second level of control is located in a built-up commercial area near downtown Los Angeles. Here there is definite concern about development sequence and prior rights. A version of whole-building access is used that allows variations in the amount of solar access to unlike faces of surrounding buildings, such as window walls, party walls, roofs, and ground floors. This does not assure equal amounts of sunlight to each property, as did the Wilshire development, but at least the solar access for each site is clearly defined, bringing a degree of certainty to the planning process. The principles generally apply to all sites and to future development.

The result of the downtown project is an approach to whole-building or roof-top access for medium-to-high-density commercial development. The envelope's shape is no longer based on a uniform edge condition, but on the variety of buildings and land uses that surround it. The relationship of one envelope to another is not uniform either, but structured, or differentiated, as an adaptation to the surroundings. Each parcel is regulated individually, but with respect for a more complex set of rules.

An expanded set of urban design issues attends this level of regulation. Because envelopes are interdependent, building qualities as well as streets can be generally controlled by setting envelope constraints. As conditions surrounding a site change, future envelopes for the same site will automatically adjust to sustain the prescribed qualities of buildings and streets.

The Third Level of Regulation

The third, or maximum, level of regulation is the most complex and requires the highest level of control. This is appropriate when a project is so large and its relationship to the surround so complex that its specific nature can only be determined over time. It is the kind of project that may be phased over long periods of time in a manner analogous to urban growth generally. This level of solar access control is also characterized by a great potential for internal diversification of building, open space, and mixed-use development, as well as by a diverse set of edge conditions. The envelope's scale is such that sets of buildings, rather than individual buildings, may push against its limits.

This level of solar access regulation is most applicable to large-scale urban sites with a variety of surrounding land uses. A typical situation might be a cleared redevelopment area of one or more whole blocks, surrounded by a variety of sites that will also change if the project's design and construction extend over several years.

The potential complexity of this level of regulation in combination with diverse edge conditions can be seen in a diagram of adjacencies. The central point, representing the large site's envelope, meets many surrounding conditions. If they are varied, the envelope's shape is likely to be complex; if the large project takes time to plan and construct, the envelope itself may change over time.

If one looks back to the first and second levels of solar access regulation, one can see a progression from many simple envelopes toward larger and increasingly more complex envelopes. Diversity is increasingly internalized by the envelope, requiring greater levels of control.

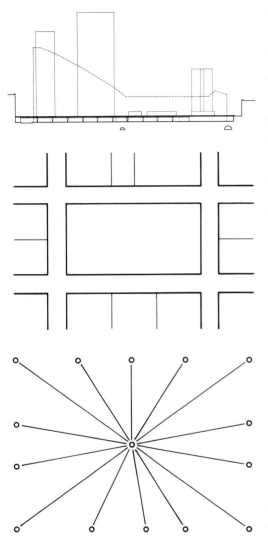

The project illustrating the maximum level of control has a known, but highly varied, set of surrounding conditions. It involves a nine-acre site on Bunker Hill, in Los Angeles, with a program calling for mixed-use development that includes housing, commercial office space, retail stores, and a museum. The scale and complexity of the project calls for the application of all modes of solar access, including whole-site, whole-building, and roof-top access, and the generation of a single solar envelope for the entire project.

At this scale, the envelope actually plays a planning role in matching the scale and land use on the site with the scale and land use in adjacent areas. Complex associations among on-site functions and between on-site and off-site functions are also handled by the envelope zoning. Various clusters and interconnections are possible, depending on the attitude toward solar access adopted in the generation of and subsequent development within the envelope.

Urban design issues within the site are uncontrolled by the envelope at this level of regulation. Building and street qualities are generally controlled on the site's perimeter and on adjacent sites, but not inside the large site itself. Here, the designer and developer bear responsibility for both specific design qualities and exploiting the enhanced potential for energy equilibrium on so large a site.

Seeking to control solar access at this scale also introduces some uncertainties. Since adjacent conditions may actually change while the project is being built, there must be a policy as to whether the envelope should change.

Shifting values and development patterns may affect any level of envelope regulation. But a large-scale application involves more assumptions about the surroundings. Internal development may take a very long time, during which values may change regarding solar access, land use, or economic feasibility.

The sequence of envelope transformation then must be controlled. It will be a function of perceived community needs and therefore of new phases of project development, regulated by a changing set of conditions for solar access to the surround. Clearly, the level of control that would be required under such circumstances may generally discourage such large projects in favor of smaller ones that can be regulated more simply.

The levels of control required for the regulation of solar access on an urban scale must be carefully considered in the formulation of public policy. The following designs have been chosen to clarify the issues surrounding envelope zoning and its implications for urban design. Through them, I will explore the issues of urban quality as well as issues relating to energy conversion.

The Wilshire Housing Project

Housing designs for the Park Mile area of Wilshire Boulevard demonstrate the first level of solar access regulation and the concepts of solar design applied to large-scale problems. The objectives are not significantly different from those for individual buildings described in chapter 9, but the proximity of several sites takes this project into the realm of urban design. The accumulated building forms have an impact on the size and shape of streets and on the rhythms of their spatial qualities and start to provide images of solar zoning at urban scale.

The project is representative of the first level of solar access regulation in that each site comprising the project is defined by its own boundaries, rather than by adjacencies, for solar access purposes. Its design concerns are internal; the design of one site is not dependent on another. Its replication is by increment.

The program for design focuses on three primary objectives, consistent with maximizing development potential and assuring pleasant living environments: (1) to provide the maximum number of dwelling units, preferably 40 to 60 dwelling units per acre; (2) to provide a living environment with good qualities of sunlight and cross-ventilation, with private and shared open space for each unit; and (3) to minimize shadowing and to protect the privacy of adjacent single-family houses.

Sites

There are undoubtedly countless areas within a city the size of Los Angeles that are suitable for demonstrating the envelope's applicability to urban design, but the locale selected has several unique attributes. First, several vacant land parcels in close proximity to one another are under extreme pressure for development. Second, the parcels front on or relate to Wilshire Boulevard, which has become an important transit link between downtown Los Angeles and the city of Santa Monica on the ocean. Throughout its history, this boulevard has been the location of prestigious apartment and commercial structures, ranging in height from 1 to 20 stories. Third, the land parcels are surrounded by single-family housing of high quality, and the residents of the area are adamantly opposed to high- or even medium-density development, particularly commercial development. At the same time, developers are exerting enormous pressure on the city planners to allow relatively high-density housing, commensurate with land costs.

The obvious compromise for these sites is a medium-density housing project that has minimum impact on the surrounding neighborhood. The six parcels, A through F, are part of the original residential platting, each being of similar geometry and only somewhat larger than the adjoining lots. The full block between sites B and F is also vacant land, but is not being considered for immediate development and is therefore not included in the project.

Each of the six study sites has its own solar envelope, consistent with the minimum level of regulation. The conditions for generation are simple: All edges are the same with reference to an 8-ft. privacy fence. (This results in shadowing equivalent to that from a $1\frac{1}{2}$-story detached single-family house with the usual side yards.) Public rights-of-way are shadowed. Solar access to each site is provided throughout the year from 9 A.M. to 3 P.M.

These rules produce significantly different envelope bulks on either side of Wilshire Boulevard. The envelopes constrain the three sites to the north more severely because of their proximity to adjacent, built-up properties.

Sites to the south of Wilshire have greater envelope bulk because they may cast shadows northward, across Wilshire, to properties on the opposite side.

When all envelopes are in place, the effect is one of great variety. The locations of sites make the greatest differences. Lesser differences of size and shape result from the relationship between the sites' plan geometry and the sun's movement.

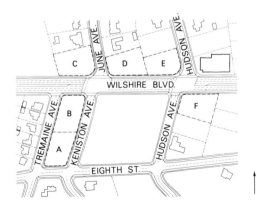

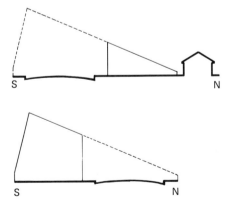

The envelope shapes, in combination with the existing buildings, display the properties of a well-fit puzzle. This is the habitual architectural way of relating forms in space. But forms in time belong to the real order of things as well.

By day, shadows migrate from west to east; by season, from north to south. The full effect of these cycles is caught better here in contiguous development, where forms specifically relate to each other within a set, than where an isolated shape casts shadows without a context.

Heliodon studies reveal this constantly changing aspect of form. This is especially true at cutoff times in winter when shadows are longest and fit precisely into the streets located between sculpted envelope shapes.

Further studies of shadows from envelopes on sites A, B, and C indicate the precision with which changing shadows fit the total environment of a site. Shadows can be seen to maneuver around the corners of adjacent houses without touching them during the period of assured access. This rhythmic addition to the dimensioning between sites suggests a profound connection between them that can be experienced only over time.

View from west; 9 A.M., winter.
Solar envelopes over six sites, A−F.

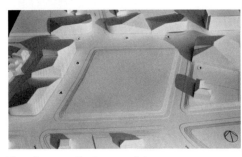

View from south; 9 A.M., winter.

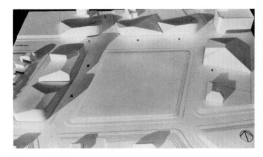

3 P.M., winter.

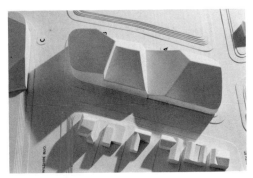

View from west; 9 A.M., December.

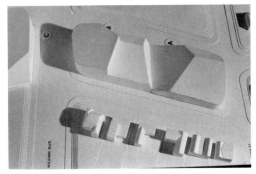

1 P.M.

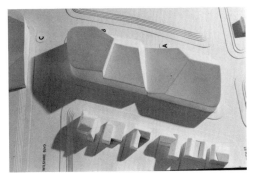

10 A.M.

2 P.M.

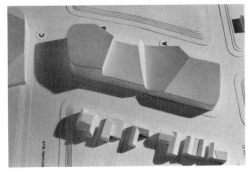

11 A.M.

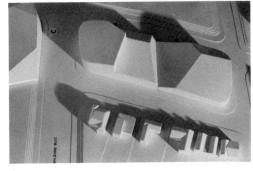

3 P.M.

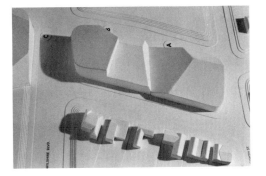

12 noon

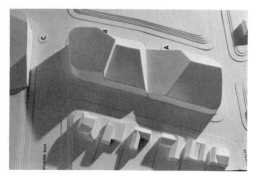

View from west; 9 A.M., December.

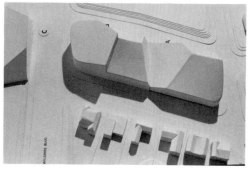

April/August

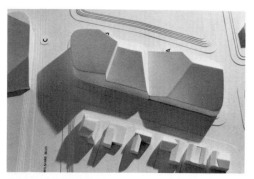

January/November

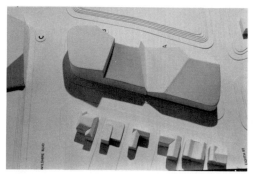

May/July

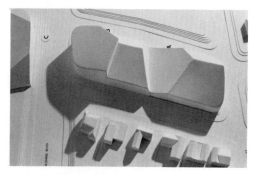

February/October

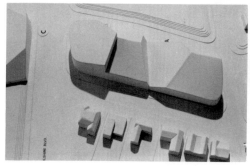

June

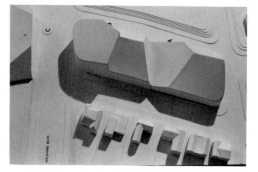

March/September

Building Designs

The average number of units on each of the six demonstration sites is 28, not very large by some standards but sufficient to encourage the active interest of developers. This number amounts to a density of 52 dwelling units per acre.

The trade-off usually required to attain such densities in low-rise structures (2 to 6 stories) is to increase land coverage and decrease open space. In this, the designs are surprising; the average building covers only 56 percent of its site area. But the results are even better than implied by this average coverage, for the total open space, counting private terraces and patios as well as setbacks and courtyards, comes to 67 percent of the site area.

Such figures can, of course, be equalled by the conventional high-rise strategy, but only by sacrificing solar access. On the other hand, most conventional low-rise development done at roughly 25 to 35 dwelling units per acre provides far less open space.

The results for all the building designs are summarized in table 1, in a form that facilitates detailed site comparisons.*

*Tables 1 and 2 were prepared by Richard D. Berry and, together with some of the design examples in this chapter, have appeared earlier in a different form in Ralph L. Knowles and Richard D. Berry, *Solar Envelope Concepts: Moderate Density Building Applications* (Golden, Colorado: Solar Energy Research Institute, 1980).

Site C
Site C is typical of all three of the sites (see the site map on p. 235) located on the north side of Wilshire, and the building examples are similar to approaches taken on the other sites, D and E.

The solar envelope for site C is characteristic of these sites. Its south, or street, side is high and its north side is low in order to protect neighboring single-family residences from winter shadows. On the east, the envelope has small, sloping faces that protect the sites across June Avenue, and sloping faces on the west protect adjacent property. The envelope's dominant feature is a large face that slopes down to 8 ft. above grade on the site's boundary. This last characteristic, common to envelopes over sites C, D, and E, sets stringent development and design limits.

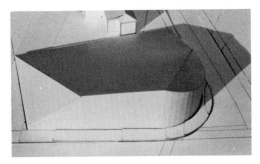

View from south; 3 P.M., winter. Envelope over site C.

Table 1 Building and Development Data for Prototype Design Studies of Multifamily Condominium Housing on Six Land Parcels

Development Parcels			Dwelling Unit Densities Achieved[a]				Average Size of Dwelling Units[b]		On-Site Parking[c]	Open Space Characteristics[d]	
Site No.	Area (sq. ft.)	Area (acres)	Designer's Name	Total No. of DUs	Land Coverage (as % of site)	DUs (per net acre)	Enclosed Space (sq. ft.)	Outside Space (sq. ft.)	Average Stalls per DU	Total Open Space (sq. ft.)	Total Space (as % of site)
A	22,430	.51	Alonzo	25	54	49	1,540	380	1.9	17,700	69
			Myers	30	62	58	1,270	250	1.6	16,300	67
			Pica	26	48	50	1,270	250	1.6	20,200	89
B	23,970	.55	Gehring	32	43	58	1,180	145	1.9	18,000	75
C	26,000	.60	Aguilar	27	55	45	1,200	240	2.3	14,600	56
			Gutierrez	29	50	48	1,080	370	1.9	18,400	70
			Quon	25	52	42	1,350	330	1.8	19,700	75
D	23,700	.54	Liu	22	55	44	1,310	320	2.4	18,100	76
			Stockus	27	65	49	1,360	300	2.1	13,700	56
			Sullivan	26	70	50	1,280	360	2.2	13,600	57
E	20,000	.46	Marquez	25	65	54	1,240	330	1.8	10,800	54
			Stockwell	25	59	54	1,180	180	2.4	10,400	52
F	23,960	.55	Kearns	30	50	55	1,160	270	1.8	17,000	71
			Lisiwicz	40	55	73	1,200	130	2.0	17,200	72
			Wallace	27	65	49	1,280	230	2.3	15,100	68
Averages for all sites	23,340	.535		28	56	52	1,260	272	2.0	16,000	67

a. Land coverage is based on building bulk above grade and excludes subterranean parking and building overhangs above the first floor.
b. Program requirements specified a mix of unit sizes, ranging from efficiency to 3-bedroom units, and all units were specified to have some private outside space: decks, balconies, or patios.
c. All parking was placed below grade and conformed to current Los Angeles zoning requirements for on-site parking.
d. Total open space includes private outdoor spaces as well as courts, walkways, and setbacks.

One design for residential units within the envelope employs a strategy first discussed in chapter 9. Two rows of units are arranged parallel to Wilshire so that each has south exposure. As the southern units rise to fill the envelope's greatest height, the courtyard also broadens, thus assuring sunshine on the back row. This fortuitous relationship of building height to area of shadow is the automatic result of the envelope's proportional relationship to site dimensions. Twenty-five units are included in this design for a density of 42 dwelling units per acre.

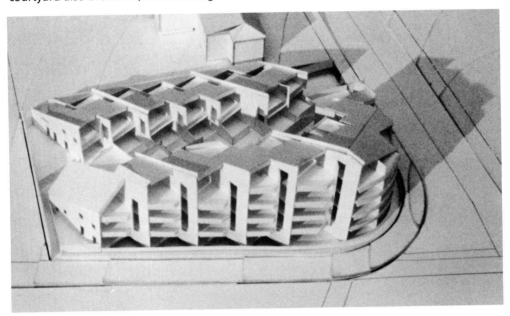

Designer, Jeannette Quon.

View from west; 3 P.M., winter.

A second design under the same envelope follows a different strategy that provides less south exposure, but greater density. Almost all units are arranged in three north-south rows instead of two east-west rows. By a combination of clerestories and terraces, some south exposure has been provided to every unit, but the rows of units have major east and west exposures. While this orientation does not have the energy-conversion advantage of a south exposure, it does offer development advantages. Twenty-nine units are included in the complex for a density of 48 dwelling units per acre.

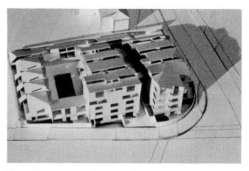

View from south; 3 P.M., winter.
Designer, Paul Gutierrez.

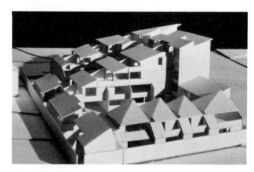

View from west; 3 P.M., winter.

The accumulation of building designs for sites C, D, and E begins to suggest the character that Wilshire's north side would assume with solar zoning. Building profiles rise and fall with each site's envelope; transitions are graceful, without abrupt changes in scale from one new project to another, or between old and new projects. Within this overall, unifying order, there is a diversity resulting from the self-expression of individual designers.

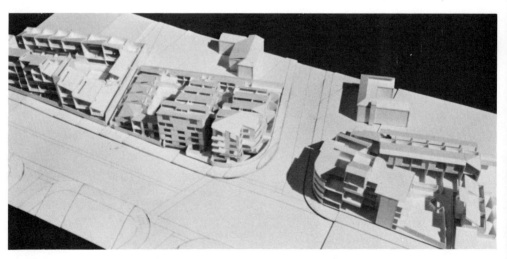

View from southeast; 9 A.M., summer.
Designers on sites C, D, and E, from left to right:
Mary Stockus, Paul Gutierrez, and Barry Sullivan.

Site B

Site B, to the south of Wilshire, is unique in that it is surrounded by streets on three sides and its scale seems more typical of the very old parts of eastern cities, where block size is significantly smaller than that found in mid-west or west-coast cities.

The envelope, as it faces north to Wilshire, is relatively high because shadows may extend quite far. Across Tremaine to the west are single-family residences that must be protected; a similar condition, for future development, occurs across Keniston to the east. These two situations require that the envelope's southern portions be dropped below the northern portion.

Shadows cast from the building on a winter morning indicate how closely the design approximates the shape of its solar envelope. If winter and summer views are compared, the importance of south orientation becomes clear. On winter mornings, the sun penetrates deeply into the main living spaces of every unit. The designer retains this sunlight throughout the day by the skillful use of courtyards, terraces, and sun-screens. The form and orientation of the building protect interior spaces from the summer sun.

The project includes 32 units, for a density of 58 dwelling units per acre, a characteristic number for sites to the south of Wilshire, where envelope bulk is greater than it is on the north.

View from south; 9 A.M., winter. Envelope over site B.

Designer, Michael Gehring.

9 A.M., summer.

A more complete image of Wilshire evolves with the accumulation of projects on both sides. Designs for sites B and C face one another across Wilshire; each is constrained by a solar envelope. Yet, because the envelopes are unique and because individual designers are involved, the solutions are quite different.

Both designers have made good use of courtyards that harken to an earlier tradition of southwestern building. The Spaniards used courtyards, and architects of the 1920s and 1930s developed them further into an extraordinarily rich vernacular. Only after World War II did that development give way to the single-family ranch house we seem less and less able to support.

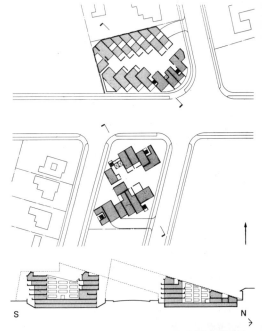

View from south; 9 A.M., winter.
Projects are shown on all sites to demonstrate the character of streets.

The Downtown Commercial Project

Commercial development in the Olympic-Figueroa district near downtown Los Angeles represents a project organized at the second level of control, involving more complex constraints on the solar envelope and a greater concern for development sequence.

Adjacent building and site conditions, rather than a site's own uniform boundaries, variously determine the envelope's edges. If, for example, existing buildings surrounding a vacant site are high on one side and low on another, the envelope will exhibit a marked directionality.

Sequence is an issue, as solar access is based more on prior right of access than was the case for the first level of control. Equal access among sites is not assured, but everyone knows what he is entitled to. In this case, the envelope assures solar access to buildings on adjacent properties, rather than to the whole site as in the case discussed in the preceding section.

The design objectives for each site are as follows: (1) provide the maximum amount of rentable floor area that can be obtained; (2) provide sufficient on-site parking to comply with city zoning requirements; (3) provide natural light to all offices, with maximum office depths not to exceed 35 ft; (4) prevent direct penetration of sunlight through windows during normal office hours; (5) provide an appropriate structural framing system; (6) comply with all fire and building codes.

The project also encounters some new design issues in relation to solar access. New buildings interact with existing ones through controlled shadowing; thus, buildings on separate sites become interdependent parts of a larger arrangement. Buildings on one site cannot be conceived independently of their surround. Design concerns are no longer exclusively internal. Replication is structured directionally with reference to the built and unbuilt surround.

Sites

The demonstration sites are on the southwest fringe of the Los Angeles central business district. This portion of the downtown contains a large number of vacant parcels and parking lots. These open parcels occur between buildings of different sizes, ranging from 1 to 13 stories. The average FAR is 3 compared to 3.6 for the downtown as a whole. The area contains new buildings, as well as a significant number of older ones that have limited economic viability.

The area appears likely to attract medium- to high-density development over the next ten to twenty years. Land values are comparatively low and land assemblage appears to be relatively simple to accomplish. Also, the city's planning department recently reduced the allowable FAR from 13.0 to 6.0, in recognition of what was actually being built within the commercial core of the city.

Nine sites (A–I) are shown along two major arterial streets, Olympic and Figueroa. Five of the sites (A–E) range in size from 22,000 to 35,000 sq. ft. The other four (F–I) are significantly larger, about 50,000 sq. ft., and two, sites H and I, have complex shapes resulting from modification in public rights-of-way or land assemblage.

As a set, the nine sites represent the range of conditions that potential developers confront when they attempt to build office space anywhere within this part of Los Angeles, or within similar commercial areas in other cities.

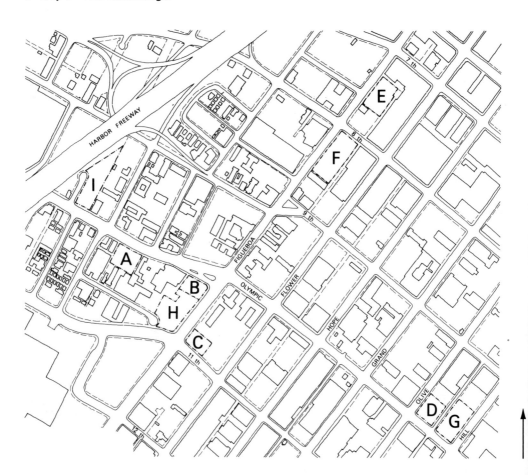

Results of Conventional Zoning

Before proceeding with the discussion of solar zoning and design on the nine sites, I shall describe the development implications of existing zoning as a basis for comparison. Future development under present zoning will result in conventional structures ranging from 6 to 30 stories; none can exceed the allowable FAR of 6.

A model helps us to visualize a scenario of twenty years of growth without solar zoning. In two views from the west, one at 9 A.M. and the other at 3 P.M. during winter, shadow impacts can be seen. Streets receive sunlight either in the morning or afternoon, but new high-rise buildings severely shadow neighboring properties.

In the morning view, Olympic Boulevard is the long vertical street that can be seen receiving direct sunlight along its full length. All streets paralleling Olympic receive morning light. The other street, Figueroa, runs left-to-right across the picture, and is shadowed by the buildings located on its southeast side.

In the afternoon view, the sun sweeps up streets from the southwest (from the right) and shadows Olympic Boulevard and the streets running parallel to it. Figueroa and the other streets that run from southwest to northeast are bathed in sunshine.

A comparison of the two preceding views provides a dramatic illustration of how the pattern of light over a cityscape changes as the sun moves from morning to afternoon over a Spanish grid. Every street receives the sun's light and heat during some part of the winter day. Shadowing also occurs early in the morning and late in the afternoon, when shadows move quickly.

There are obvious advantages in providing solar access to a commercial district where shopping and other pedestrian activities are enhanced in direct proportion to the light and warmth in the street itself. The portion of the downtown core that already contains 20- to 40-story buildings has lost most of the qualitative advantages provided by the Spanish grid, along with much of the street life that once existed.

View from west; 9 A.M., winter.

3 P.M., winter.

Rules for Envelope Generation

The rules for envelope generation reflect the specific characteristics of the district, as well as an explicit set of premises designed to assure useful insolation and to encourage, or at least not inhibit, new development over time.

The basic premises can be stated as follows:

1. Each building is a total system with the potential to utilize solar energy through either passive or active means (sunlight or shadow on open space is not relevant here).

2. Solar irradiation must be available for at least 6 hours per day in order to provide a sufficient amount of energy for practical conversion within a building.

3. Existing development patterns in the area, in combination with real estate values, suggest that FARs for new construction should in no case exceed 6, but new development could probably be encouraged even with an FAR as low as 4.

4. Solar zoning, consistent with current zoning, imposes no setbacks on commercial properties.

The rules following from these premises make envelopes dependent on the buildings surrounding a site. Consequently, as surrounding buildings change, so do the conditions of generation. Thus time, as measured in years and decades as well as seasons and hours, becomes another determinant of form.

The rules used in generating all zoning envelopes for the commercial sites can be stated as follows:

1. Sunlight shall be provided to all surrounding buildings at all times of the year between the hours of 9 A.M. and 3 P.M. solar time. (This interval, at the latitude of Los Angeles, provides maximum heat gain at winter solstice, while mitigating heat gain in the summer; or, in other words, it provides about 77 percent of the aggregate daily energy that is theoretically available at the winter solstice and about 45 percent of what is available at the summer solstice.)

2. The solar envelope for a land parcel cannot shadow above the roof parapet of any existing building during the specified hours of the day. This protects future placement of solar collectors on nearby roofs.

3. If a development parcel adjoins one or more vacant sites, then a single envelope may be constructed under the assumption that firewalls will be built at the common property lines when new building occurs.

4. Parcels of land containing only temporary structures whose bulk is 10 percent or less of the allowed FAR may be treated as vacant parcels for purposes of establishing a solar envelope.

5. Walls of surrounding buildings that serve as firewalls or that have no significant windows may be totally shaded by a solar envelope as they have little or no potential for using solar radiation. (The possibility that such walls may be used to store heat or to mount energy-conversion devices is precluded by this rule. Here, a judgment is made favoring development over energy conversion.)

6. Walls of nearby buildings that function as window walls or that have window openings that exceed 25 percent of the wall area may be partially shadowed by the solar envelope as long as no more than 33 percent of the wall is shadowed during the specified hours on any day of the year. For example, on a midwinter morning, the lower one-third of an office building may be shadowed, since such shadows are transitory and would allow solar access to most of the building wall most of the day at most times of the year.

7. Vacant parcels located on the opposite side of a public right-of-way (a street or alley) from a development parcel shall be treated as if they already had buildings on them (as they will in time). Any future building on the vacant land must necessarily fit within its own solar envelope. First, the solar envelope is generated for the vacant parcel, assuming that a full-height window wall will eventually be built on the property line fronting the right-of-way. Under this condition, the solar envelope for the developable parcel may shadow one-third of the assumed window wall. If a solar envelope cannot be determined for the vacant parcel, then the envelope for the parcel being developed may cast a shadow on the bottom 20 ft. of the hypothetical future wall.

8. If the walls or roof of an existing building are being shadowed by an existing tall building to a greater extent than what is imposed by an intervening solar envelope, then the solar envelope may be raised vertically until its shadow equals, but does not exceed, that of the existing tall building.

Following these rules, which were written in enough detail to serve as a sample ordinance, growth tends to be dynamically regulated by the solar envelope in such a way that scaling is a continuous process and always relative to the current stage of growth, rather than to some constant constraint, either of height or FAR. Resulting adjacencies are between elements of more nearly equal size, thus avoiding the abrupt height differences that sometimes accompany conventional development. Over time, the city is able to increase its density, but at a slower rate and without the discontinuities that disrupt neighborhood scale and vitality.

The sequence of development also becomes important as each envelope, with its contained buildings, successively becomes the generating reference of the next. The envelopes are thus interdependent in an urban context and, if the sequence changes, so will the envelopes and the development potential within. One example of how this may occur can be demonstrated by looking at two related commercial sites out of the original nine.

In the accompanying drawing, the order of development (site D or G first) is arbitrary, but the envelopes are interdependent, and the order in which they are generated has development and design consequences. Let us presume that site D, located to the northwest of site G and across the alley from it, is developed first.

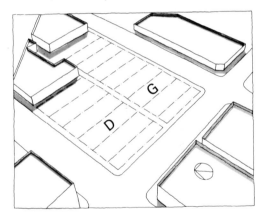

View from west; 9 A.M., summer.
Sites D and G with original platting.

Both envelopes have generating references on all sides except across the alley from each other; it is here, at the alley, where the effects of sequence are seen. Generation of an envelope for site D initially requires that a reference, a 20-ft.-high shadow line, be drawn at the property line of site G. An envelope can now be generated for site D and a building can be designed.

Presuming that the designer puts few windows on the alley and, instead, opens the offices to an interior court, the envelope over site G can be generated to protect only the roof of the building on site D. But if the designer had used a window wall on the alley, the outcome would be quite different; the envelope over site G would have been considerably smaller. Obviously, who comes first makes a difference.

Building Designs

Before showing examples of building designs for the Downtown Commercial Project, I will here summarize the planning, design, and development attributes for each site (table 2).

The data provided by table 2 suggests the range of building densities that may be expected for infill development. For example, the designs on site A achieve an average FAR of only 2.5 on 0.66 acres. The smaller site B, with only 0.45 acres, produces an average FAR of 3.5.

To achieve the specified solar access, the zoning envelope must reflect the existing conditions surrounding a site, and these variable conditions are what impose variable limits on the building potential of any site. Site A has buildings on three sides, while site B is situated on a corner.

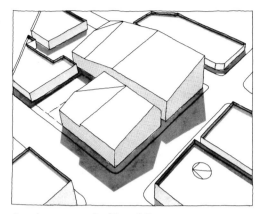

Envelopes over sites D and G.

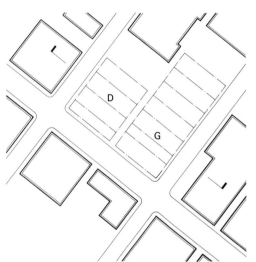

Plan showing sites D and G.

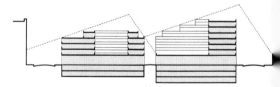

Section through sites D (left) and G (right).

Table 2 Envelope, Building and Development Data for Prototype Design Studies of Commercial Office Buildings on Nine Land Parcels

Development Parcel		Solar Zoning Envelope (max. development potential)[a]			Building Design and Development Feasibility				Building/Envelope Relationships	
Site No.	Land Area (sq. ft.)	Gross Floor Area	FAR	Enclosed Volume (cu. ft.)	Building Design and Development Studies[b] Designer's Name	Gross Bldg. Floor Area (sq. ft.)	FAR	Building Volume (cu. ft.)	FAR (bldg.) / FAR (env.)	Vol. (bldg.) / Vol. (env.)
A	28,675	90,900	3.17	1,022,289	Alizor	66,154	2.31	793,852	.73	.776
					Carmichael	64,563	2.25	884,916	.71	.866
					Lew	81,167	2.83	908,802	.89	.889
					Magno	80,180	2.80	962,160	.88	.941
B	19,435	94,000	4.84	1,158,107	Assef	68,784	3.54	931,464	.73	.804
					Suberville	67,308	3.46	876,076	.71	.756
C	21,650	113,313	5.23	1,407,250	Murabata	80,630	3.72	1,075,998	.71	.765
					Steele	98,116	4.53	1,298,436	.87	.923
D	27,630	136,940	4.95	1,801,400	Mitnick	129,295	4.68	1,605,580	.95	.891
					Lowinger	97,589	3.72	1,328,568	.75	.738
E	35,200	156,200	4.44	2,440,047	Reza	131,835	3.75	1,694,020	.84	.694
					Pina	141,200	4.01	1,888,800	.90	.774
F	53,664	288,756	5.38	3,890,640	Reza	236,448	4.41	3,143,748	.82	.808
					Pina	206,863	3.74	2,633,745	.69	.677
					Alizor	194,724	3.63	2,608,074	.67	.670
G	49,500	295,000	5.96	3,579,425	Suberville	222,146	4.49	2,931,360	.75	.818
					Assef	229,854	4.64	3,137,697	.78	.877
					Lowinger	224,250	4.53	2,962,512	.76	.828
H	50,702	224,010	4.42	5,799,813	Steele	210,951	4.16	2,821,206	.94	.486
					Mitnick	196,473	3.88	2,536,468	.88	.437
					Murabata	184,465	3.64	2,401,712	.82	.414
I	49,500	310,875	6.28	4,746,833	Magno	233,899	4.73	3,103,788	.75	.654
					Carmichael	188,349	3.81	2,172,072	.61	.457
					Lew	232,867	4.70	2,819,232	.75	.594

a. Potential buildable floor area and FAR calculated for above-grade building bulk, assuring constant floor-to-floor height of 12 ft.
b. Building floor area, FAR, and building volume excludes below-grade parking.

On the other hand, the highest building FAR, about 4.5, occurs on two quite dissimilar land parcels of roughly equal size (sites G and I). Both have the same general orientation, but site I has an unusual geometry and envelope form.

The buildings on all the combined sites range in size from about 65,000 sq. ft. up to roughly 230,000 sq. ft., differing by a factor of 3.5 from smallest to largest. By comparison, land parcel size differs by a factor of only 2.7.

This second level of control clearly regulates density, and development potential, in ways that are quite subtle but always related to the specific conditions that surround a building site. Why and how this happens can be understood, at least in a general way, by looking at the following design examples.

Sites B, C, and H

The most complex set of interrelated sites occurs at the corner of Figueroa and 11th Street. Here, by removing a few small buildings (rule 4), two adjacent sites (B and H) are formed to extend a full block. Across the street to the southeast is site C.

The envelopes for sites B and H are generated together (rule 3). Their combined volume is 7 million cu. ft., a considerable development potential. The most distinguishing feature of these envelopes is their surface complexity, a result of variable heights and locations of existing roofs that must be protected (rule 2).

The envelope for site C is generated next. It contains 1.4 million cu. ft. Its major slope responds to the envelope height and presumed window wall on site H across Figueroa (rule 6). Its high, vertical face on the opposite side meets an adjacent, vacant site that is included under an extension of the same envelope (rule 3).

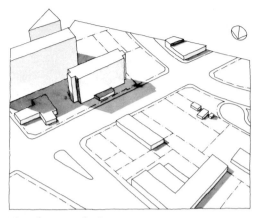

View from north; 9 A.M., summer.
Sites B, C, and H with original platting and small buildings to be removed.

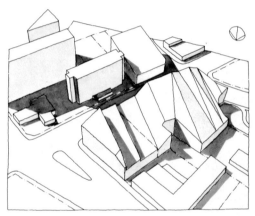

Envelopes over sites B, C, and H.

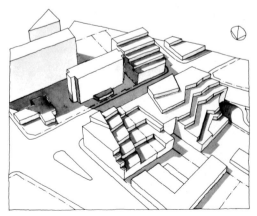

Topographies B, C, and H.

At 12-ft. intervals, a topographic interpretation of the three envelopes provides useful development information. For example, if the full potential floor area of 94,000 sq. ft. could be realized on site B, the resultant FAR would be 4.84. On site B, the potential floor area is 113,000 sq. ft. which converts to a FAR of 5.23; and on site H the potential floor area is 224,000 sq. ft., converting to a FAR of 4.42.

Of course, this information only provides a picture of relative development potential, since most designs would need to trade off envelope volume for sunshine and fresh air to offices.

Site C provides a typical example of lost volume in the conversion from envelope to building design. The envelope contains 1.4 million cu. ft. with a development potential of 113,000 sq. ft.

A design under the envelope contains only 1.0 million cu. ft., or 76 percent of the envelope's volume. The floor area is 80,000 sq. ft., or 71 percent of the envelope's potential. The possible FAR of 5.23 has dropped to a designed FAR of 3.72.

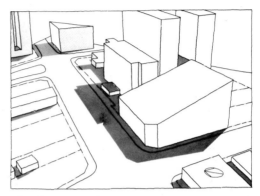

View from west; 9 A.M., summer.
Envelope over site C.

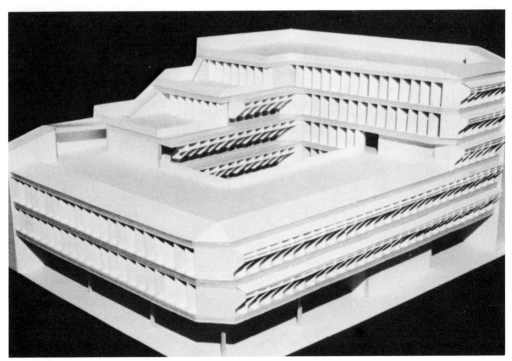

3 P.M., summer.
Designer, Roy Murabata.

Design consequences can be interesting when the envelope's shape is complex, as on site B. Here, the designer has found it necessary to follow closely the envelope's contours for a satisfactory FAR.

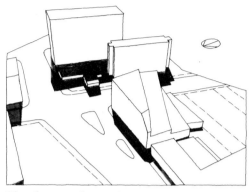

The envelope has a series of faces, separated by vertical cuts that fit exactly with the variable building heights surrounding the site.

The design makes an almost literal translation of the envelope's form. The result is a building that not only provides solar access to neighboring buildings but scales to them as well.

View from northwest; 9 A.M., summer. Envelope over site B.

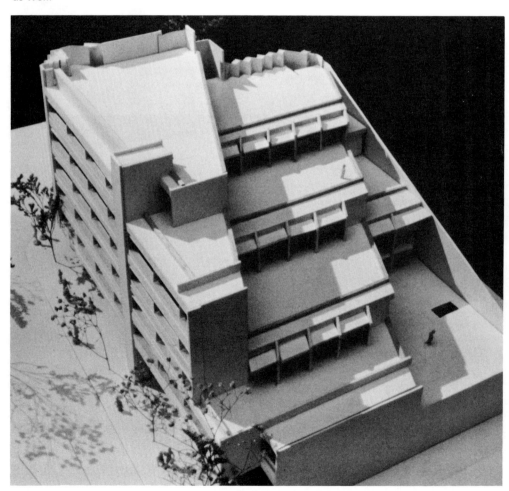

Designer, Mark Suberville.

Site I

Site I, because of its proximity to the Harbor Freeway, provides the largest FAR for the solar envelope. The situation is extreme but not uncommon in a modern city like Los Angeles. And except for a small, but new, building, chosen here to be protected on a nearby site, the envelope would be much larger than it is pictured.

The main bulk of the envelope extends over a vacant site to the northeast and rises to cast long winter shadows across the freeway. Both strategies gain envelope volume, but the envelope must be cut away to protect a small neighbor on the west.

If bulk were not removed, summer morning shadows would be cast over the roof area of the small building, thus breaking rule 2.

This case stretches rule 4 in favor of protecting the small neighbor, but proves the need for clear policies with respect to the minimum set of conditions to be recognized and protected at this level of control.

A final design, if it is to meet requirements for daylighting of offices, trades envelope volume for a larger S/V ratio. The freeway's impact is mitigated by using a relatively inefficient, single-loaded corridor to acoustically insulate the offices. As a result, the building contains 65 percent of the envelope's volume, with a FAR of 4.74.

Only a few sites in the Downtown Commercial Project have been shown here, but they are indicative of the urban design issues under discussion for the second level of control. They also offer the opportunity to re-examine the general applicability of courtyards and terraces at building and urban scales. Valuing the sun precludes large-plan buildings that isolate their interiors and inhabitants from the natural world. It encourages designers to cut into the envelope and articulate open spaces that provide access to sunlight and heat. The direct

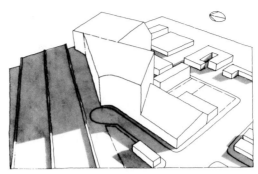

View from west; 9 A.M., winter. Envelope over site I.

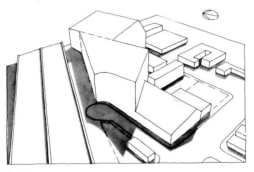

9 A.M., summer.

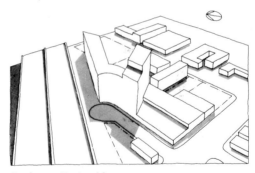

Designer, Hector Magno.

or indirect connection of such spaces can enrich the city, providing a series of public and private spaces that are shared by more people and add another way to experience the city.

Consistent with designs in chapter 9, roof terraces usually result here when the rectilinear geometry of conventional construction meets the sloping limits of the envelope. As mentioned before, terraces may be open or closed according to function or climate, but, in either case, if well-designed, terraces will enhance the potential for recreation, agriculture, and community.

Courtyards result when daylight is valued. Particularly in the case of office buildings with large plan dimensions, courtyards and atria, enclosed or open to the sky, provide an effective combination of lighting quality and other amenities. The courtyard is also a way to expose the building interior to the heat of the sun, thus increasing the possibilities for passive thermal design by natural heating and cooling.

When solar access is assured to cities, rhythmic change in the qualities of light and dark, warm and cool, become controlling design elements. The designer need no longer build indifferent boxes that are plugged into life-support systems at huge energy costs. Assuring solar access allows buildings to be tuned to natural recurrences and urban forms to be generated without fear that the light will be turned out by future development.

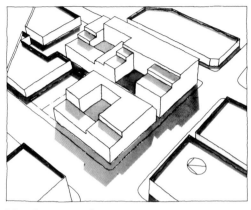

View from west; 9 A.M., summer.
Designs for sites D and G showing courtyards and terraces.

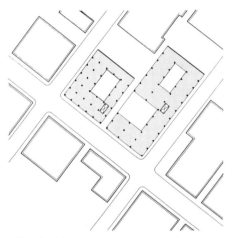

Office building plans on sites D and G.

The Bunker Hill Project

The last project is the mixed-use development for downtown Los Angeles in the portion of the city called Bunker Hill. A well-known community in the early part of the century, Bunker Hill was cleared for redevelopment during the 1960s and is today one of the largest vacant sites in a downtown American city. It is presented here as a project organized at the third level of regulation for solar access.

Bunker Hill is still connected to the older, established parts of Los Angeles, as well as to the more recent commercial burgeoning of the area. Large hotels, office, and commercial complexes are turning the area from an underdeveloped district into the most vital part of the city.

Bunker Hill is also the highest point in downtown Los Angeles and was famous, in early days, for the Angel's Flight cable car that took residents up and down the hill. Now, plans for this last undeveloped portion of Bunker Hill are being made and Angel's Flight may yet be restored.

The whole site is under the control of the Community Redevelopment Agency (CRA), which plans to proceed with development, estimated at $1 billion.

Program

A preliminary program for the nine-acre site was made available to the University of Southern California by the CRA in the fall of 1979. A similar program later became the basis for a competition among five invited developer-architect teams.

The mixed-use program called for a total developed area of 3.0–3.9 million sq. ft. (not counting parking, which needed to be on site) on a land area of 393,000 sq. ft., or nine acres. Of the total developed area, the CRA called for 70 percent in commercial and retail (2.1–2.7 million sq. ft.) and 30 percent

in housing (0.9–1.2 million sq. ft.), or about 800 to 1,000 dwelling units. In addition, there was to be a museum of about 100,000 sq. ft.

Land coverage was not to exceed 60 percent of the site, or 5.4 acres. Of the remaining 3.6 acres, 1.5 acres was designated a public park.

The competition program also called for energy-conscious design; and, as an aspect of that concern, the CRA became interested in the studio results of the Bunker Hill Project at USC and consequently included solar access as a factor in the evaluation of final entries.

The winning team, Bunker Hill Associates, was announced in July 1980: the developers were Cadillac Fairview California (a subsidiary of Cadillac Fairview Ltd., Toronto), Goldrich & Kest of Los Angeles, and Shapell Government Housing of Los Angeles (a subsidiary of Shapell Industries, Los Angeles); the architects were Arthur Erickson Associates, of Vancouver, with Kamnitzer Cotton Vreeland and the Gruen Associates, both of Los Angeles.

In its July 1980 majority report, the CRA cited the winning entry for its attention to scale and to solar access with regard to neighboring properties: "The massing is sensitively handled, with the highest office masses at the south end where they will not overwhelm the much smaller scale senior citizen housing to the east and the proposed housing to the west on Parcels L and M. The lower scale residential development central to the site relates well to its neighbors, and permits sun access to its neighbors to the east and west for much of the day during most of the year." *

*Taken from a memorandum: To Agency Members; from the Agency Bunker Hill Task Force—Majority Report of Alan Goldstein and Dr. Everett Welmers. (CRA of Los Angeles, California, July 14, 1980), p. 2.

With respect to the issue of solar envelope zoning being discussed here, the size of the Bunker Hill Project far exceeds any study project previously described. The urban design and control choices take into account the land uses and solar access needs of a complex surround. Boundaries are constrained by spatial and temporal adjacencies. The project not only has a complex relation to the surround, but there are also complex problems of urban interaction within the limits of the Bunker Hill Project itself.

The rules for the solar envelope need to recognize existing off-site housing and off-site commercial and institutional development. And different attitudes about solar access are taken for each of these. In general, the most generous attitude is taken about solar access for housing and the least generous for existing or proposed large-scale commercial structures.

Within the site, design choices are made about housing and commercial development that relate them systematically to each other and to their surroundings, both by size and by use. The scale of this project is such that, for the first time, it becomes clear that such decisions within the project limits may be a matter for public regulation and not the sole decision of an individual developer.

The large size of the Bunker Hill site suggests that the sequence of development might also be publicly regulated. In the context of the USC project under discussion here, the limited purposes of that regulation are solar-energy conversion and quality of life.

Many larger questions of public policy—for example, regulation of the sequence, as well as the size and complexity, of development—remain unanswered after this work. Surely, the answers must be based on a sound understanding of community values and existing land uses. But if energy self-sufficiency and community stability are to be purposes for new growth, answers must be found to the question: What comes first, then second, and so on, through to the completion of a well-balanced project that serves the community?

No precise answers are suggested by this project as to exactly what sequence should occur. The project was not based upon sufficient information about energy and community needs. Nevertheless, a strategy of relatively small buildings was followed. No attempt was made to design a megastructure.

The strategy of dealing with relatively small increments of development and of breaking the major functions into smaller physical parts has the obvious advantage of maintaining more options for the developer. In such a large project, the time for construction may be so great as to involve changing community needs and policies; the developer may need options that only phasing can provide.

Site

The Bunker Hill site is in a key location, with major downtown shopping to the south, the music center to the north, and the civic center to the northeast. All of these are within a few blocks of the site and thus within walking distance.

The slope of the site is pronounced. The grade falls generally from high on the north to about 35 ft. lower on the south.

The properties immediately surrounding the site vary in two ways. First, not all of them are occupied by buildings; therefore, a degree of uncertainty exists about future de-

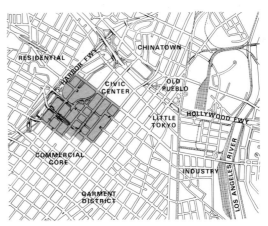

District map locating Bunker Hill Redevelopment area.

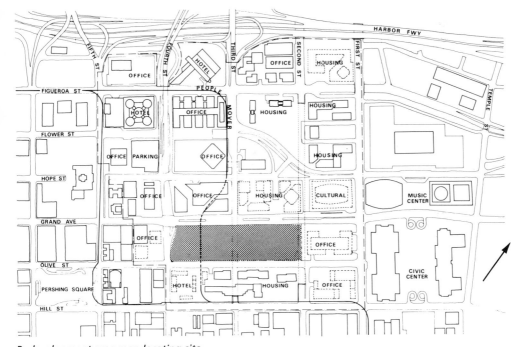

Redevelopment area map locating site.

velopment along the perimeter. Second, adjacent land uses are varied. Some existing and proposed buildings are major commercial structures. Some housing in the 12-story range is already under construction. And the CRA has proposed additional housing ranging from 3 to 30 stories.

Commercial development is concentrated at the southwestern end of the site. It is composed of older 15-story buildings directly across Fourth Street to the southwest, and soon-to-be-built 50-story highrise office towers across Upper Grand Avenue to the northwest. Across Olive Street to the southeast is a proposed hotel of about 15 stories.

Housing is generally grouped on the site's long sides. Twelve-story housing under construction for the elderly takes up most of the southeastern boundary to the lower right of the plan; proposed housing from low- to high-rise is slated for the northwestern edge on the upper left. The low-rise sections are proposed to be two-story housing over retail shops at ground level. The tallest proposed apartment house is 30 stories.

The least certain part of the surroundings takes up the site's narrow northeastern end, in the direction of the music and civic centers. The presumed uses here are institutional, either a cultural facility or a county municipal building about 12 stories high.

Rules for Envelope Generation

Before describing envelope generation for the Bunker Hill site, I shall give a short description of shadows from surrounding buildings.

This site, like the earlier commercial building sites, is on the Spanish grid. Consequently, the description of seasonal variation given for those streets is relevant here. In addition, the shadows from surrounding buildings change by season. The

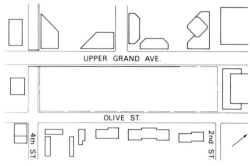

Site and immediate surroundings.

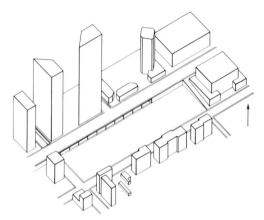

View from south; Bunker Hill site.

View from south; Bunker Hill site. Summer, 9 A.M.

Winter; 9 A.M.

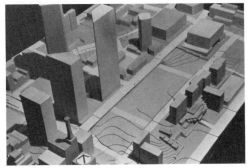

11 A.M.

11 A.M.

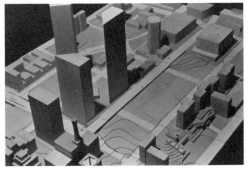

1 P.M.

1 P.M.

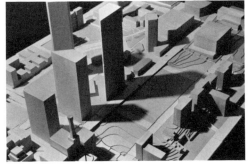

3 P.M.

3 P.M.

site is barely affected at all in summer until about 3 P.M. when tall buildings across Grand Avenue cast diagonal shadows from the west.

The winter shadowing is entirely from buildings rimming the site on the southeast, across Olive Street, and southwest, across Fourth Street.

A corollary is that buildings on the site would tend to cast shadows across perimeter streets and onto surrounding properties in summer, but only onto properties to the northwest and northeast in winter.

Following the rule of least shadow on housing and most on commercial office buildings, a general picture of acceptable shadows emerges. Thus, the rules for envelope generation make distinctions in the magnitude of acceptable shadowing of surrounding properties.

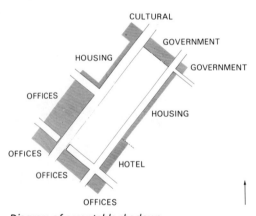

Diagram of acceptable shadows.

The Envelope's Shape Varies With Surround
Whole-site access, above 20 ft. at the property line, is required to protect the housing for the elderly. But only whole-building or roof-top access is required for most other buildings. This is consistent with rules applied in the earlier two projects as follows: Commercial office buildings may be shadowed to 33 percent of their window wall areas; buildings with less than 10 percent window area are assured only roof-top access. (The hotel is classified as a commercial building; cultural and government buildings proposed near the northeastern end of the site have less than 10 percent window and thus qualify only for roof-top access.)

The final envelope that emerges from the application of these rules is indeed of variable height. Its profile rises and falls along with that of the surrounding skyline. Lateral sections through the site and surrounding buildings show generally how the sun's rays define envelope volume.

Starting at the southwestern end of the site, the envelope is determined by commercial office buildings on one side and a hotel on the other. It peaks at 500 ft. in this section, but slopes steeply to avoid casting summer shadows onto more than an allowable proportion of the hotel's window wall.

The envelope is lowest farther along the site, toward its midsection. Here, it scales to housing on one side and low retail on the other. Its height is between 100 and 150 ft.

Still farther on, toward the northeastern end of the site, the envelope is moderately high. A proposed 30-story housing tower over retail stores on one side, and an intersection on the other, allow additional height. The extreme end of the envelope is in the same moderate range. At 200 ft. it scales to proposed cultural and government buildings about 150 ft. high.

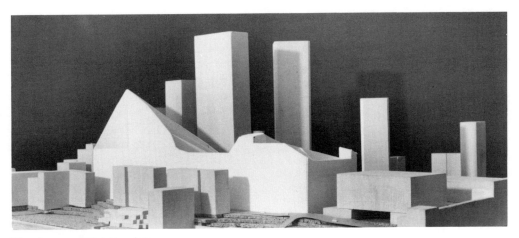

View from east; 9 A.M., winter.
Solar envelope over Bunker Hill site.

Cross section at southwestern end of site.   *Cross section at mid-site.*

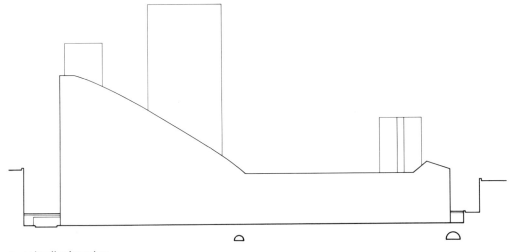

Longitudinal section.

Hour-by-Hour Envelope Generation
Simple generation techniques, detailed in chapter 4, suffice for most situations where sites are smaller and the surround is less varied than is Bunker Hill. But when adjacent buildings change size abruptly, as they do across Upper Grand where a 50-story and a 3-story building stand next to each other, an hour-by-hour check of the envelope is preferable to plotting only the cutoff times.

When only the cutoff times are plotted, the resulting envelope alternates sloping planes with vertical, connecting planes as it steps up and down to meet a varied surround. The refinement of time-checks produces more facets. Some of the envelope's surfaces become warped because they are generated by the sun's moving rays rather than by rays at a single instant.

As the envelope becomes more refined, it gains volume. When sites are small, this gain is insignificant. But on Bunker Hill and similarly large sites the additional volume can be well worth the more detailed generation effort.

Greater envelope refinement strongly suggests the desirability of high-speed computation to provide a more reliable legal description of large-scale development rights. But, even when sophisticated computer capability is available for envelope generation, initial work on the heliodon is advisable to determine approximate massing.

A first cut on the heliodon strengthens the designer's sense of the site. Also, a physical model can act as a check on the more precise, but sometimes less perceptually pertinent, computer output.*

View from east; 12 noon, winter.
Envelope showing generation planes.

---

*The heliodon analysis and accompanying generation drawings were done by Daniel T. Reza at the University of Southern California in partial fulfillment of a contract with the Solar Energy Research Institute, Golden, Colorado.

Generation Steps on the Heliodon
A preliminary inspection of a site model on the heliodon indicates that, if the rules are followed as outlined, the envelope will generally rise and fall with the surround; and further, that sharp changes of building height or use will require comparable adaptations of envelope size and shape.

More precisely, these changes can be determined in a series of steps taken with physical models on the heliodon. As in chapter 4, planes are used to represent the bearing and azimuth angles of the sun's rays. Appropriate surrounding heights are shown for reference at each set of generating steps.

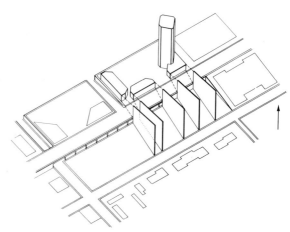

View from south; 9 A.M., winter.

The first series of steps analyzes each hour of the winter solstice between 9 A.M. and 3 P.M. The northeast half of the envelope is defined principally by the sun's low rays at 9 A.M. But toward the envelope's southwest half, where the greatest height differential occurs, a moving ray generates the surface in hourly intervals until 1 P.M. By that time, moving shadows from 50-story office towers cover the roofs of 3-story retail shops being protected by the rules of generation. When that happens, the envelope's height can increase. Its shadows fall harmlessly, duplicating those of the tall building.

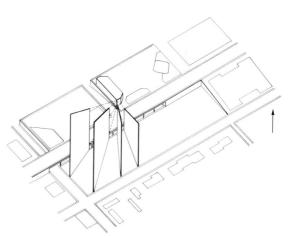

10 A.M. to 1 P.M., winter.

The next critical time is 3 P.M., the cutoff; only at the far northeastern end of the site does this time of a winter day control the envelope's height to assure rooftop access for a county government building.

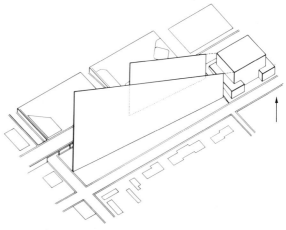

3 P.M., winter.

The next series of steps analyzes each hour of the summer solstice, but only at 3 P.M. do they act to limit the envelope's height. At that time, rays crossing the site strike housing for the elderly. If solar access is to be assured, the envelope may not rise above a sharply inclined plane.

The next steps combine seasonal planes. The summer rays are critical over some parts of the site because they pass below the winter rays; over other parts of the site, the winter rays control. While the equinox rays are not shown in this demonstration, heliodon studies indicate that they are critical over a very small portion of the site at the north end.

The final steps eliminate all but the essential plane dimensions to indicate the envelope's upper limits. The result is an implied set of boundaries, described by the top edges of vertical planes.

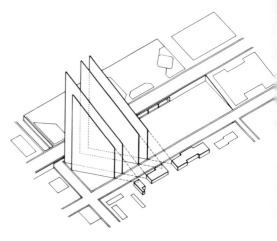

3 P.M., summer.

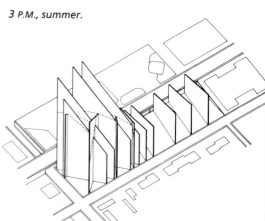

Summer and winter planes.

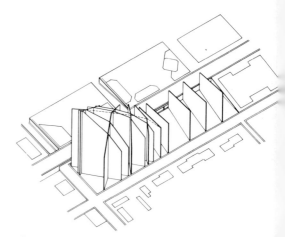

Eliminate redundancy.

When the actual boundaries are drawn, the envelope appears as a faceted shape. To the extent that its variations of bulk match surrounding buildings, there is a tendency for on-site land uses to group with those off the site. The solar envelope thus becomes a planning tool that aids in the regulation of growth.

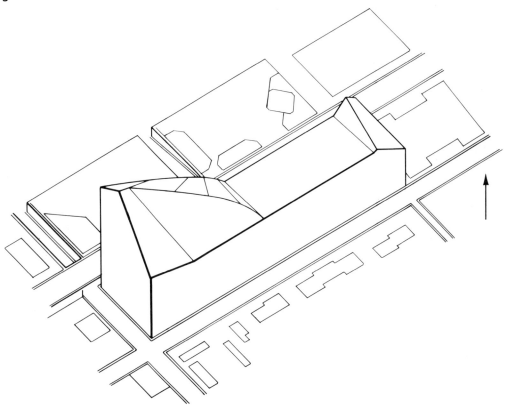

Final envelope.

Winter shadows (cast every two hours; 9 A.M., 11 A.M., 1 P.M., and 3 P.M.) provide a revealing picture of how the envelope fits its surround. As the shadows move, they phase in and out of critical relationships with surrounding building features.

The envelope shadows itself later in the afternoon—an important reminder that the envelope, as an instrument of public policy, assures solar access only to surrounding properties; the designer must resolve problems of shadowing within the site.

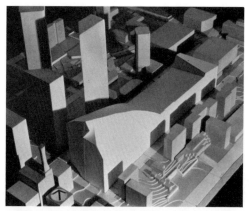

Winter shadows. View from south; 9 A.M.

1 P.M.

11 A.M.

3 P.M.

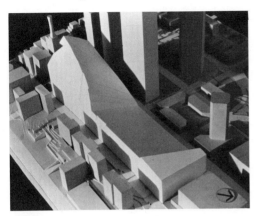

View from east; 9 A.M.

1 P.M.

11 A.M.

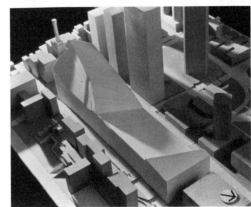

3 P.M.

Summer shadows become critical only at 3 P.M. They are cast from the envelope across Olive Street, toward the hotel and housing for the elderly. The envelope does not shadow itself in summer, but tall office towers on Upper Grand cast long, diagonal shadows across the envelope's midsection by 3 P.M.

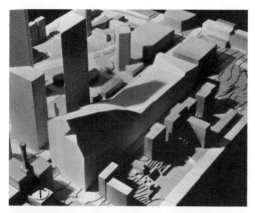

Summer shadows. View from south; 3 P.M.

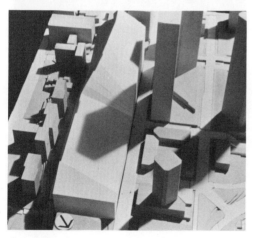

View from northeast; 3 P.M.

Shadows on the envelope signal special problems, and perhaps opportunities, for the designer. The winter shadows here indicate that buildings placed to take advantage of the envelope's high volume will tend to block winter afternoon sun from other buildings and open spaces on the site. The summer shadow, on the other hand, may provide an opportunity for the designer to ease the hot summer afternoon. But, as a general rule, we must remember that while people may choose to stand in shadow, they will resist a developer's mandating it.

I shall now proceed with a few design examples to demonstrate how, at this level of control, the envelope's shape suggests the disposition of land uses and how, within a composite urban form, distinct buildings and open spaces can adapt by location and form to achieve solar access.

Building Designs

The solar envelope is an expression of the freedom to choose whether or not to shadow one's own land and buildings. Shadowing of neighboring property, either inadvertently or willfully, is forestalled.

To satisfy the public policy constraint, the envelope shape must match the surrounding scale. To satisfy the option of solar energy and environmental quality, the designer must work within the envelope. The designer's option, rather than the policy constraint, inflicts the greatest development price on Bunker Hill.

The solar envelope has a potential FAR in excess of 20, based on a vertical increment of 15 ft. per story. Within such a huge volume, the CRA's programmed FAR of 8–10 could easily be met by following standard development procedures.

The average FAR for the following designs is 6.7, less than what was called for. As a trade-off, they provide sunshine to housing and to public open spaces within a mixed-use project. For this design choice, they fall 16–33 percent below the CRA program.

The designs that I will exhibit here achieve an average total of 2.63 million sq. ft. of floor space: 1.67 million for commercial offices and retail stores, and 868,000 for housing. As would be expected where the sun is used as a source of heat and light for buildings and open spaces, land coverage is only 50 percent instead of the 60 percent allowed by the CRA.

The envelope for the Bunker Hill site tends to be large in a large-scale environment, small where the surroundings are scaled down. In general, designs follow the envelope's outline; that is to say, there is a positive correlation with the surroundings. Tall buildings generally group together at the site's southwestern end, and those of moderate height at the northeastern end, with the shortest buildings taking up the site's midsection.

View from east; 11 A.M., equinox. Solar envelope over Bunker Hill site.

Designer, Randall Hong.

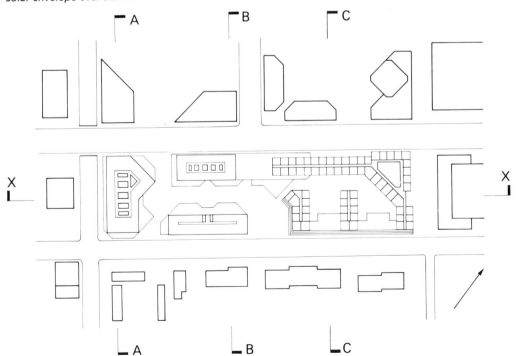

Designer, Scott Beck.

To the extent that building size and function are related, there is a match between major on-site functions and surrounding land uses. Commercial office buildings are located on the site's southwestern half, under the envelope's high peak. Not only is the greatest volume here to develop large commercial structures, but this end is surrounded by neighboring office buildings. Housing is generally located on the northeast half, under the low and moderately high parts of the envelope. Here, too, there is a scale match with neighboring land uses in the area.

More variety appears in the choices of location for the museum and retail stores. The museum and the stores require relatively small volumes and, consequently, their placement is less influenced by the shape of the overall envelope.

Three Urban Design Strategies
The museum and retail stores, along with the disposition of public open space, generate linkages within the site and between the site and other parts of the city. Different strategies for handling these components demonstrate the designer's feelings about how the site should perform as an urban entity with its own character. I have selected three designs to illustrate quite different points of view.

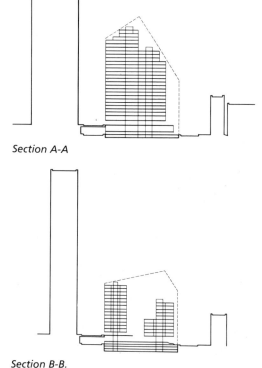

Section A-A

Section B-B.

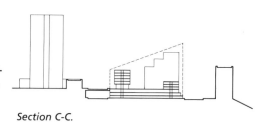

Section C-C.

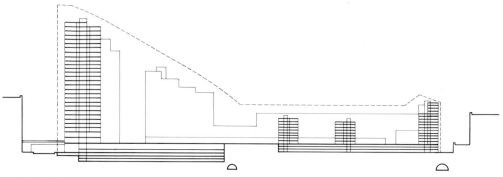

Section X-X.

The first design locates the major public open space, the museum, and the shops at the site's lower, southwestern end along with the major commercial office buildings. The effect of this grouping is to separate public activities from housing at the higher, southeastern end. A large plaza, open to the street at the juncture of a proposed subterranean "people-mover" and at the head of Angel's Flight, invites the public onto the site and focuses pedestrian traffic. People living in the adjacent, but somewhat removed, housing can choose between participation and privacy as and when they choose.

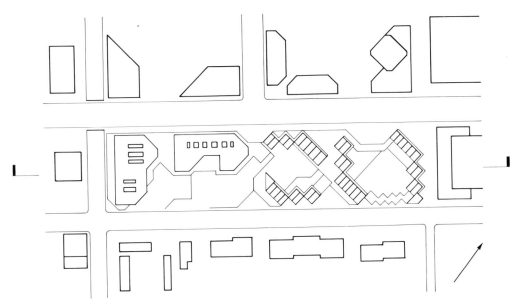

Designer, Robert Tyler.

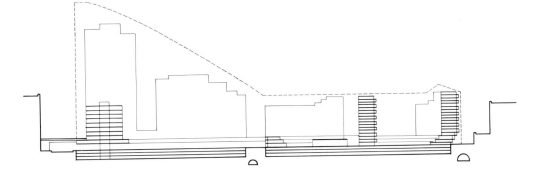

The second design follows a completely different strategy. The general disposition of office space and housing is the same, but the museum, shops, and open space are changed.

This design consists of an internal and separate "street" composed of a sequence of large and small, broad and narrow plazas. The shops rim this street, which runs from the office buildings on one end to the museum on the other. Sometimes the shops are below the offices, sometimes below housing. In this scheme, people walking from the commercial development to the museum would pass shops and housing.

Living above such a street would surely provide different experiences of the city than would living in the previous scheme, where the housing is more isolated. The first scheme invites people into the site, whereas the second scheme turns its back on the original streets and makes a new one.

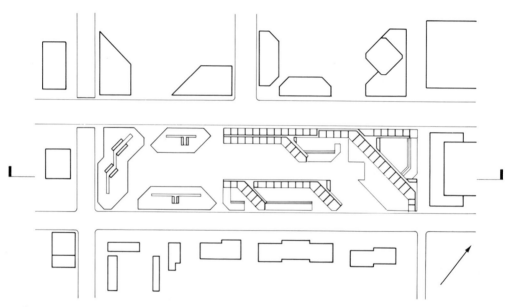

Designer, James House.

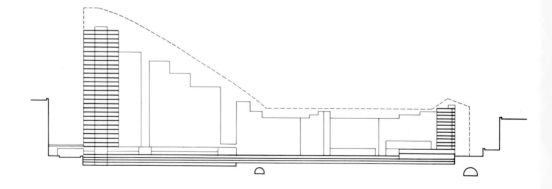

The third design also uses an internal pedestrian street rimmed with shops below, offices and housing above. What distinguishes this scheme as a separate strategy is that it links parts of the city. The street cascades diagonally across the site from its higher edge to its lower edge, thus connecting housing and the music center on the north with shopping, commerce, and Angel's Flight on the south. Instead of connecting to the city at only one major point or making primarily internal connections, this third scheme encourages passage through the district, linking it to the larger community.

Three different schemes thus represent different urban values, all within the tenets of solar access for the surrounding city.

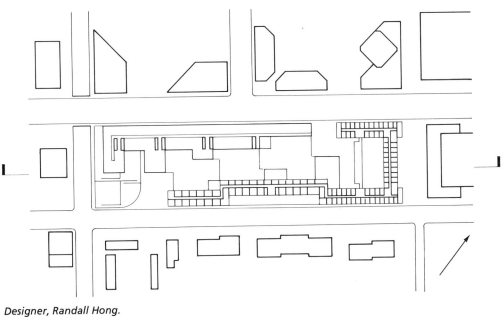

Designer, Randall Hong.

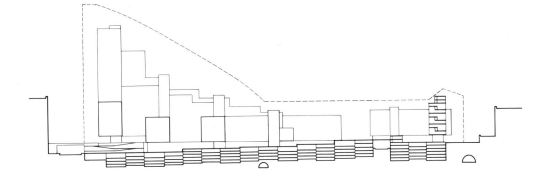

Observations Made Over Time
When viewed at an instant in time, the designers' models reveal a picture of potential richness. But with observations made over time, the continuity and rhythm of urban events can be seen. As days and seasons pass, impressions of the whole site swing to and fro—buildings and the spaces between them go from light to dark, from warm to cold. If the designers had carried the pro-gram's intent into construction, the pulse of human activity would be reinforced by these light and heat cycles of buildings and spaces.

As described earlier, multiple views of a project over time provide a stronger sense of the space-time fit of the buildings with their surroundings. The accompanying pictures are of three designs at different times of day and year.

View from south. Designer, Robert Tyler. Summer; 9 A.M.

1 P.M.

11 A.M.

3 P.M.

The first design shows seasonal and hourly shadow changes in its public space just northwest of Olive, near Fourth Street. Large commercial office buildings and shops rim the open space; housing can be seen in the background.

A sequence of images demonstrates the first designer's concern for sunlight. During the midday hours, when commercial activity and shopping would be at their peak, the design assures that the plaza is in full sun-light. If summer shadow is desired at mid-day (and such is not often the case during the month of June in Los Angeles), there are many temporary ways to provide it while maintaining a choice in the matter. During winter afternoons, the designer is unable to avoid shadowing the public space, but does avoid casting shadows from large commercial buildings onto the housing.

Winter; 9 A.M.

1 P.M.

11 A.M.

3 P.M.

The second design values south exposure for housing units over large, sunlit plazas. To achieve this, the housing occupies more of the site and has single-loaded corridors that allow almost all units to face south or southeast. In the winter, existing housing across Olive shadows the new housing from about 9 A.M. to 10 A.M.. And in the summer, the off-site 50-story office towers across Grand Avenue shadow two-thirds of the housing from about 3 P.M. until sunset. Otherwise, the designer has skillfully arranged the housing so that one set of on-site units rarely shadows another.

View from south. Designer, James House. Summer; 9 A.M.

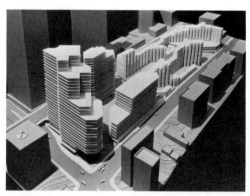

1 P.M.

11 A.M.

3 P.M.

Winter; 9 A.M.

1 P.M.

11 A.M.

3 P.M.

The internal street of the third design allows solar access in winter to on-site buildings. To accomplish this, the heights of buildings are matched with the width of the internal street so that where the street is narrow, the buildings along Olive Street are low and cast short shadows to the northwest across open space. Farther along Olive, toward Second Street, where the buildings become taller at the site's northeast end, the interior street widens and finally opens where the shadows can be cast across Grand Avenue.

During the midday hours, the sun sees down the entire length of the interior street because it runs more nearly in a

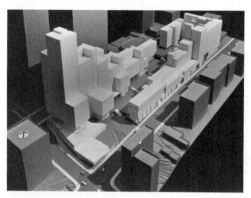

*View from south. Designer, Randall Hong.
Summer; 9 A.M.*

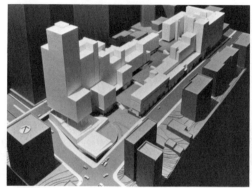

1 P.M.

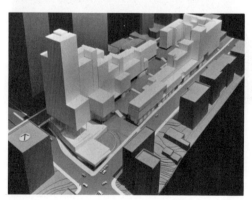

11 A.M.

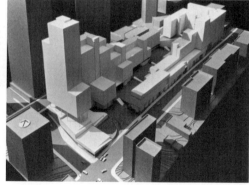

3 P.M.

north-south direction, diagonally across the site. The major public space provided at the corner of Fourth and Olive is half in sunlight and half in shadow at noon.

At 3 P.M. in the winter, the public space is still in sunlight, as is the entire length of the interior street on its southeastern side. The designer captures the sun's late winter rays by cutting away some of the envelope's pyramid that would otherwise cast shadows the length of the site.

Such sensitive tuning of the building's location and form combine the best aspects of both the Spanish grid and the Jeffersonian grid. Some volume is lost, but at great qualitative gain.

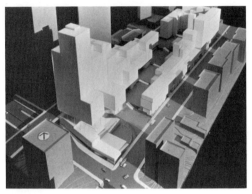

Winter; 9 A.M.

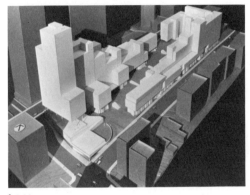

1 P.M.

11 A.M.

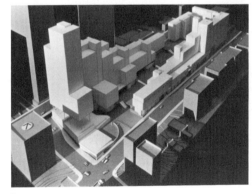

3 P.M.

This chapter has shown how a feeling for the rhythmical nature of light and heat can reach its greatest amplification and expression in urban design. In *The Structure of Verse,* Harvey Gross wrote, "Rhythm itself is a mysterious fact of aesthetic experience." * Of course, he was writing about poetry, not architecture and urban design. But he strikes a sympathetic chord when he goes on to say, "Rhythm is the way our bodies and our emotions respond to the passage of time. Seasons recur, autumn follows summer. . . ."

And, as the old Piute said in referring to seasonal migrations across Owens Valley, "Then, it is winter again." When I have spoken about rhythm as a design strategy, I have meant to describe a strategy extending beyond adapting our buildings to use solar energy. My references to the quality and rhythms of life have come closer to my actual intentions.

Certainly, I do not mean to imitate physical action or simply to describe solar phenomena by architectural means. Rhythm as a design strategy, as a medium of the designer, can express our most delicate feelings and moods. It can bring us closer to what the poet Allen Tate called "a sense of nature as something mysterious and contingent."

When significant groups of buildings are designed in direct response to natural recurrence, when daily and seasonal rhythms are reiterated and intensified by our built surroundings, then the city will offer as strong a sense of place and time as did the Owens Valley for the Piute. The city will then become a ceremonial affirmation of life.

---

*See the introduction and commentary by Harvey Gross, ed., *The Structure of Verse* (Greenwich, Connecticut: Fawcett, 1966).

Index